EDGAR HEAP OF BIRDS

EDGAR × HEAP OF × BIRDS

BILL ANTHES

DUKE UNIVERSITY PRESS
DURHAM & LONDON 2015

Printed in the United States
of America on acid-free paper ∞
Designed by Amy Ruth Buchanan
Typeset in Whitman by Copperline

Library of Congress Cataloging-in-Publication Data
Anthes, Bill.
Edgar Heap of Birds / Bill Anthes.
pages cm
Includes bibliographical references and index.
ISBN 978-0-8223-5981-4 (hardcover : alk. paper)
ISBN 978-0-8223-5994-4 (pbk. : alk. paper)
ISBN 978-0-8223-7499-2 (e-book)
1. Heap of Birds, Edgar—Criticism, interpretation,
etc. I. Title.
N6537.H383A58 2015
709.2—dc23 2015009508

Cover art: Edgar Heap of Birds, *Neuf* series, *Nuance of Sky #3*, 2012. Acrylic on canvas, 36 × 44 inches. Artwork © Edgar Heap of Birds.

DUKE UNIVERSITY PRESS GRATEFULLY ACKNOWLEDGES THE CHEYENNE AND ARAPAHO TRIBES AND PITZER COLLEGE, WHICH PROVIDED SUPPORT TOWARD THE PUBLICATION OF THIS BOOK.

PUBLICATION OF THIS BOOK HAS BEEN AIDED BY A GRANT FROM THE WYETH FOUNDATION FOR AMERICAN ART PUBLICATION FUND OF THE COLLEGE ART ASSOCIATION.

For Kelly and the girls

CONTENTS

ILLUSTRATIONS

ACKNOWLEDGMENTS

In completing this book, I am indebted to many individuals and organizations who supported my work over the past five years, materially, intellectually, and psychically. In particular, I would like to thank Edgar Heap of Birds and his wife, Shanna Ketchum-Heap of Birds, and their family. Without their generosity and hospitality, this book would not have been possible. An award from the Creative Capital | Warhol Foundation Arts Writers Grant Program supported early work on the project, and faculty research awards from Pitzer College helped sustain the writing process. Pitzer College and the Cheyenne and Arapaho Tribes of Oklahoma also contributed subvention funds toward publication. Thanks to Dean of Faculty Muriel Poston of Pitzer College and to Cheyenne and Arapaho Governor Eddie Hamilton for their support.

Ana Iwataki provided invaluable research assistance at an early stage, and this project has also been enriched by dialogue with my students at Pitzer and the Claremont Colleges. In Claremont I have also enjoyed an ongoing conversation with a diverse community of supportive colleagues and friends including Ahmed Alwishah, Brent Armendinger, Michelle Berenfeld, Tim Berg, Bruce Coats, Jud Emerick, Ciara Ennis, Paul Faulstich, Sarah Gilbert, George Gorse, Todd Honma, Kathleen Howe, Carina Johnson, Alex Juhasz, Tim Justus, Brian Keeley, Juliet Koss, Tarrah Krajnak, Jesse Lerner, Ming-Yuen Ma, Milton Machuca, Mary MacNaughton, Leda Martins, Stu McConnell, Jessica McCoy, Kathryn Miller, Lance Neckar, Harmony O'Rourke, Susan Phillips, Frances Pohl, Katie Purvis-Roberts, Brinda Sarathy, Andrea Scott, Dan Segal, Katrina Sitar, Erich Steinman, Ruti Talmor, Andre Wakefield, and Kathy Yep.

The installation of *Native Hosts* in Claremont in 2013 was funded by art+environment, a four-year interdisciplinary program at Pitzer College, supported by the Andrew W. Mellon Foundation. Thanks to Larry Burik, assistant vice president of campus facilities, and his staff, Jim Stricks of the Office of College Advancement, and President Laura Skandera Trombley for their support. My Pitzer colleagues Tessa Hicks-Peterson, Gina Lamb, Scott Scoggins, and Erich Steinman worked to connect the project to local indigenous groups. Tongva educator Julia Bogany worked closely with us on the project, and Lorene Sisquoc opened her classroom at the Sherman Indian School in Riverside for a workshop with Edgar and her students. Simultaneously, at the Pomona College Museum of Art, Kathleen Howe, Steve Comba, and Terri Geis (with research assistance from Pomona undergraduate intern Ben Kersten) organized *Nuance of Sky: Edgar Heap of Birds Invites Spirit Objects to Join His Art Practice*. I am very grateful to all those who helped connect my work with Edgar to the broader community.

My career as a scholar of Native North American art has been deepened by many years of my participation in networks of other scholars and artists, including the Native American Art Studies Association, but extending beyond that organization to emerging groups focused on indigenous arts in global perspective. The readings of Heap of Birds's work and the broader ideas that animate this book have evolved in conversations and collaborations with colleagues and friends including in particular Kathleen Ash-Milby, Janet Berlo, Chris Dueker, Candace Greene, Jessica Horton, Elizabeth Hutchinson, Carolyn Kastner, Kate Morris, Ruth Phillips, Dean Rader, Jack Rushing, Karen Kramer Russell, Damian Skinner, Charlotte Townsend-Gault, Norman Vorano, Mark Watson, and Mark White.

I presented a preliminary version of some of the ideas developed in chapter 1 to the Department of American Studies and the Native American Initiatives program at the University of Notre Dame in January 2011. Thanks especially to Laurie Arnold, Annie Coleman, Brian Collier, Erika Doss, and Sophie White for their engaged conversation. An early version of chapter 1 was published as "Ethics in a World of Strange Strangers: Edgar Heap of Birds at Home and Abroad" by the College Art Association in the fall 2012 issue of *Art Journal*. Thanks to Katy Siegel and Joe Hannan for their facilitation and support. Some material in chapter 3 was discussed in different form in my article "Contemporary Native Artists and International Biennial Culture," published in *Visual Anthropology Review* in fall 2009. I first presented this material at the College Art Association Ninety-Seventh Annual Conference, Los Angeles, in February 2009, in a session organized by Kathleen Ash-Milby and Kate Morris. My copresenters, Jessica Horton, Jolene Rickard, and Paul Chaat-Smith, offered important feedback and perspective. Other parts of chapter 3 were presented at the 2013 meeting of the Native American Art Studies Association in Denver. Thanks to my copresenters Netha Cloeter, Alex Marr, and Kate Morris for their collegiality.

Several individuals and organizations assisted in supplying images for his book, including Kathleen Ash-Milby of the National Museum of the American Indian; Nancy Blomberg, Eric Berkemeyer, and Liz Wall at the Denver Art Museum; Andrea Felder at the New York Public Library; Cat Kron at the Paula Cooper Gallery; Catherine Belloy at the Marian Goodman Gallery; Ron Warren at the Mary Boone Gallery; Jessica Lally and Bettina Yung at the Casey Kaplan Gallery; Steve Comba at the Pomona College Museum of Art; Hannah Rhadigan at Artists Rights Society; Robert Warrior in the American Indian Studies Program at the University of Illinois; Melissa VanOtterloo at History Colorado; Coi E. Drummond-Gehrig at the Denver Public Library; Gordon Hookey of the Boomalli Artists Collective in Sydney, Australia; Nicole Wittenberg; Elizabeth Sisco; Louis Hock; David Avalos; Veronica Passalacqua; Lorna Brown; and Sharon Irish.

From our first conversation, Ken Wissoker at Duke University Press saw the importance of a book on Heap of Birds's critical art practice, which has been insufficiently recognized in the contemporary art world. I am very appreciative of the diligent work and advocacy of Ken and his staff, especially Jade Brooks and Liz Smith. Jane Blocker offered welcome encouragement and particularly helpful suggestions about framing Heap of Birds's work vis-à-vis the historiography of contemporary art. Her comments and those of another anonymous reader helped shape the present book, and it is much better for their insightful criticisms.

Kelly Newfield read and offered important comments at every stage of the writing process, was there for pretty much everything, and, as always, did so much more than was required.

My royalties for the book are being donated to a Cheyenne and Arapaho scholarship fund named for Edgar's father, Charles Heap of Birds, who died in 2013 at the age of eighty-four. I am particularly grateful to Edgar and his family, who hosted Kelly and me in Oklahoma when we attended the Earth Renewal Ceremony in 2010. In writing this book, I enjoyed an ongoing conversation with Edgar over the course of several years. The final product has benefited enormously from his input and openness to my inquiries, as well as his attentiveness to checking my drafts for errors of fact and protocol. Any lapses that remain are mine alone.

INTRODUCTION

Making a Puncture

In 2009, Hock E Aye Vi Edgar Heap of Birds (b. 1954, Wichita, Kansas), a contemporary artist and enrolled citizen of the Cheyenne and Arapaho Tribes of Oklahoma, installed a temporary public artwork titled *Beyond the Chief* on the campus of the University of Illinois in Champaign. Heap of Birds's artwork comprised a series of twelve commercially printed steel panels, each eighteen by thirty-six inches, deployed around the campus and looking very much like official signage posted by the university's administration. *Beyond the Chief* was based on Heap of Birds's signature series of public installations, *Native Hosts* (begun 1988), which name the displaced indigenous nations that once enjoyed sovereign ownership of the lands now claimed by settler nations such as the United States and Canada. *Beyond the Chief* greeted visitors to the campus: "FIGHTING ILLINI" (in backward type) "TODAY YOUR HOST IS" followed by the name of a tribe with traditional territories in Illinois, including Peoria, Kickapoo, Myaami, Meskwaki, Kaskaskia, Potawatomi, and six others. Today there are no federally recognized Indian tribes residing in Illinois; nations listed on the panels in *Beyond the Chief* had been relocated to Indian Territory—present-day Oklahoma—and other far-flung places in the nineteenth century.

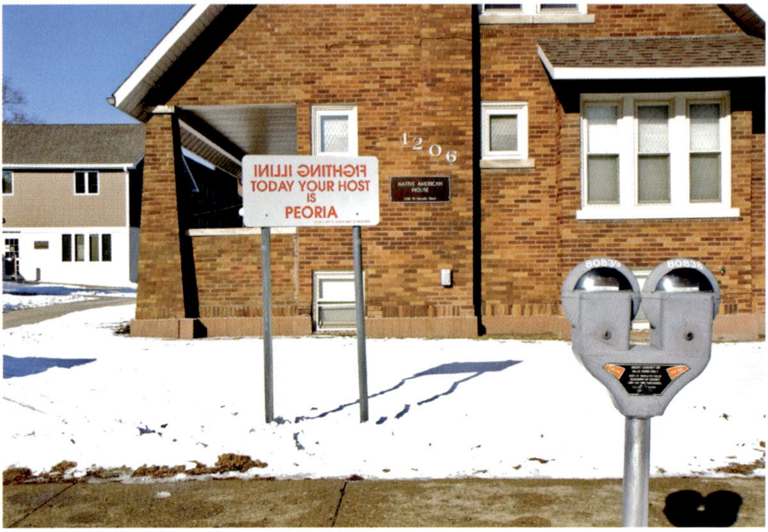

I.1 Edgar Heap of Birds, *Beyond the Chief*, 2009. Twelve commercially printed steel panels, 18 × 36 inches each. Installed at the University of Illinois, Champaign-Urbana. Photo: Durango Mendoza. Artwork © Edgar Heap of Birds. Heap of Birds was invited to create *Beyond the Chief* by the university's American Indian Studies Program, which collaborated with other campus organizations including the African American Cultural Center, La Casa Cultural Latina, Asian American Cultural Center, Department of African American Studies, and Asian American Studies. The installation included panels with text in English, Spanish, and Chinese, with the names of twelve Native tribal nations with traditional territory in what is now the state of Illinois.

Heap of Birds has been an influential presence in the contemporary art world for over three decades. Based in Oklahoma, where he is a professor of Native American studies at the University of Oklahoma, he is sought after as an artist, lecturer, and visiting critic. Since completing his art studies at the University of Kansas, the Tyler School of Art at Temple University in Philadelphia, and the Royal College of Art in London in the late 1970s, he has traveled the world producing site-specific artworks and gallery exhibitions including numerous locations in the United States and Canada; Sydney, Australia; Derry, Northern Ireland; Cape Town, South Africa; and Hong Kong, China. He has participated in major international art exhibitions such as Documenta 8 in Kassel, Germany (1987), and the Fifty-Second Venice Biennale in Venice, Italy (2007). He has maintained a disciplined practice in multiple genres: public art installations, both temporary and permanent, in multiple media; the abstract landscape paintings of his ongoing *Neuf* series; large-scale, text-based drawings; and prints and multiples. Taken as a whole, his body of work comprises a trenchant and thoroughgoing critique of the loss of land and autonomy endured by Native North Americans under the heel of settler colonial expansionism. His art also embodies a distinctly indigenous epistemology as regards place, nation, and identity.[1]

Beyond the Chief exemplifies Heap of Birds's practice in many ways. The sign panels installed throughout the campus were not labeled as artworks. There were no explanatory plaques or didactic text other than the credit line "Hock E Aye Vi Edgar Heap of Birds 2009" at the bottom of each panel. The panels were left to be encountered by passersby, like other official notices and directional signs. Heap of Birds has explained that he intends for his artworks to create a "puncture." His public projects are not explicitly identified as art because, as he explains, he is interested in making psychic inroads before a viewer has time to cordon off the experience as just an artwork. The intervention has already commenced its work as the viewer begins to wonder about the unfamiliar message she has just read. As Heap of Birds explains, "The idea of it being art or not being art . . . well it's too late to worry about that."[2] His works are less a political statement than a platform for discussion; they need to be completed by an engaged public. These unannounced interventions into shared spaces, he hopes, will engender a critical conversation and allow new understanding to emerge.

Heap of Birds first appeared in the contemporary art world alongside a cohort of radical artists such as Elizabeth Sisco, Louis Hock, and David Avalos, who installed advertising placards reading "Welcome to America's Finest Tourist Plantation" on public buses in San Diego during the Super Bowl in January 1988, introducing the issue of labor exploitation in the border city's hospitality industry; or the artist-collective Gran Fury, whose public posters sought to raise awareness of the AIDS crisis in the 1980s. *Welcome to America's Finest Tourist Plantation* played the part of an unlikely local chamber of commerce campaign of truth telling; Gran Fury's well-designed productions appropriated the look of public service announcements in the years before government and the nonprofit sector took action to address the growing epidemic.

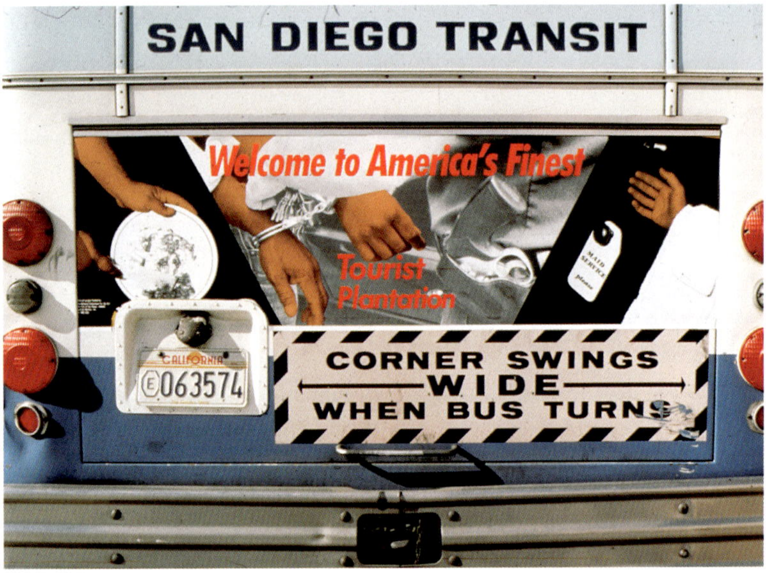

I.2 Elizabeth Sisco, Louis Hock, and David Avalos, *Welcome to America's Finest Tourist Plantation*, commercially silk-screened posters mounted on one hundred San Diego Metropolitan Transit buses, January 4–31, 1988. Photo: Elizabeth Sisco. Sisco, Hock, and Avalos created a site-specific and time-specific public art ambush that exploited the relationship between two notions of public space: physical space (the streets of a city) and informational space (the mass media). As intended, during the month of San Diego's first Super Bowl, the bus posters provoked enough political and media controversy to enable the artists to gain access to informational space and stimulate dialogue and debate about the exploitation of Mexican immigrant labor by the city's tourist industry.

The stern appearance of Heap of Birds's panels masks their subversive intent. His public artworks have avoided the slick look of advertising, instead adopting a bare-bones layout and text set in Helvetica or Avant Garde—typefaces favored by government agencies and other bureaucracies because they convey essential information transparently, without calling attention to their artifice, their presumptiveness. Such objects speak with an authority that appears natural, partaking of the anonymous authority of the state and institutional power that art historian Benjamin Buchloh, describing an earlier generation of conceptual artists, termed the "vernacular of administration."[3] An official-looking sign hails viewers, enlists them

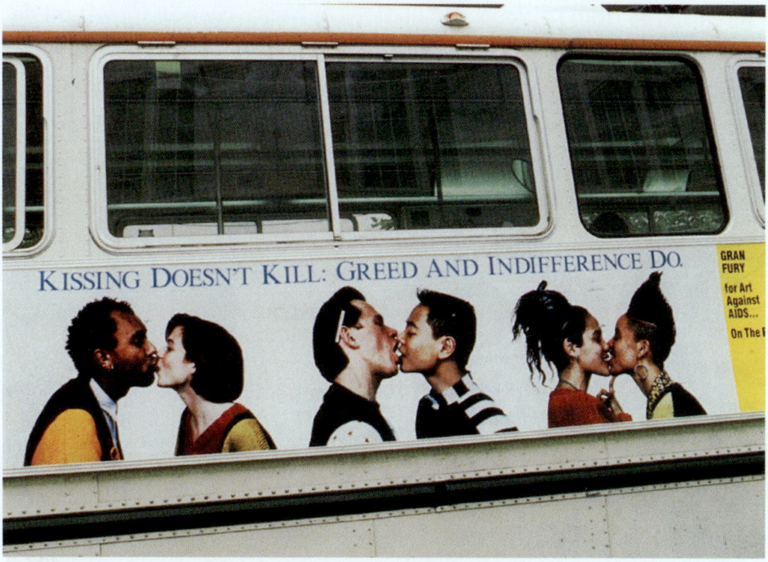

I.3 Gran Fury, *Kissing Doesn't Kill*, 1989. Color postcard, 8½ × 4 inches. Gran Fury Collection, Manuscripts and Archives Division, New York Public Library, Astor, Lenox and Tilden Foundations. Gran Fury's postcard, an easily circulated multiple, depicts the 3 × 12-foot posters that the group installed on buses in New York City, Chicago, and San Francisco.

as obedient subjects. Information presented in this format seems beyond question; signs announce that we are on the campus of the University of Illinois, for example, or that parking is prohibited between the hours of eight and ten in the morning. There is, apparently, no reason to question such simple directives. But whereas institutional signage demands compliance, Heap of Birds's projects aim to provoke critical thinking. As he explains of his choice to assume the mode of official signage: "People tend to believe a sign. I ask them to also learn to question other 'official' signs, which they may see in the future. All signs, laws, and histories are editorials."[4]

Beyond the Chief also exemplifies the serial nature of Heap of Birds's practice. In Illinois, he adapted the format of his ongoing series *Native Hosts*, much as he has produced abstract paintings and text drawings in new situations and varied locations throughout his career. While the formula is spare and simple, unchanging in layout and design, each installation is attentive to its context, requiring time on the ground for research with local informants and other resources and collaborators. *Beyond the*

Chief differed from previous installations of *Native Hosts* in important details. In other locations Heap of Birds has used place names, generally states or provinces—"NEW YORK" or "BRITISH COLUMBIA," always in backward type—to address passersby. In Illinois, in collaboration with students and faculty, Heap of Birds chose to break from this pattern and make an artwork that engaged with the university's recent decision to retire Chief Illiniwek, a costumed performer whose half-time dances in ersatz Plains Indian regalia had made the University of Illinois's Fighting Illini sports teams (named for a powerful regional confederacy of indigenous nations in the upper Mississippi valley) the subject of some controversy.

Heap of Birds's project in Champaign, Illinois, also resonates with what art historian Miwon Kwon has termed "site-oriented" art, in that it operates outside the gallery and art's conventional institutional spaces, outdoors in public spaces. The content of the work merges with the physical site itself—the university and its charged history—revealing voices and perspectives that have been obscured by official public representations.[5] Moreover, this and all of Heap of Birds's public works have been exemplary of what artist Suzanne Lacy has termed "New Genre Public Art," a movement that might best be described as a social interventionist practice, in which artists use varied forms to engage diverse audiences about the meaning and function of shared spaces, and the often turbulent histories of those spaces, as well as the notion of the "public" itself.[6] Hailing passersby as "FIGHTING ILLINI" (backward) implicated all who viewed the piece in the university's troubled culture of sports fandom. The public placement and deliberate address encouraged viewers to think about the complex history of a shared space, as well as their own investment in and attachment to the institution and state.

Addressing the viewer in backward text is one of Heap of Birds's signature artistic strategies (along with his use of commercially printed signage), and it has several effects. Critic Jean Fisher has written that the "use of mirrored English words . . . disrupts legibility, forcing us to relinquish our mastery over language and read it 'otherwise.'"[7] Lucy Lippard locates an indigenous precedent: "The reversed words," she writes, "also recall the historical 'Contraries'—Tsistsistas [Cheyenne] warriors who rode their horses backwards, said hello for goodbye, and washed in the mud."[8] Interestingly, this links an indigenous trickster practice to a warrior tradition—which has relevance for what Heap of Birds calls his "insurgent messages."[9]

For his part, Heap of Birds describes the use of reversed text as an embodiment of an imperative that viewers and readers learn to see and think historically—an injunction against cultural amnesia and forgetting. Indeed, it is not just the address to the viewer—a proxy for the occupying state or offending institution—that is reversed. Heap of Birds's text also reverses expectations. It is commonplace to speak of indigenous peoples in the past tense—as an artifact of a lost culture, denizen of the historical museum—but *Beyond the Chief* is insistent in its use of the present tense: "TODAY YOUR HOST IS POTAWATOMI." Here the *Native Hosts* live beyond the chief, outlasting the obsolete colonial stereotype, demanding recognition and deference. But as the reception of *Beyond the Chief* would demonstrate, not everyone in Champaign was willing to take up Heap of Birds's challenge to think historically. The backward text in this case might be seen as a metaphor for irreconcilable viewpoints.

Heap of Birds's historical imperative links his practice to other contemporary artists who share what art historian Hal Foster has termed "an archival impulse." Foster describes a number of artists, including Thomas Hirschhorn, Tacita Dean, Sam Durant, and others, whose projects since the 1990s have explored historical experiences that have been forgotten or actively suppressed, offering "counter-memories" that might offer salutary "points of departure" in the present.[10] Heap of Birds's projects, including *Beyond the Chief*, which make available a history of indigenous struggles for homeland and sovereignty and provide historical background for a dialogue about the uses of images of Native peoples, might be seen to offer such a point of departure—an occasion for critical conversation about the burden of the past and the power of representation. If the artists Foster describes as embodying an archival impulse have explored alternative histories in a moment when the notion of a shared historical inheritance seems outmoded or reactionary, Heap of Birds's work, which makes use of indigenous knowledge and oral traditions, challenges ideas of what comprises history and who claims the right to define it—what histories matter, as it were.

The controversy over the use of Indian names and images bespeaks a deep divide between Native Americans and non-Native people—a fundamental and incommensurable disagreement about the meaning of history and the right to use and control symbols and Native American heritage. Heap of Birds has argued that "no human being should be identified as

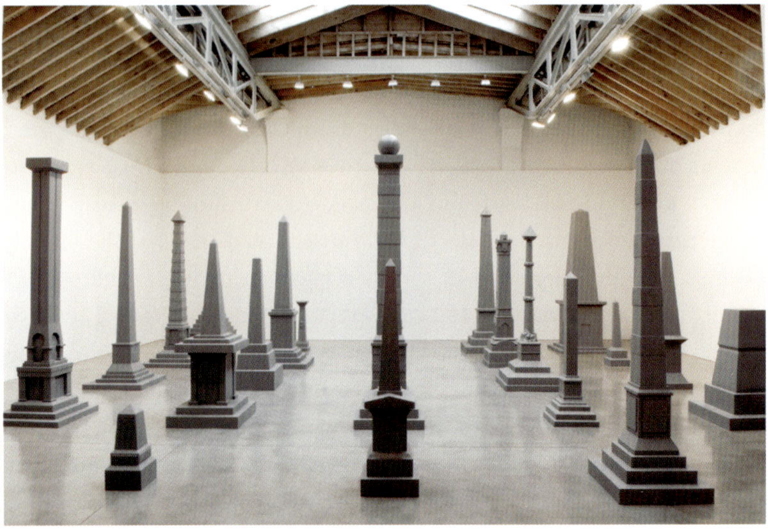

I.4 Sam Durant, *Proposal for White and Indian Dead Monument Transpositions, Washington D.C.*, 2005. Thirty monuments and one architectural model: MDF, fiberglass, foam, enamel, acrylic, basswood, balsa wood, birch veneer, copper. Dimensions variable. Installation view from Paula Cooper Gallery, New York. Artwork © Sam Durant. Courtesy of Paula Cooper Gallery, New York. Collection Los Angeles County Museum of Art. Exemplary of contemporary art's archival impulse, Durant's artwork comprised a proposal to relocate a selection of monuments erected across the United States to commemorate massacres—from the colonization of the Americas to the end of the Indian Wars in 1890—to the National Mall in Washington, DC, making a grim demonstration of the foundational role of violence in American history. Durant noted that the overwhelming majority of the monuments memorialize white deaths, even though the toll for Native people was far greater. In his conceptual proposal for redeploying the historical markers to Washington, DC, Durant planned to separate the memorials to whites from those memorializing Native American dead—a vivid demonstration of the bias inherent in national histories.

subservient to another culture. To be overpowered and manipulated in such a way as to become a team mascot is totally unacceptable."[11] Yet many non-Native sports fans have argued that Native team names such as the Indians or the Braves, logos, and costumed performances are intended not as insults, but as honorific celebrations of America's Indian culture. Indeed, throughout the Midwest and across the country, Native names and other references to indigenous culture and people are an important part of non-Natives' sense of place and history—instilling feelings of rootedness and community for many.

Many other universities, responding to protests by Native American activists and their supporters, had quietly relegated their cartoonish Indian mascots to the dustbin of history. However, the University of Illinois kept Chief Illiniwek on the field until 2007, longer than most of their peer institutions, bowing to pressure from sentimental alumni. (A number of professional sports franchises, including the Kansas City Chiefs, the Washington Redskins, and the Cleveland Indians, have persisted in using Indian mascots and stereotypes, although newspapers in cities including Minneapolis, Portland, Salt Lake City, and Seattle have editorial policies against publishing "Indian" team names, referring instead to the team by city.) The controversy continued to mount; several schools in the Big Ten Conference would no longer allow Illinois's mascot to perform at their home games, and an accreditation report for the university recommended that the chief be retired out of respect for Native Americans who found the image offensive. Ultimately, the university retired the chief—but retained the name Fighting Illini for the sports teams—when faced with increasing public pressure, lost revenues from the athletic programs, and the threat of being banned from conference play.

In creating *Beyond the Chief*, Heap of Birds sought to highlight an authentic, historical indigenous presence in Illinois. When Heap of Birds's panels appeared on campus in the winter of 2009, they touched a nerve that was still quite raw. The panels became targets for multiple incidents of vandalism—they were defaced with permanent marker, the metal bashed and creased at the corners—prompting Heap of Birds to have the panels refabricated with heavier-gauge material. Melissa Merli, writing in the Champaign-Urbana *News-Gazette*, linked the incident to the university's recent retirement of the mascot, and a popular backlash in some quarters. She quoted Heap of Birds's explanation of the artwork and the public re-

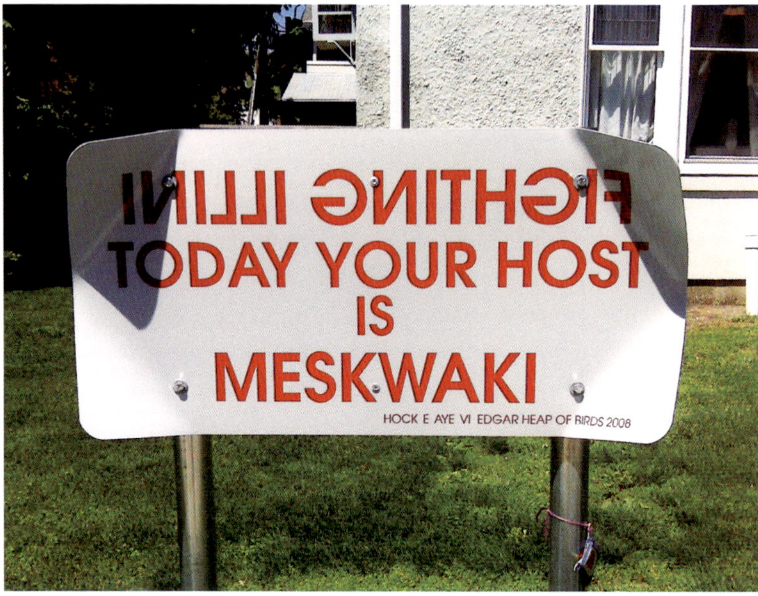

I.5 Edgar Heap of Birds, *Beyond the Chief*. Sign panel defaced in spring 2009. Artwork © Edgar Heap of Birds.

action. "It's really a memorial to the tribes that are gone," the artist said. "People . . . take it as a sort of an affront to the sports team. The signs are self-referential. When natives make memorials to themselves or their losses that's more important than a college mascot or other issue. Everything doesn't have to be about the dominant white culture."[12]

The vandalism revealed a divided campus. Commentators linked the incidents of vandalism to what they described as a climate of racism on campus, citing fraternity parties with ethnic slurs as themes, as well as other incidents of threats and intimidation of minorities. Moreover, Chief Illiniwek managed to linger even after his official retirement in 2007. Diehard fans still brandished chief paraphernalia as a sign of solidarity with the former mascot; their tenacity was taken as an affront by those who struggled to end the use of the chief. Teresa Ramos, a PhD candidate in cultural anthropology at the University of Illinois, penned an editorial critical of the continued appearance of the image after the university's official retirement of the chief, arguing that the "lack of response to the vandalism

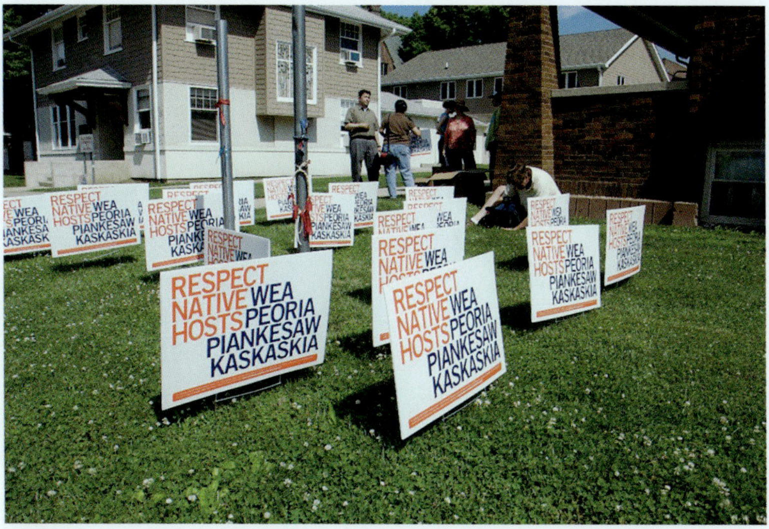

I.6 Yard signs in support of *Beyond the Chief*, 2009. Photo: Sharon Irish.

contributes to a culture of tolerance of racist action." Ramos wrote, "Upper administration's management of these incidents displays similar ethics to CEO's who are more concerned with profit than their responsibility to their clients and the people they serve."[13] Heap of Birds returned for an open campus meeting on Wednesday, April 29. Robert Warrior, the director of the American Indian Studies Program at the university and one of the project's sponsors, was quoted in the *News-Gazette* linking the incident to a larger pattern of institutional racism: "This meeting will provide an opportunity for people on campus to discuss the significance of the recent vandalism and other crimes directed toward American Indians and other people of color in an open forum."[14] But the incidents of vandalism continued unabated in the summer; two panels were stolen in the early morning of Saturday, June 13, 2009. A group of local artists and activists started a campaign, concerned by the lack of a public response from university administrators. The group printed free yard signs with the text "RESPECT NATIVE HOSTS: WEA, PEORIA, PIANKESAW, KASKASKIA," the names of the tribes on four of the damaged panels.[15]

An anonymous tip left on the Crimestoppers hotline led police to a recent graduate who was identified as the early morning thief, but nabbing one vandal did little to repair the rift in the university town that Heap of Birds's artwork—and puncture—revealed. The thief was arraigned on a single misdemeanor (rather than a felony) charge, as the combined value of the two panels was placed at less than $300.[16] Heap of Birds and several supporters voiced concerns that the vandalized artworks were undervalued—appraised only for the cost of their fabrication, rather than as artworks. Previously, a similar installation of twelve *Native Hosts* panels in British Columbia had been valued at $10,000 per panel (for a total of $120,000) by two independent art appraisers.[17] One of the appraisals had been furnished to the Champaign County state's attorney's office. However, state's attorney Julia Rietz disregarded the art appraisal and based her charge on the costs to manufacture the pieces—$88.65 per panel, which Heap of Birds paid to American Logo and Sign, Inc., in Moore, Oklahoma, who produce most of his panels. Of course appraised values of artworks are never based solely on cost of materials and fabrication, but rather on other factors, not least of which is the value of other comparable work by the artist. John McKinn, assistant director of the American Indian Studies Program, interviewed in the *News-Gazette*, linked this latest insult to a climate of institutional racism, and also university officials' ignorance of contemporary art. "We see it as a pattern of behavior of treating American Indians as second-class citizens, both on campus and in the community," McKinn argued. "It's just another attempt to devalue American Indians and their experience. It also speaks to the lack of education we all have for what constitutes art."[18] Travis McDade, writing for the *News-Gazette*, noted that Illinois law considers "fair market value" in determining charges for theft and property destruction and reasoned that perhaps state's attorney Rietz calculated that she could not win a felony conviction: "In central Illinois, in this economy, it's not a stretch to think a jury of local folks would have a hard time believing that what appears to be a collection of street signs could be worth anywhere near six figures." McDade also suggested that if the thief, for example, "had stolen an Anasazi pot or vandalized a Hopi petroglyph, for instance, he would be in real trouble," under the provisions of federal Cultural Heritage Resources Guidelines.[19] For his part, the thief sent a letter to the editor of the *News-Gazette*, in which he apologized for the incident and said he had been drinking and "made an extraordinarily bad decision." He was fined $200, sentenced to one year of court supervision, and ordered to perform one hundred hours of community service and to submit to a substance abuse evaluation. No conviction will appear on his permanent record.[20]

Sharp Rocks

As *Beyond the Chief* illustrates, Heap of Birds's public art practice—grounded in local history and context, critical and at times antagonistic—is also generative of dialogue and engagement. The agonistic and hostile responses to the artwork when it was installed at the University of Illinois revealed a public not merely unprepared for a concept-driven and political art, as John McKinn argued, but also in some quarters unable to fathom the fact of living, contemporary Native people. Heap of Birds's text-based works are insistently in the present tense ("TODAY YOUR HOST IS . . ."), rather than focused on nostalgic representations of Native people in the past—gone and no longer threatening. Native people continue to claim the right to their lands, their cultures, and their images.

While the formal strategies that Heap of Birds employs in his artwork—from text-based conceptual and public works to painterly abstractions—do not draw from indigenous aesthetic traditions, his art continues a warrior tradition specific to the Cheyenne and other Plains peoples.[21] For Heap of Birds, art making is a kind of symbolic or semiotic warfare, undertaken for community protection. Heap of Birds has compared his art to the "sharp rocks" or flint-knapped arrow points that are easily found on the ground of the Cheyenne reservation and elsewhere in North America—physical evidence of historical indigenous presence on the land, and of the struggles to sustain and defend Native homelands. In an early essay, Heap of Birds noted that these "sharp and strong weapons" were used traditionally as weapons by the Cheyenne people. They were instruments of self-defense in warfare against human aggressors, and as "tools of preservation" in the hunt, which brought sustenance to Native communities: "The sharp rocks idea came to me from living out here on the reservation land. I find stone arrowheads hunting as we have arrows within the tribe that are very important throughout our history."[22] In contemporary times, however, the strategies of community protection have shifted from armed resistance to struggles in the symbolic realm. "At this time, the manifestation of our battle has changed," Heap of Birds wrote. "The white-man shall always project himself into our lives using information that is provided by learning institutions and the electronic and print media. . . . Therefore we find that the survival of our people is based upon our use of expressive forms of modern communication. The insurgent messages within these forms must serve as our present day combative tactics."[23]

Native Artist in the Contemporary Art World

To date, Heap of Birds's work has been discussed primarily in relation to Native American art history. Notwithstanding his background and education in mainstream institutions, the situation of Heap of Birds and other Native North American artists resonates with Néstor García Canclini's critique of interpretations of artworks created in sites peripheral to the metropolitan centers of the contemporary art world: "While works created in the centers are looked at as aesthetic deeds, the works of African, Asian, and Latin American artists are typically read as part of their visual culture or cultural heritage."[24] This is somewhat understandable given that his work in large part addresses the experiences of Native North American peoples, and he is best known as a member of a cohort of contemporary Native American artists including Rebecca Belmore, Bob Haozous, Hulleah Tsinhnahjinnie, Jimmie Durham, George Longfish, James Luna, Jaune Quick-to-See Smith, Shelly Niro, and others, who first garnered acclaim in the 1980s and early 1990s, and who were included in a spate of exhibitions mounted in 1992 to counter official quincentennial commemorations of the European discovery of the New World. Moreover, Heap of Birds has spoken of being mentored by Native artists including Blackbear Bosin while growing up in Wichita, Kansas, and he attended Haskell Indian Junior College (now Haskell Indian Nations University) in Lawrence, Kansas, before enrolling at the University of Kansas and pursuing graduate studies in art in Philadelphia and London.

But like other Native American contemporary artists, Heap of Birds has pursued a career in the wider contemporary art world at a key moment in its history. He is a member of a generation of artists who, beginning in the late 1970s and early 1980s, broke from the strictures of late modernism, and who, driven by the social and political movements of the 1960s, pushed beyond formalist explorations to address issues of power and identity. Heap of Birds's works, as art historian W. Jackson Rushing III has noted, "helped define their moment in time."[25] The generation of artists that came of age in the era of pluralist postmodernism—and was influenced by Black Power, the Chicano movement, the American Indian movement, feminism, and gay liberation—produced the multicultural art of the post–civil rights era, a period of contemporary art history that was crystallized in such watershed exhibitions as *The Decade Show: Frameworks of Identity in the 1980s* (mounted in 1990 by the New Museum, the Museum of Contemporary Hispanic Art, and the Studio Museum in Harlem, and in which Heap of Birds was featured) and the controversial 1993 Biennial Exhibition of the Whitney Museum of American Art.

Moreover, since the early 1990s and coinciding with the emergence of a global contemporary art world, critical attention and not a little commercial energy have been expended on a cohort of artists who, as described by the editors of a roundtable published in *Art Journal* in 1998, "travel widely to create and exhibit their work, much of which derives from their experience of homeland, displacement, migration, and exile."[26] Indigenous contemporary artists certainly fit this description, and they have, to an extent, engaged with the new institutions of the transnational art market, exhibiting in venues including the Venice Biennale and pursuing careers as what Miwon Kwon describes as "itinerant artists."[27] Since the late 1990s, new support structures and Native-led critical and curatorial efforts have been launched to advocate for Native artists on the global stage. Yet, with few exceptions, Native artists are absent from most accounts of global contemporary art. Notably, Terry Smith's otherwise expansive classroom textbook *Contemporary Art: World Currents* (2011) fails to address a single Native North American artist.[28] In *Mapping the Americas: The Transnational Politics of Contemporary Native Culture*, Shari M. Huhndorf identifies a similar lack of attention to Native North America in the larger project of cultural studies. Huhndorf argues that this invisibility has the effect of "extending the colonial erasure of indigenous peoples" even as the historical experience of indigenous peoples in North America might otherwise be seen as a key example and implicit critique of imperialism.[29]

A possible explanation for the lack of visibility of Native American artists in the contemporary art world—of their lack of standing vis-à-vis the discourses of contemporary art and contemporaneity—is the lingering stereotype of Native Americans as a people of the past. But perhaps more critical is the failure on the part of the institutions of the art world to engage with issues of land and sovereignty, language and culture, and

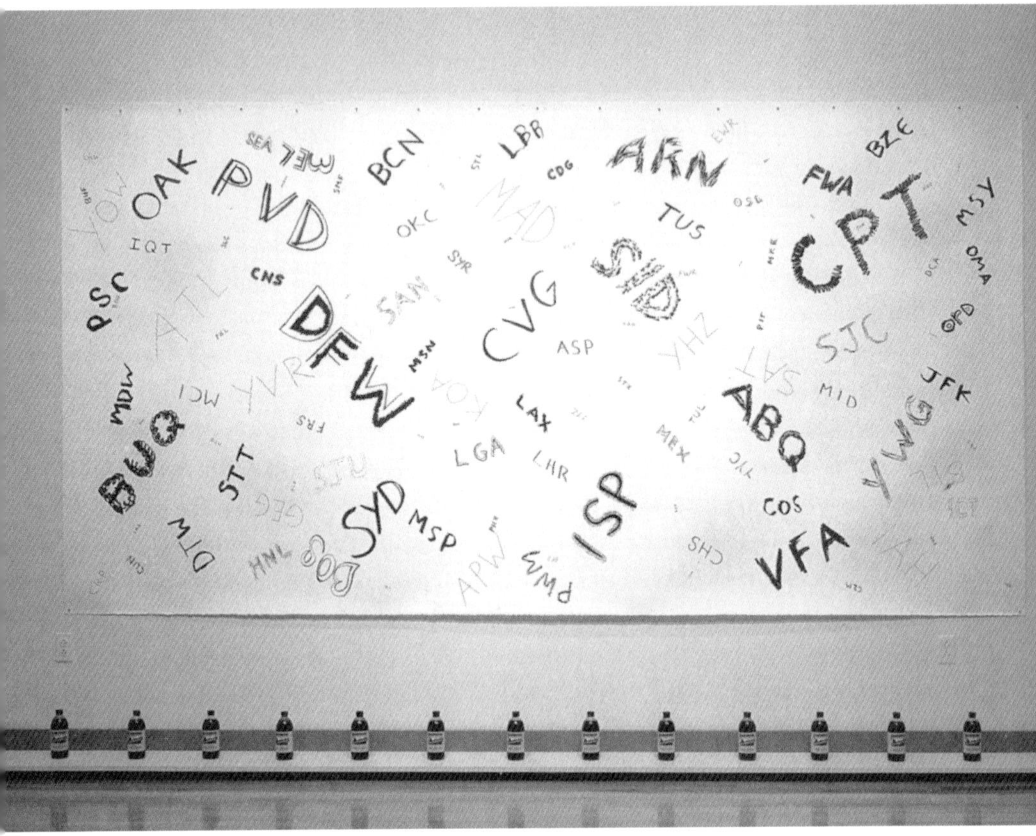

I.7 Edgar Heap of Birds, *CPT*, 2002. Marker on rag paper, 6½ × 13 feet. Artwork © Edgar Heap of Birds. A 2002 text drawing created for *Eagles Speak*, a traveling exhibition mounted in collaboration with indigenous artists from New England and artists from South Africa, Heap of Birds's drawing is an accumulation of the three-character codes for the many international airports through which he has traveled in pursuing his career as an artist. The code CPT stands for Cape Town International Airport in South Africa. For the exhibition, Heap of Birds installed the drawing with bottles of blackstrap molasses, to reference the triangular trade in sugar, rum, and slaves between New England, the Caribbean, and Africa, a previous and far more tragic history of the traffic in human bodies and commodities, which ironically prefigures the global itineraries of contemporary artists.

the burdens of history in terms employed by Native artists. To be sure, Heap of Birds's artwork, like that of his cohort of Native American contemporary artists, needs to be considered in light of indigenous cultures, histories, and epistemologies. The work of indigenous artists and critics such as Jolene Rickard as well as important indigenous writers such as Vine Deloria Jr. and Gerald Vizenor is crucial to understanding his work in this context, and this book is organized thematically to illuminate Heap of Birds's practice in this light.

But just as important is an attention to the work of Native artists vis-à-vis the practice of art today globally, and of the theories and debates that animate the wider contemporary art world. Moreover, such an approach must also recognize the problems of attempting to engage Native artists solely as contemporary artists, that is, in terms of a set of discourses and institutions that have misrepresented and disadvantaged indigenous and other marginalized peoples, even as the art world has sought to open up and redress its past exclusions and erasures. Indeed, one of the challenges faced by Native artists and other artists from marginalized communities is the fact that they have often been accorded only a delimited space within art history and criticism, appearing primarily in museums and galleries devoted solely to Native art, or included in mainstream institutions only in occasional surveys of "multicultural art" or engaging in issues of "primitivism," or in exhibitions such as those mounted in 1992—worthy endeavors, of course, but critical typecasting is inherently damaging. As performance artist James Luna recounted of the attention he received in the build-up to the quincentennial year, "Curators want a certain kind of Indian and a certain kind of Indian art. . . . They want you to be angry, they want you to be talking it up. So when people call me I have to ask 'Why didn't you call me before? You're calling me now, but will you call me in '93?'"[30]

The most relevant question to ask about Heap of Birds's connections to contemporary art—or about the work of any indigenous artist in the contemporary art world—is how his work grapples with those discourses and institutions, and how they are challenged and transformed in his practice. It is not so much a matter of lobbying for Heap of Birds's inclusion in a familiar history—arguing that he too was a participant in key moments and that he too has made works in recognizably contemporary modes and in conversation with contemporary theories of art, although this is certainly true. Rather, as was the challenge for the first generation of feminist art historians writing in the 1970s and 1980s, the question concerns the inherent problems of seeking to add neglected figures to a received canon, which in its structure—its assumptions and key terms—has perpetuated exclusionary habits of thought. Heap of Birds's work, in bringing new perspectives to bear, suggests other key terms for a critical history of contemporary art: an attention to place, land, and sovereignty, which suggests a different take on the contemporary art world's fascination for works that thematize global itinerancy; questions of language and power, which illuminate still-unfolding postcolonial and neocolonial histories; questions of historicity and notions of history (or histories), which should inform current thinking about the meaning of contemporaneity in global context; and a commitment to a notion of renewal, which suggests a different model of futurity from that traditionally associated with artistic modernism, but also distinct from ideas of being-in-the-present that have informed much of the thinking on contemporary art—particularly relational aesthetics or other modes of social practice that currently command critical and institutional attention. In describing a 2009 artwork, *Please the Waters*, which, in part, referenced the spectacular emergency landing of a commercial airliner in the Hudson River near Midtown Manhattan after a flock of Canada geese flew into an engine of the Airbus A320, Heap of Birds has suggested that the downing was a result of "the birds asking the plane to land."[31] US Airways Flight 1549 was brought down, remarkably, without human injury; perhaps this is a metaphor for the present project. Not geese, but another Heap of Birds asks us to ground the plane, rather than add names to the passenger manifest—to reimagine the work of art history and art criticism as platforms for discussion of and across differences.[32]

Renewal

A significant and critical point of difference for engaging with Heap of Birds's work is the degree to which his practice is grounded in Cheyenne ceremony. Heap of Birds has been a participant in the Earth Renewal—or Sun Dance, as it is more commonly known—an annual event undertaken during the summer solstice by Cheyenne and other Plains people. Over the years, Heap of Birds has assumed greater responsibilities within the ceremony, taking on the role of headsman of the Elk Warrior society and, having completed numerous cycles as a dancer, as an instructor for new participants. The philosophy and iconography of the Earth Renewal ceremony resonate throughout Heap of Birds's art in all media—from the repetition of elements in multiples of four, to specific personages such as Lizard and Eagle, to the description of songs and phrases as offerings. His works echo the ceremony's message of the individual's responsibility to the community, land, and universe.

In July 2010, I traveled with my wife, Kelly, to Oklahoma, to be with Edgar and his family as he danced in the annual Earth Renewal on the Cheyenne-Arapaho reservation, thirty miles west of Oklahoma City. Edgar invited me to attend the Earth Renewal ceremony when we first began discussing this book. The ceremony is practiced widely among Plains people, although the Cheyenne may have originated it. They have traditionally referred to the ceremony as the New Life Lodge; the object of the ceremony is to make the world new again each year. The ceremony takes place over four days, during which time participants dance to a cycle of four songs, repeated four times. For the duration of the ceremony, dancers (traditionally male) fast and take no water. The ceremony is a feat of endurance—a sacrifice, even though Cheyenne dancers no longer pierce the skin of their breast as a flesh offering as part of the ordeal. Daytime temperatures can reach one hundred degrees or more; humidity is high, and afternoon thunderstorms are not uncommon in the summer on the Southern Plains. Participants commit to dance each solstice for four years, and at the end of a four-year cycle earn a "paint," a sequence of body adornment in which the dancer embodies an animal spirit or totem, which grants them the right to instruct others in the correct protocols of the ceremony. As the participants dance to renew the earth, they also earn the privilege to maintain and perpetuate the ceremony. The renewal is thus renewed.

Over the course of the ceremony, Kelly and I drove each morning from our hotel in Oklahoma City thirty miles west to Concho, on the Cheyenne-Arapaho reservation north of the historic railroad town of El Reno (and nearby historic Fort Reno) on U.S. Route 81, which follows the old Chisholm Trail, used for cattle drives from Texas, across Indian lands, to railheads in Kansas in the years following the Civil War. Northwest of the tribes' smoke shop and the busy Lucky Star Casino, along Black Kettle Boulevard, we pulled into an open field that is part of the rangeland on which the tribes' herd of bison is grazed, but which serves each year as the campsite for one of three Earth Renewal ceremonies held on the reservation. We were taken aback by the beauty of the setting: a high hilltop surrounded by rolling hills; individual farm plots defined by rows of trees planted as windbreaks; trees growing along Turtle Creek and the Washita River in the distance. The drama of the gathering thunderstorms, which always seemed to skirt the campsite; the breezes which, for the most part, made the hot summer days tolerable and the nights lovely. By day, the buzzing of insects, and the pungent smell of the fire and the sage; at night, in the distance could be seen the lights of houses and farms beyond the casino, and above it all a full moon in a clear sky. At the center of a circular gravel drive rose the lodge, rebuilt each year with freshly felled timbers arranged in a circle—a cosmic diagram linked through the generations to the ancient medicine wheels, marked with stones in the landscape by the ancestors of the Cheyenne and other Plains people. Heap of Birds referred to the lodge as a "spacecraft" or a "time machine" that carried the participants through the universe and through the generations in the course of the ceremony.[33]

Through his participation over many years in the Earth Renewal, Heap of Birds has earned four paints: Cheyenne, Eagle, Lizard, and Deer. These spirits appear regularly in Heap of Birds's work—a clue to how deeply the experience of and commitment to the ceremony inform his art. As we sat with Edgar's family and friends, I was struck by the realization that this ceremony—this place—is at the heart of Edgar's identity as a Cheyenne and as an artist. The Earth Renewal and the reservation ground his sense of himself and inform his practice as a contemporary artist. Heap of Birds has cautioned, "Being indigenous should not be a curious fantasy open to the public."[34] However, it is undeniable that this identity, and the perspective it affords, is foundational to the work that Heap of Birds has created for over three decades.

As a non-Native scholar, my focus for many years has been on writing and teaching about indigenous art, and on modern and contemporary art in terms of intercultural exchanges and multimedia practice. Building on my earlier work, in which I argued that Native American art in the twentieth century was an important story within the histories of American modernism, my initial plan in undertaking a book on Heap of Birds's work was to argue for his place in the history of contemporary art generally, and in particular in terms of developments in the global art world of the 1980s to the present.[35] And while this is very much the case here—and absolutely true to Heap of Birds's career in the contemporary art world—time spent in dialogue with the artist and with his work has led me to write a book that foregrounds Heap of Birds's practice as grounded in Cheyenne spirituality and local indigenous knowledge. I have come to recognize that Heap of Birds's grounding in Cheyenne epistemology—through which he reckons his place in terms of the local and the global, and between past and future—is the crux of his contemporaneity.

Neuf

This book is not a catalogue raisonné—I do not discuss or account for all of Heap of Birds's works. It is not organized chronologically, following his aesthetic evolution as an artist, nor are the chapters based on the media in which he has worked—although readers will learn something about these subjects and many of Heap of Birds's artworks. Instead, I have imagined the chapters in this book as interrelated essays, each of which focuses on themes that cut across Heap of Birds's practice—exploring in detail several of the major bodies of work that he has produced. For readers who are unfamiliar with Heap of Birds's art—or know only a few pieces—I hope the book will introduce a major figure in the contemporary art world and provide an introduction and background to his practice and the commitments that inspire his artworks. For those readers who are well acquainted with Heap of Birds's art, and with other Native American contemporary artists, I hope the book will suggest some new ways of engaging with his important work, in the context of contemporary art, but also in terms of how his practice explores critical ways in which indigenous artists' work can be understood as sharp rocks—weapons for community protection—as well as interventions in the institutions and discourses of the contemporary art world, openings to new and transformative dialogues about the meaning of art in a global culture.

Resonating with the importance of the number four in Cheyenne and other Plains Native cultures, the book comprises four thematic sections addressing the importance of land, language, history, and future generations in Heap of Birds's art. *Neuf*—the Cheyenne word for the number four—is a key concept in Cheyenne culture relating to the four sacred colors, the seasons, or the four directions, and to the process in which a ritual is performed four times, as in the commitment made to undertake the Earth Renewal ceremony for a cycle lasting four years. Neuf resonates throughout

Heap of Birds's practice. Elements appear in multiples of four, linking his diverse works in his varied artistic practice back to the ceremony, to the four directions that define a center and a homeland, and to the renewal of the earth and its inhabitants.

In chapter 1, "Land," I argue that Heap of Birds's art must be seen in the first instance as an expression of his Cheyenne-Arapaho identity and grounding in indigenous conceptions of place and identity. I focus on Heap of Birds's series of abstract *Neuf* paintings in terms of the particular resonance of the landscape for indigenous cultures and for understandings of indigenous sovereignty. I also describe *Native Hosts* and other text-based public art installations that address the history of Native land claims and a deeper view of environmental history, in particular as it relates to indigenous nationhood. Chapter 2, "Words," explores Heap of Birds's development of text-based strategies, such as large-scale wall drawings, prints, and public art installations and "insurgent messages" in relation to the history of conceptual and activist art, as well as to Heap of Birds's critique of the use of language as a weapon of domination—and its potential as a medium of expression and tool of resistance.

Chapter 3, "Histories," takes up a question asked by Heap of Birds in several artworks: "Who owns history?" It explores what his projects suggest about the meaning and power of history, and of competing notions of historicity. A concluding chapter, "Generations," brings the book full circle, as it were, exploring Heap of Birds's commitments—in his art and as grounded by his practice of the Earth Renewal ceremony—to a notion of "new growth," or a sense of time as distinct from Eurocentric historical thinking, investing in the next generations through creative processes that are collaborative and global, as well as insistently local.

This book, then, does foreground the extent to which Heap of Birds's practice is based in a Native way of seeing and being in the world. Rather than following a conventional chronology, the book traces a circular path; it begins with Heap of Birds at home, as a participant in tribal ceremony, then follows his work across multiple media and through the global spaces of the contemporary art world, and returns to the Cheyenne-Arapaho lands in Oklahoma to focus on the artist's commitments to new growth, which are renewed each year. I see this book's underlying narrative structure in terms of a circle, or perhaps a spiral, much as Heap of Birds's work is deliberate in its outward reach—engaging with other histories and senses of time and place—even as it always seeks to return to a place of origin. The book begins with Heap of Birds's profound sense of being-in-the-world, in terms of land, community, and sovereignty, and ends with a consideration of time, history, and futurity—with a practice committed to renewal and grounded, again, in place. This circular motion and concomitant conception of time in terms of a returning, rather than a departure, resonates with Heap of Birds's work as an artist and with indigenous epistemologies and perspectives.

Ceremony, History, and the Contemporary

But the significance of Heap of Birds's practice is not limited to the embodiment and expression of Native perspectives, even as I argue that articulating that mode of seeing and being in the context of the contemporary art world is in itself a radical proposition. Indeed, Heap of Birds's practice makes a puncture in the discourses of contemporary art and contemporaneity, and I hope that this book will make those stakes clear, as his work's engagement with the discourses and spaces of the contemporary art world offers a critical challenge with the potential to transform those institutions and habits of thought. The historical project—the archival impulse—in Heap of Birds's work also links to questions of temporality, which are current in contemporary art practice, as well as art criticism and theory, and the periodization of the contemporary as a historical epoch.[36] Heap of Birds's engagements with history, and with notions of historicity and time as lived and imagined, should be read alongside the work of other artists whose practices since the 1960s have been described by Pamela Lee in terms of a prevailing anxiousness about being-in-time, or the work of Robert Smithson, whose fascination with "continuance" across deep time has been examined by Jennifer Roberts.[37]

Christine Ross, citing the proliferation of "time-based" practices since the 1960s—including performance, site-specific installation, film, video, and emergent media—notes a refutation by contemporary artists of "presentness," or timelessness, as espoused and some would say fetishized in the criticism of Michael Fried and other late modernists. Ross describes what she terms a "temporal turn" in contemporary art, as works in various media thematize "endlessness . . . entropy, ephemerality, repetition, and real time; contingency and randomness . . . slowing down, condensation or acceleration." Moreover, she notes that many artworks since the 1960s have also sought to depict and embody experiences of different temporalities: "the unproductive—unrecognized—times of modernity ('women's time,' the time of the 'other')."[38] With Ross, I argue that this is a crux of contemporary practice, as artists whose experiences and perspectives are formed by and embody nonnormative positionalities (feminists, queer artists, artists of color) express nonnormative (more than merely postmodernist) modes of being-in-time; and these modes foretell a notion that the contemporary (and isn't foretelling an expression of being-out-of-time?) is characterized by "the coexistence of distinct temporalities, of different ways of *being* in time, experienced in the midst of a growing sense that many kinds of time are running out," as Terry Smith writes.[39] For Smith, the contemporary "proliferation of asynchronous temporalities" is a product of relatively recent processes of globalization—largely understood through the discourses of political economy, that is, in terms of market liberalization and technological and communications breakthroughs since the late 1980s.[40] Heap of Birds's works, and those of other artists who articulate "different ways of *being* in time," expand Smith's time horizon for the contemporary into the deep past and into a future understood as a cycle of return and renewal.

This sense of being-in-time from different positionalities raises the stakes of Smith's and other writers' periodizations of the contemporary and of the larger question of contemporaneity—as a mode of being-in-time distinct from modernist notions of time as history, and of postmodernist notions of the end of history. And it is here (deliberately figured as a spatial "here" rather than a historicizing "now"), with the temporal experience of difference—of different temporalities—that I argue the radical potential of Heap of Birds's work in imagining contemporaneity is evident. Heap of Birds's work allows us to imagine the contemporary not (or not only) as a moment of ascendant neoliberalism and always-on individualized connectivity, but in terms of nonnormative positionalities vis-à-vis temporality and historicity. Artists who embody and express these nonnormative positionalities create works of art that are at once repositories of and engagements with collective memories—of sovereignty and displacement, freedom and enslavement, genocide and renewal—and in which the past remains vital and alive in the present, through and across time. The contemporary might be figured as a spiral. Indeed, as Ross writes, contemporary art is "a pivotal site of temporal experimentation," especially to the degree that art history (along with criticism, theory, and curatorial practice) seeks to engage with artists and art traditions that are not, as the tired stereotype would have it, "people without a history," but who express other relationships to temporality and historicity.[41]

My argument here resonates, deliberately on my part, with Keith Moxey's discussion of "heterochrony," or the possibility that there might be multiple temporalities, many different and incommensurable experiences of time. Moxey ruminates on the problem of art historical periodization as the discipline's purview becomes ever more global. Recently, art historians have become aware of the multiple modernisms forged by artists in locations far from the metropolitan centers that have been conventionally seen as privileged sites of artistic foment, recombinant experimentation and innovation, and decisive break with tradition. Recognizing multiple temporalities, Moxey suggests that modernity's clock, which has been assumed to be universal and unidirectional in its linear progress ever forward (to the "end of history" as some theorists of art and political scientists have argued), might not "run at the same speed and density" in all places.[42] Western Europe and the settler states of North America have been decentered, have lost their privileged pride of place vis-à-vis art's histories, and might no longer be seen as the mean or standard time to which all clocks—all chronologies—can be set. Moxey conjectures, "Is the time of modernity the same in London and Johannesburg?"[43] We might also ask the same of the Southern Cheyenne and Arapaho homelands: What time is it here? And what about an artist such as Heap of Birds (or indeed, any number of artists from locations formerly seen as peripheral to art history) who has accessed the temporalities of the contemporary art world yet still keeps his feet firmly grounded in the circular temporalities of indigenous ceremony?

But art historical narratives valorize primacy, and accord status, prestige, and value based on an assumption of history as universal and unidirectional—that while time moves in the same speed and direction everywhere, progress lags in some locations, which are cast as backward, or merely derivative of innovations made in those places that drive history ever forward. Geeta Kapur has pointed to art history's problem with time lag across global spaces, citing temporal differences between Western Europe and South Asia, asking, "When was modernism in Indian art?"[44]

Kapur suggests that terms like "modernism" cannot be the same in all locations. Indeed the historical processes of modernization do not unfold at the same rate across frictionless surfaces, but make uneven progress over uneven ground, or may make idiosyncratic false starts and detours in varied contexts. And of course power matters. As Moxey writes, art historical attempts to account for multiple temporalities—other modernisms—have failed to account for and destabilize historical imbalances and inequalities, and the legacies of unequal power relations in the present. "What are the implications," Moxey asks, "of such unequal power relations for historical narratives? Even if the historical record attempts to interlace the various narratives of global art in an effort to produce a richer tapestry of the past and the present, these threads will inevitably be woven together according to the idiosyncrasies of a particular loom."[45]

Smith's notion of the contemporary describes a congeries of "asynchronous temporalities" that might seem to promise a world in which the legacies of inequality are upended by a "pregnant present," defined by the experience of "multiplicitous complexity," and in which the "*constant experience of radical disjunctures of perception, mismatching ways of seeing and valuing the same world . . . in the jostling contingency of various cultural and social multiplicities* [are] *all thrown together in ways that highlight the fast-growing inequalities within and between them*."[46] But does contemporaneity—the pregnant present—ameliorate the inherent problem of modernity and the exclusionary ways in which the modern and modernism have been historicized? Heralding the contemporary in this way seems very much like diagnosing the present as the end of history, rather than as merely one possible point from which a story about time—and about people, power, and place—might be constructed. Perhaps, Heap of Birds might help us to see, the problem is with history itself, or rather, with modern (read: imperial, colonial) modes of historical imagining and in parochial notions of historicity.

Smith identifies the contemporary in a break with modernist historicism, and the modernist presumption that art—like time—moves ever forward, as exemplified by Clement Greenberg's insistence in 1939 that the role of the avant-garde was to "keep culture *moving*."[47] As Boris Groys has noted, this historicist project was future oriented. "Modern art," Groys writes, "is (or, rather, was) directed towards the future. Being modern means to live in a project, to practice a work in progress."[48] The precise contents of that futurity might have been up for debate—consider the competing utopias proposed by twentieth-century modernisms—but modernism was characterized by what Smith terms a "contract with the future," which contemporary artists have decisively broken.[49] And as Ross writes, contemporary art after the temporal turn "does not seek so much to provide a new content to the future. It doesn't have that type of utopian drive. It rather activates the inconsistencies and vicissitudes of temporal passing to remove the future from its modern role—the role of initiator of change—and make room for the reimagining of the future. The temporal turn is non-progressive: its progressiveness lies in the reconsideration of modern progress."[50]

To be sure, this book is not an attempt to definitively answer the question asked by Smith and others: "What is contemporary art?" However, I do suggest that close attention to Heap of Birds's practice over three decades, and to the work of other Native North American artists, affords a unique purchase on the question. Looking at the question of the contemporary as framed from the perspective of the Earth Renewal lodge in Oklahoma—a position that is marginalized in most accounts of the contemporary art world and art historical narratives generally—suggests the importance of Heap of Birds's practice. But, more important, the view from the Earth Renewal lodge—and recall that Heap of Birds called the lodge a "time machine"—prompts me to argue that the question of the contemporary might be framed differently as different histories and modes of historical thinking, other artists, and nonnormative perspectives are brought to bear. From the perspective of a hilltop in Oklahoma, indigenous thought, a grounded expression of another temporality, might be seen as a compelling example for the present moment's critical investigation of notions of the past, modernity, progress, and the future.

Of course Heap of Birds was trained in and travels among the institutions of the art world. But he did not make the temporal turn out of a sense of modernity's crisis—even though modernity's crises have been felt deeply by indigenous people. Nor is Heap of Birds's practice based in an anxiety about a crisis in art history's narratives, or any narrative of crisis. From the perspective of the Earth Renewal lodge, it becomes clear that his practice is grounded in and embodies an altogether different temporality.

For Heap of Birds, there was no temporal turn but a sense of temporal return, a career-long commitment to Cheyenne cosmology and sense of time and histories as circularities: a spiral that reaches outward and back to the center simultaneously. A practice of renewal and new growth requiring respectful attention to ceremony. Looking outward from a lodge on a hilltop in Oklahoma to the global spaces of the contemporary art world, we might begin a different conversation about the contemporary.

1 LAND

Home Place

Since the early 1980s, Edgar Heap of Birds has produced an ongoing and open-ended series of abstract paintings that he has given the name *Neuf*—the Cheyenne word for the number four, a key concept in Cheyenne culture. Heap of Birds made the first *Neuf* painting around the same time that he became an Earth Renewal participant, as he moved to the reservation to live in his grandmother's cabin on the family property near Geary, in western Oklahoma, which he has called "the old home-place."[1] The first *Neuf* painting was small and completed outdoors—quickly and spontaneously—in acrylic paints on canvas board. Interlocking impasto forms in white, black, and gray play against shapes in shades of green, salmon, and earth tones—a field of related but discrete bodies in which no individual predominates, and which suggests extension beyond the edge of the canvas. While it is, to be sure, an abstract painting, Heap of Birds has described the painting as his response to the rugged canyon that he was coming to know as he lived on the land, taking daily hikes and hunting with his dogs to make a living and find his way as an artist.

For Heap of Birds, the *Neuf* series had a beginning that was insistently local. "I was out in the canyon where my grandmother had built a house," he explains, "about 500 acres of land, and I went hiking and walking a

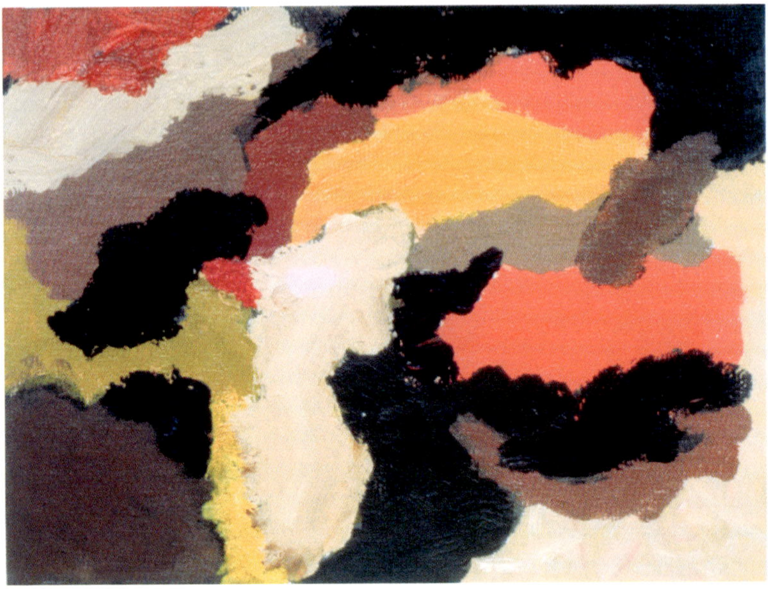

1.1 Edgar Heap of Birds, *Neuf Series #1*, 1981. Acrylic on canvas board, 8 × 10 inches. Artwork © Edgar Heap of Birds.

lot. . . . There was one lone cedar that came up out of an outcropping of rocks where you'd think nothing could survive. I went back out there and took a small 5- by 8-inch canvas and went down into the canyon and made the first *Neuf* painting. . . . It took me six years to realize I was painting this tree."[2] The recurring shapes draw from the landscape, but also Heap of Birds's sense of the land's vital energy: "Events such as water rushing after a storm, cutting the red rock, giving new form to the red earth add a natural energy to my painting, while connecting my work with a visible reality."[3] While the first painting was composed of soft, cloud-like shapes, in later paintings the forms take on jagged edges, similar to the trees that grow on the land, a comparison that Heap of Birds emphasizes in lectures, when he shows a slide of a juniper turned on its side, its serrated outline looking very much like the forms in the paintings. Indeed, for anyone who has experienced firsthand the formidable landscape of the reservation, the *Neuf* paintings will recall its rugged beauty.

Salish-Kootenai artist Jaune Quick-to-See Smith described the depth of attachment to specific landscapes felt by contemporary Native artists in an essay she authored for the 1990 exhibition *Our Land / Ourselves*. She wrote,

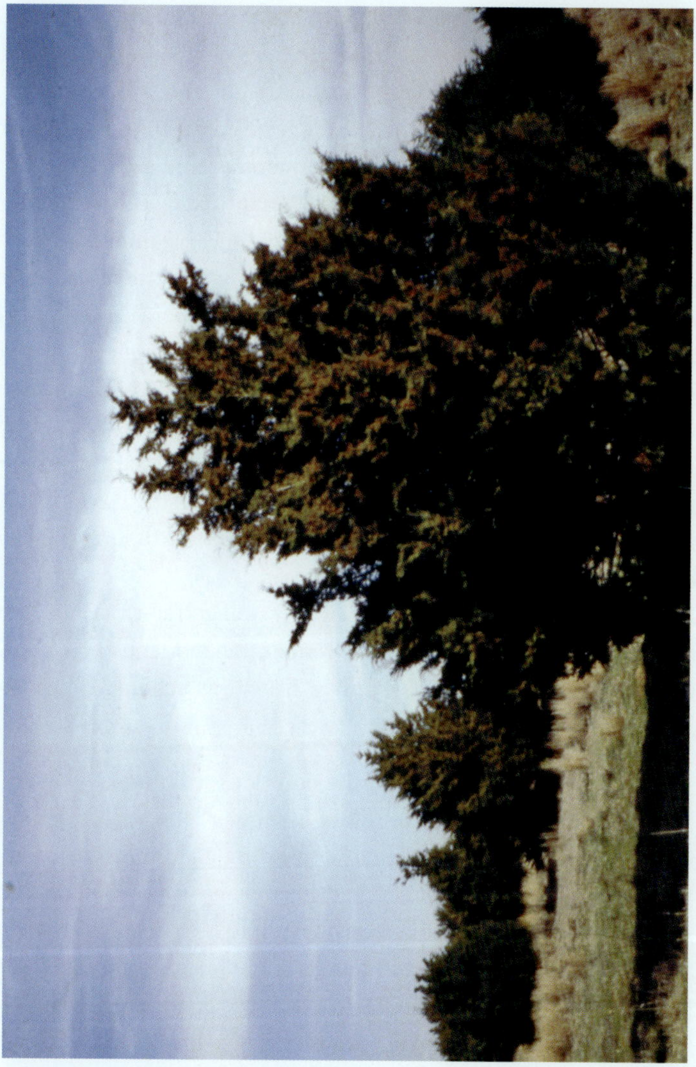

1.2 Juniper tree, Cheyenne-Arapaho Reservation, Oklahoma. Photo: Edgar Heap of Birds.

"Euro-Americans often wonder why the American Indian is so attached to the land. Even after Indians have lived in an urban environment for two generations, they still refer to tribal land as home. This continuum is made tenable by several factors. . . . Each tribe's total culture is immersed in its specific area. Traditional foods, ceremonies and art come from the indigenous plants and animals as well as the land itself. The anthropomorphism of the land spawns the stories and myths. These things are the stuff of culture which keep identity intact."[4] Similarly, Seneca-Tuscarora artist George Longfish has written of "landbase," which he defines in distinction from the European notion of landscape—as in "scenery," or sign of ownership and dominion—as "the interwoven aspects of place, history, culture, physiology, a people and their sense of themselves and their spirituality and how the characteristics of the place are all part of the fabric. When rituals are integrated into the setting through the use of materials and specific places and when religion includes the earth upon which one walks—that is landbase."[5]

Heap of Birds expressed his sense of ancestral and spiritual attachment to the family allotment and the Cheyenne-Arapaho lands in a 2004 interview with geographer Nick Blomley, his words echoing Quick-to-See Smith and Longfish:

> The land is the beginning and the end. It is to humble yourself and know that the land and earth comes first before the people: somewhat like caring for the children first because they are precious, although we are not parents of the land. . . . As someone grows to know certain sites on this earth then it can cradle you, reaffirm you, and offer you a relationship. Also the earth remains after you are gone and was here before one's distant relatives. The earth also is an instrument giving the necessary tools and plants in order to create ceremony.[6]

Land makes ceremony possible, he explained. For Heap of Birds and for the Cheyenne, ceremony is the foundation of identity. But he also emphasized that land "comes first before the people," and "remains after you are gone." Land exceeds human history.

Displacement

This close connection between artist and a specific environment is not surprising to find in the work of Heap of Birds, or any artist for whom indigenous values serve as a grounding. The words "native" and "indigenous" speak to the quality of being rooted in place or country, of being an original inhabitant as opposed to being a settler or immigrant. But it is important to keep in mind that Heap of Birds's artwork is not a passive reflection of a place, but a creative act of what anthropologist Arjun Appadurai terms "the production of locality." The term "production" is key here. Heap of Birds's paintings do not merely express a preexisting sense of place. Rather, the *Neuf* paintings actively produce it—they embody a reciprocal relationship, a process by which a sense of place is created—thus creating local subjects, who in turn contribute to the ongoing process of placemaking. Indigenous cultural practices—like those of many traditional, small-scale societies such as the Cheyenne—are aimed at the production of locality and local subjects. Placemaking is an active process of boundary marking and investment in the local even in an increasingly interconnected world, as Appadurai writes, "under conditions of anxiety and entropy, social wear and flux, ecological uncertainty and cosmic volatility."[7]

Heap of Birds began his practice of art as placemaking in the wake of the Cheyenne experience of colonialism and U.S. Manifest Destiny, and amid unextinguished claims to tribal autonomy and sovereignty. While the work of many global contemporary artists engages with issues of homeland, displacement, migration, and exile, the discourse of sovereignty as employed by Native North Americans is unique. Perhaps the most misunderstood (by non-Natives) notion in Native politics and culture generally, sovereignty in the context of Native people speaks to the claims to political autonomy of indigenous nations five centuries after the European conquest and colonization of the Americas. This abiding autonomy is grounded in a specific, bounded place in which a people reside (or once resided), and which is the basis of a shared cultural inheritance. Native sovereignty is often explained as the product of—or a reciprocal relation to—a territory or homeland, usually arrived at in primordial or legendary times after a protracted period of migration. Homeland is important, even for those peoples whose historical experience has been one of involuntary displacement and relocation; many nations experience emplacement in new lands even as they maintain profound attachments to other, ancestral places.

The Cheyenne (and other Native North American peoples) live each day in the aftermath of a traumatic displacement—but unlike the displacement felt by people living in a diaspora, for whom home might be an ocean away or more distant (and unlike decolonized nations in Africa or elsewhere), indigenous North Americans were displaced by a settler regime, which supplanted and expropriated the native nations. Today, the Southern Cheyenne homeland is thirty-five miles west of Oklahoma City along the north fork of the Canadian River, in what was established by the federal government as Indian Territory. The technical name of these lands, where many of Heap of Birds's family still live and where the Earth Renewal occurs each summer, is the Cheyenne and Arapahoe Tribal Statistical Area, as it is not a reservation created by a treaty with the U.S. government in the conventional sense. This place has been home to the Southern Cheyenne and Arapaho (as they are called in Oklahoma, to distinguish them from their northern kin in Montana and Wyoming, respectively) since 1869, when they were assigned this stretch of rolling hills and rangeland by executive order of President Grant after it became clear that the tribes could not occupy the lands in the Kansas Territory assigned to them by the Medicine Lodge Treaty of 1867.

The Cheyenne are Algonquian-speaking peoples who trace their origins to the Great Lakes region and what is now southeastern Minnesota, where they lived alongside their traditional allies the Arapaho. In historic times, they migrated across the Mississippi and into present-day North and South Dakota. Early adopters of what would become the classic Plains equestrian culture, they ranged widely across the Great Plains and developed a migratory lifestyle based around the seasonal bison hunt. They excelled as middlemen in the trade in fur and hides, building alliances with white traders and Plains nations alike. Later, they fought white incursions into their traditional territory between the Platte and Arkansas Rivers along the Front Range of the Rocky Mountains, in what was called Kansas Territory and which later became the state of Colorado, near present-day Denver and environs.

In 1851, the Cheyenne signed the Fort Laramie Treaty, which negotiated a peace between the United States and the Cheyenne and their allies the Arapaho, and other Plains nations including the Sioux, the Gros Ventre, Mandan, Arikara, Assiniboine, Blackfoot, and Crow. The treaty forbade Indian attacks on U.S. citizens and promised to protect the tribes from depredations by whites, setting boundaries for the Cheyenne territory—encompassing the lands between the North Platte and Arkansas Rivers, bordered on the west by the Front Range of the Rocky Mountains and stretching into present-day western Kansas—and that of the other sovereign signatories. The treaty demanded no cessions of land in what was still considered the "Great American Desert" and included annuity payments to the Cheyenne and other tribes to offset the loss of bison owing to increased white presence in Indian Country, which curtailed the ability of Cheyenne and other Plains nations to pursue their traditional seasonal migrations.

While the authors of the Fort Laramie Treaty hoped to quell the warfare between Plains nations, which had been exacerbated by the increasing numbers of white immigrants and settlers, the treaty did not curtail intertribal violence—particularly between the Cheyenne and their traditional rivals the Pawnee—nor did it curtail skirmishes between the Cheyenne and non-Native overland travelers, which became particularly acute in the wake of the discovery, in 1858, of gold at Pike's Peak. As the pace of white incursions increased, the Cheyenne and Arapaho sought a new treaty to protect their territory and their safety. Land- and gold-hungry whites also agitated for a new treaty to extinguish Indian title in the region.

The Treaty of Fort Wise, signed in 1861 by a delegation of Cheyenne and Arapaho chiefs, ceded most of the land recognized in the Fort Laramie Treaty, maintaining only a parcel along the Arkansas River between the northern boundary of the New Mexico territory and Sand Creek in southeastern Colorado Territory, where government officials hoped the Cheyenne and Arapaho would transition from the nomadic culture of the bison hunt to a life as sedentary agriculturalists. The 1861 reservation was a fraction of the size of the territory recognized in the Fort Laramie Treaty—not open range land, but a tract subdivided into forty-acre agricultural plots; the new agreement was opposed by a majority of the tribes, including the militant Dog Soldiers, who argued that the signatories represented only a minority faction. The militants disavowed the new treaty and continued to live on traditional Cheyenne lands—adjacent to bison migration routes—as defined by the 1851 agreement and attacked travelers making their way to the gold fields of the Rocky Mountains. Also around this time, the Southern Cheyenne and Arapaho Nations became separated from their northern kin—following the fate of the great bison herds that had been separated into distinct northern and southern populations by the new overland routes.

Tensions continued to escalate in Colorado Territory between 1861 and 1864. In the aftermath of the 1862 Sioux Uprising in Minnesota (a topic that Heap of Birds addressed in 1990 with his public artwork *Building Minnesota* in downtown Minneapolis), tensions mounted on the plains. Sioux and Arapaho raids were erroneously blamed on Cheyenne; in Colorado, volunteer cavalry clashed with Cheyenne hunting parties, leading to further retaliation on both sides. But by the fall of 1864, most bands had agreed to settle in designated camps near Fort Lyon under the American flag and the protection of Major General Edward W. Wynkoop. Colorado territorial governor John Evans pursued a policy of separating "friendly" from "hostile" Indians, offering protection to friendlies and waging war on hostiles. Evans succeeded in receiving authorization from the U.S. War Department to activate the Third Colorado Cavalry (originally formed to guard against a feared Confederate invasion) under the warmongering Colonel John Milton Chivington, a veteran of the New Mexico campaign of the U.S. Civil War, a prominent abolitionist, and a former Methodist preacher with political ambitions, then a candidate for Congress. Under Chivington, a military force comprising mostly members of citizens' militias attempted to force the tribes onto the reservation and maintain security along the Overland Route. Hard-liners whipped popular sentiment against the Indians into a frenzy, leading to an all-out war against the Cheyenne and Arapaho. The most notorious episode of the brief Colorado War occurred in 1864, as Chivington led a force of 650 Colorado volunteers to the encampment at Sand Creek of 700 friendly Cheyenne and Arapaho under the leadership of Black Kettle, where they massacred between 70 and 163 Indians, two-thirds of whom were women and children.

Following the deadly rout at Sand Creek, subsequent diplomatic efforts to bring peace to the Great Plains fell short of their mark—the 1865 Treaty of the Little Arkansas and the 1867 Medicine Lodge Treaty failed, as did the humanitarian plans of the post–Civil War Indian Peace Commission, which sought to settle Indians on reservations and provide a means for education in English, Christianity, and the fundamentals of individual landownership and agriculture, in hopes of bringing about the assimilation of Plains peoples into the mainstream. It was hoped, again, that the Cheyenne and Arapaho, relocated from their traditional territories in present-day Colorado and Kansas, where their presence presented an obstacle to overland routes to the west traveled by pioneering whites, would abandon their traditional nomadic culture and take up farming. The peace brokered by the treaties was fragile, however; raiding parties of Southern Cheyenne and other Plains tribes continued to menace white travelers and settlements across a region encompassing present-day western Kansas, southeast Colorado, and northwest Texas. A decade of bloodshed followed.

Military means to putting down the unrest on the Plains arrived in the person of General Philip Henry Sheridan, who, newly installed as commander of the Department of the Missouri, espoused a policy of total war against the nations of the Southern Plains and launched a scorched-earth strategy modeled on General William Tecumseh Sherman's brutal March to the Sea during the Savannah, Georgia, campaign of the U.S. Civil War. To deal with the Indian threat conclusively, Sheridan coordinated a winter 1868 campaign against the Southern Plains nations, including the Cheyenne, to neutralize the tribes when they were vulnerable. Under Sheridan's command, U.S. troops targeted civilians, animals, and the Indians' food supplies. The Cheyenne suffered a staggering defeat in the Washita Massacre in November 1868. (Heap of Birds made a text installation about the Washita Massacre, *Death from the Top*, in 1983.) The massacre took place as the Southern Cheyenne made their way to new reservation lands in Indian Territory (present-day Oklahoma), promised to them by the 1867 Medicine Lodge Treaty. Black Kettle's band of about 250 were the westernmost of the Cheyenne camped along the Washita near present-day Cheyenne, Oklahoma. General George Armstrong Custer's Seventh U.S. Cavalry launched a brutal attack, killing livestock and dogs as well as the encamped Cheyenne. Over one hundred warriors and an unknown number of women and children were killed, although the precise number of casualties remains disputed by historians. Tribal leader Black Kettle—who just days earlier had asked for protection for his people—and his wife were killed. They were shot in the back while attempting to flee the onslaught. The massacre was controversial—the *New York Times* and other papers condemned the army's ruthless tactics—but the killings at Washita signaled the end of the era. While there would be further battles and skirmishes, such as the Red River War of 1874–75, the Cheyenne and their allies the Arapaho would no longer be an independent nation, living free from the domination of the United States.

Sovereignty

The notion of a nation living under the domination of another is unusual, to say the least. ("Domestic dependent nations" was the phrase coined by U.S. Supreme Court chief justice John Marshall, as he explained that the court would decline to rule in the 1831 case brought by the Cherokee Nation against the state of Georgia—an outcome that precipitated the removal of the Cherokee from the state.) However, Native North American conceptions of sovereignty are founded on an altogether different principle than obtains in the modern, European-derived sense of the nation-state. While national autonomy may be a goal held by some, Native sovereignty movements depend on an idea of a people or nationhood that is fundamentally spiritual, rather than legal and political, and which has proven remarkably resilient even in the aftermath of the defeat and displacement suffered by Native peoples in the nineteenth century. A founding figure in Native North American cultural studies, the Sioux theologian and legal scholar Vine Deloria Jr., writing with Clifford Lytle in their important 1984 book *The Nations Within: The Past and Future of American Indian Sovereignty*, explained, "The idea of the people is primarily a religious conception, and with most Indian people it begins somewhere in the primordial mists."[8]

Native conceptions of sovereignty, however, while distinct from the modern European political tradition, have in the course of dealings with the settler nations taken on many aspects of the dominant model. As Deloria and Lytle wrote, "The idea of peoplehood, of nationality, has gradually been transformed over the past two centuries into a new idea, one derived primarily from the European heritage."[9] Influenced by Deloria and Lytle, the Osage intellectual historian Robert Allen Warrior described sovereignty as "a term from European theological and political discourse that finally does little to describe the visions and goals of American Indian communities that seek to retain a discrete identity."[10] However, as Deloria, Lytle, and Warrior demonstrate, the legal construct of sovereignty has been efficacious in contesting illegitimately imposed state authority over Native communities. Warrior concludes, "To simply abandon such terms, though, risks abandoning their abiding force and utility."[11]

More recently, Kahnawáke Mohawk political theorist Taiaiake Alfred, in his book *Peace, Power, Righteousness: An Indigenous Manifesto* (1999), has criticized the Native adoption of sovereignty as a political and legal construct. A veteran of the 1990 Mohawk uprising at Kanasetake (also known as Oka, Quebec, Canada), Alfred described sovereignty as "an inappropriate concept," arguing provocatively that as an artifact of European jurisprudential tradition, sovereignty has no relevance to Native values and fails to fulfill Native spiritual needs. As little more than a zero-sum contest for power, the pursuit of sovereignty reduces Native politicians to mere opposite numbers to non-Native neocolonial bureaucrats. Expedient yet deeply flawed as a model for Native community building, sovereignty is in Alfred's assessment ultimately self-defeating.[12] As the arguments suggest, "sovereignty" is a contested key term. A better term, as Deloria and Lytle suggest, might be "nationality" or "peoplehood," although the term "sovereignty" retains its currency in recent theorizations of Native art and culture.

Tuscarora artist and critic Jolene Rickard was perhaps the earliest to employ the rhetoric of sovereignty in relation to contemporary art.[13] Rickard has been clear, following the earlier work of Deloria and Lytle, Warrior, and Alfred, in arguing that the use of the discourse of sovereignty by Native people has been simultaneously an appropriation and a contestation of the European tradition of the term—an instrument wielded by Native communities in pursuit of "self-defined renewal and resistance."[14] As she writes, "The appropriation of a European notion of sovereignty was a strategy to resist the further dispossession of our land and resources. The idea that Indigenous communities would assert a call for nationhood in our own terms, not as domestic dependents as defined by the U.S. government, is at the center of the sovereignty debate."[15] Significantly for the present study of contemporary art, Rickard tracks the shift away from territorial conceptions of sovereignty to an expanded understanding of the concept as a project of cultural, intellectual, and spiritual autonomy. Sovereignty as it appears in recent writings by Native artists and critics lies beyond the limited scope of the Eurocentric framework that gave the term its original meaning. In part, this shift away from territorial notions of sovereignty may reflect a sense that commitment to specific, bounded places is at odds with the contemporary realities of globalization (in which what Hannah Arendt termed the "national trinity" of "people-territory-state" has been in large part eroded by the tendency of late capitalism to dissolve nations as concrete entities).[16] Nevertheless, Rickard cites Warrior's concept (also informed by Deloria) of "intellectual sovereignty" and the same term as employed by Lenape scholar Joanne Barker, along with other similar projects, as attempts to create "decolonized" methodologies—efforts to wrest disciplinary authority over Native histories, cultures, and identities away from colonial institutions and intellectual traditions.[17] Other recent uses of sovereignty in this expanded sense cited by Rickard include "artistic sovereignty" (Quick-to-See Smith), "cultural sovereignty" (Tewa-Diné filmmaker Beverly Singer), and "visual sovereignty" (Seminole-Muscogee-Diné photographer Hulleah Tsinhnahjinnie).[18] Following Deloria and Lytle, Warrior, and Alfred, these expanded critical projects for Native sovereignty resonate deeply with Native conceptions of nationality and peoplehood that look back to a time and place before the imposition of the European-derived legal and political tradition. They comprise what Rickard terms a "shared ancient imaginary."[19]

Moreover, Rickard argues that sovereignty—in an expanded, aesthetic, intellectual, and cultural sense—is obligatory for interpreting the work of contemporary Native artists: "Sovereignty could serve as an overarching concept for interpreting the interconnected space of the colonial gaze, deconstruction of the colonizing image or text, and Indigeneity."[20] Attention to this "emergent space," she writes, is a critical and theoretical imperative. Indeed, a more complete understanding of indigenous conceptions of sovereignty would help clarify the status of Native artists in the contemporary art world, which has been inattentive in large part to the perspectives on the experience of contemporaneity that indigenous artists—with their unique historical experience of homeland, displacement, migration, exile, and daily life under a neocolonial settler regime—might offer.

Landscapes

Indigenous ideas of—and attachments to—land are complex, and often conflicted. Heap of Birds's series of *Neuf* paintings are, fittingly, unconventional landscapes. Their bold abstraction aside, what distinguishes them from the European tradition of the landscape as it has evolved since the seventeenth century is the absence of a horizon. The horizon line, which figures so prominently in landscape paintings, might as well stand in here for the rationalized system of perspectival rendering that creates the illusion of a view into deep space. The horizon—the point where land meets sky—is the limit of our vision in a landscape painting. It corresponds to the eye-level view of the perceiving subject—the viewer of the painting, who occupies, at least in theory, the same vantage point as the painter, or the imagined individual whose gaze we momentarily inhabit when we look at the painting. From the first *Neuf* painting, made on-site in the canyon, Heap of Birds has pushed the horizon line out of the frame, so that the effect is of being plunged into the canyon—engulfed in an environment—rather than viewing it from a commanding distance.

Scholars in recent years have argued that the techniques of perspective encode an ideology of dominion over the landscape and those that inhabit it. The limit of our vision corresponds to the limit of our domain. Perspective, it is argued, creates a distinction between surveyor and surveyed—between subject and object—a gaze that distances and objectifies, enabling policies of colonial expropriation, territorial expansionism, and wanton environmental devastation. It would take much more space to flesh out this argument, but, suffice to say, the modern, Euro-American acquisitive individual, the argument goes, is constructed by this panoramic view, this fantasy of mastery. Malcolm Andrews, in his history of landscape in European art, writes that such paintings offered a combination of "information and invitation."[21] Art historians have argued for the close connection between the development of landscape as a genre in early modern Europe and the project of colonialism. The geographer Jay Appleton has sought to naturalize such a notion with his "habitat theory," which argues that the aesthetic pleasure we take in a landscape painting derives from "atavistic modes of valuing territorial advantage that were almost instinctive to hunter-gatherer societies. The strategic importance of seeing the hunter's prey or hostile forces without being seen oneself translates naturally into a sense of greater security. Land forms that offer images of prospect and refuge, therefore, satisfy ancient survival needs that are buried deep in the human psyche. An appealing landscape is a single view of aptly disposed prospect-refuge opportunities."[22] Appleton links these features to the "visual field of violence . . . hunting, war, surveillance." Appleton's theory has its limits. There exist other, nonexploitive positions that one might take in relation to the landscape, such as that figured by Heap of Birds.

In this regard, it is significant to note, as Heap of Birds mentioned in a 1992 interview, that his grandmother's cabin does enjoy such a commanding view. "As you saw from the top of our place here," Heap of Birds recounted, "you can see twenty or thirty miles in every direction."[23] Yet, for the *Neuf* paintings, the view that Heap of Birds has sought is from

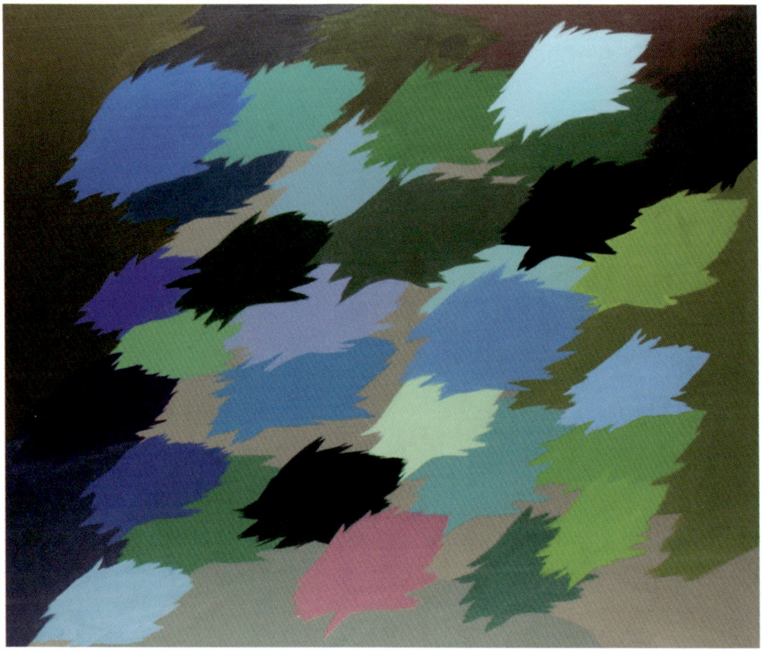

1.3 Edgar Heap of Birds, *Neuf* series, *Nuance of Sky #1*, 2012. Acrylic on canvas, 36 × 44 inches. Artwork © Edgar Heap of Birds. Heap of Birds created four *Neuf* series paintings in shades of blue and green for the exhibition *Nuance of Sky: Edgar Heap of Birds Invites Spirit Objects to Join His Art Practice*, at the Pomona College Museum of Art. This exhibition brought together all aspects of Heap of Birds's practice, including a public artwork, *Native Hosts*, mounted at nearby Pitzer College in conjunction with the exhibition. Heap of Birds's exhibition statement referenced *wougim*, the ceremonial Cheyenne word for the sacred blue of the sky, as well as the name of his youngest son. He wrote, "This precious atmosphere covers the world in protection from harmful rays. It also becomes the serene reflection we see in fresh waters and seas that can create and replenish being. Water is the significant spirit without which no one can exist, now a valuable world commodity and human right. Blue, flowing at our feet and flying above our heads, brings a positive, all-encompassing, life-giving presence in 'Nuance of Sky.'" Edgar Heap of Birds, "Curatorial Statement," *Nuance of Sky: Edgar Heap of Birds Invites Spirit Objects to Join His Art Practice* (Claremont, CA: Pomona College Museum of Art, 2013).

1.4 (*opposite, top*) Edgar Heap of Birds, *Neuf* series, *Nuance of Sky #2*, 2012. Acrylic on canvas, 36 × 44 inches. Artwork © Edgar Heap of Birds.

1.5 (*opposite, bottom*) Edgar Heap of Birds, *Neuf* series, *Nuance of Sky #3*, 2012. Acrylic on canvas, 36 × 44 inches. Artwork © Edgar Heap of Birds.

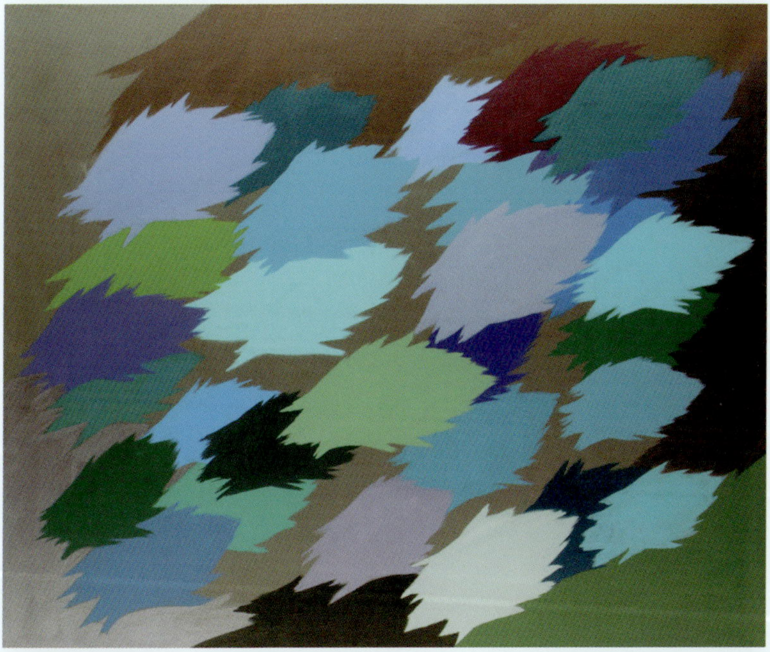

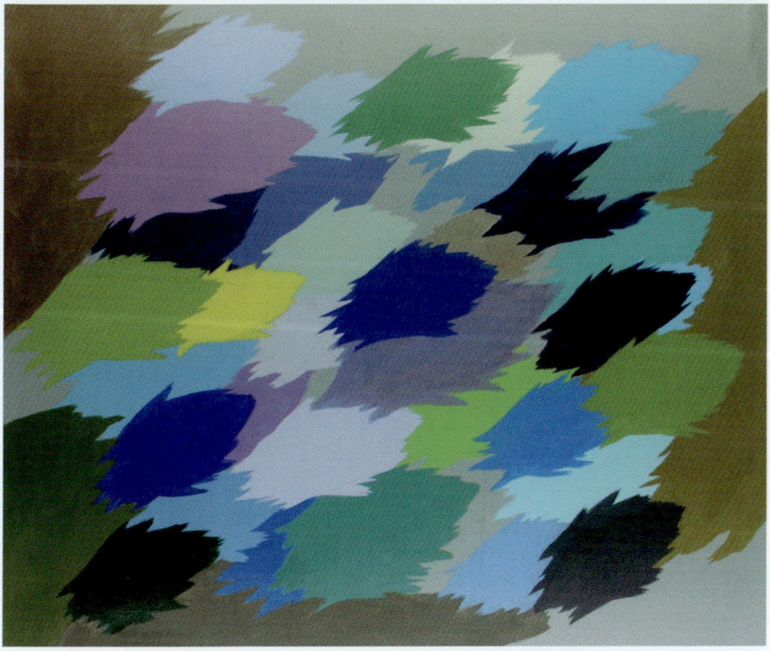

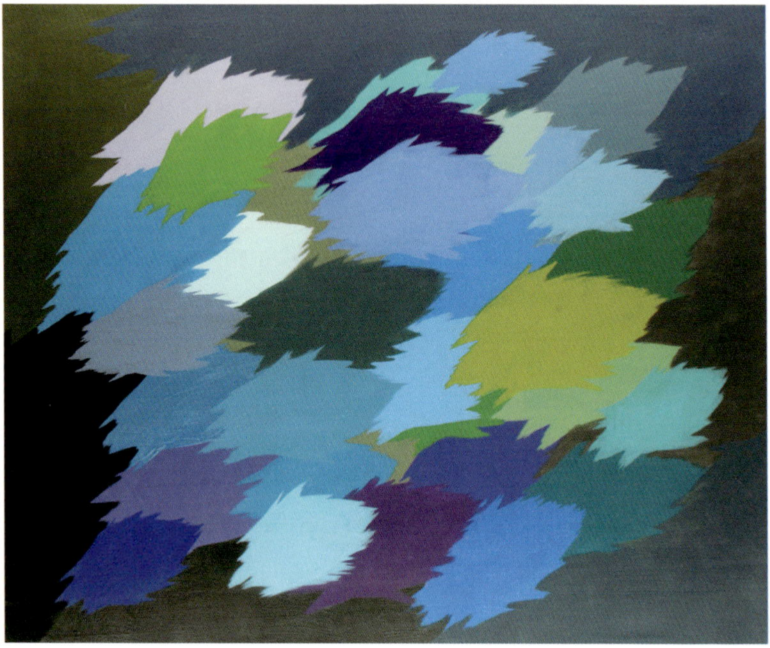

1.6 Edgar Heap of Birds, *Neuf* series, *Nuance of Sky #4*, 2012. Acrylic on canvas, 36 × 44 inches. Artwork © Edgar Heap of Birds.

down in the canyon, with the horizon pushed out of frame—not a gaze that surveys the landscape like a predator, but the view of an inhabitant of that landscape. In a sense, as the horizon line disappears, so does the perceiving subject. Not separate from the landscape, the subject is part of a larger collective of human and nonhuman actors.

Recognizing the landscape as a vital collective and as a set of reciprocities and relations is in turn helpful in understanding sovereignty from a Native, rather than Eurocentric, perspective. Describing practices of visual sovereignty, the Seneca scholar of Native literature and film Michelle Raheja writes, "Native nations prior to European contact theorized about the concept of sovereignty in order to discursively distinguish themselves from the other human, spirit, animal, and inanimate communities surrounding them through performance, songs, stories, dreams, and visual texts such as wampum, pictographs, and tipi drawings."[24] Here, Raheja invokes a tradition of imagining the indigenous nation that predates the imposition of a European notion of the nation as state. For Raheja, sovereignty (and following Deloria and Lytle, a better word to capture this sense might be "peoplehood") is asserted by a human population across and against a field or network of human and nonhuman relationships—from which a nation and an identity are forged. This reading resonates with the idea that most Native peoples' names for themselves translate as "the people," or "the real people." As Deloria and Lytle write, "Tribal names generally reflect the basic idea that these particular people have been chosen from among the various peoples of the universe—including mammals, birds, and reptiles, as well as other humans—to hold a special relationship with the higher powers."[25] We may see this sense of the interrelation between human and nonhuman as embodied in the permeability between human and nonhuman realms that is an important part of many Native worldviews—for example, the nonhuman or "shape-shifting" supernatural personages that figure in many Native spiritual practices and stories of origin. The *Neuf* series pictures such a view of the self and the human community of which it is part as also embedded in a broader network. The landscape is not a thing out there, but a continuous field alive with energy of which the artist is part. There are no edges, no sure footing, no borders. Nevertheless, we will see that Heap of Birds's vision is very much committed to the idea of a bounded, specific space of the family allotment, the reservation, or the tribal nation, which coheres and abides despite the exigencies of history—human and nonhuman—even though it has been uprooted and displaced.

For an artist so well known for his neoconceptual, text-based, and often critical political artworks, it is striking that Heap of Birds has so regularly pursued abstract painting drawn from the experience of landscape. Perhaps because of this fact, some critics have interpreted the *Neuf* series as embodying the artist's commitment to a concept of place that is at odds with the contemporary experience of globalization. They see the *Neuf* paintings as central to understanding the artist's commitment to tradition and emplacement—to being rooted in a specific, bounded homeland. The art historian Charlotte Townsend-Gault, for example, argues that there is "a certain logic to the repetition of the *Neuf* sequence. There are fixed places, there *are* great certainties, everything is *not* relative."[26] Moreover, this sense of being grounded in a fixed place is seen as central to a project that critics have termed "defending the homeland" and "picturing sovereignty," which they argue characterizes Heap of Birds's artistic practice more generally.[27]

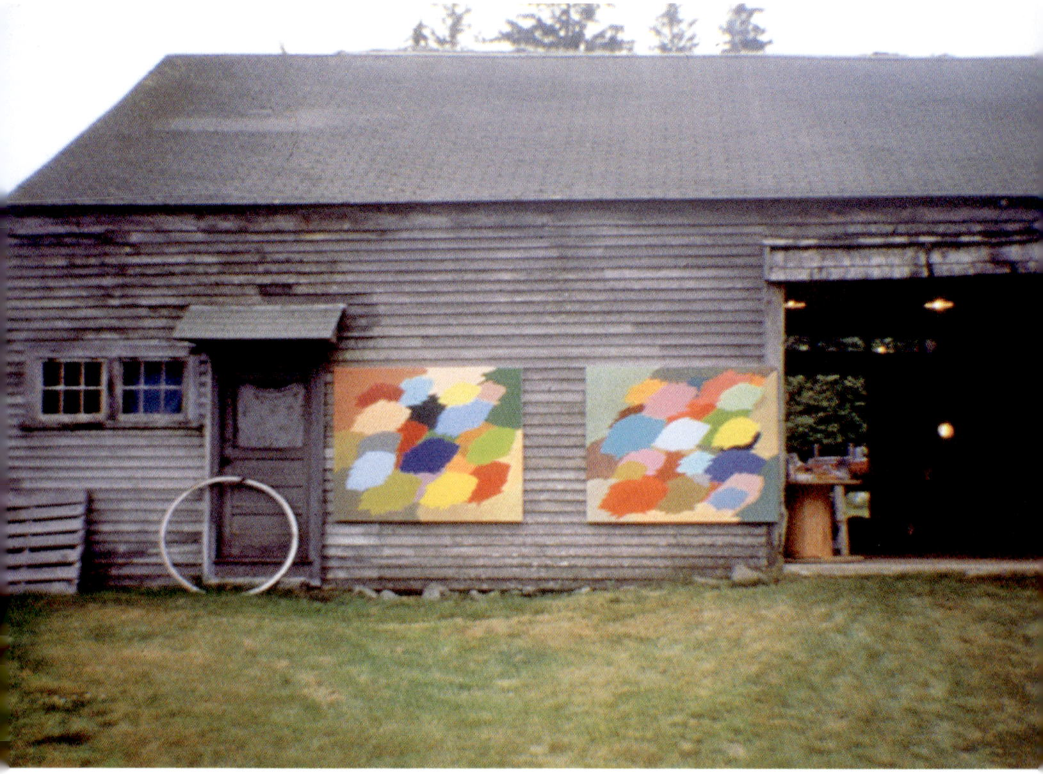

1.7 Edgar Heap of Birds, *Neuf* paintings at Acadia Studio, Bar Harbor, Maine, 1998. Artwork © Edgar Heap of Birds.

However, such readings elide (or perhaps merely fail to recognize) the degree to which the *Neuf* forms have developed into a pictorial language, a flexible artistic syntax that enables Heap of Birds's increasingly global practice. Heap of Birds has continued to make *Neuf* paintings for over three decades. The later paintings have become larger—and perhaps more schematic—as Heap of Birds transformed his initial response to the "old home place" into a repeatable pattern that can be picked up again and again, as an autonomous studio practice, regardless of the artist's location. He has produced *Neuf* paintings "for Arizona" and "for Maine," as well as "for Oklahoma," and in such far-flung sites as Australia. Far from grounding the artist, the *Neuf* series has become a language of shapes that suggest the interchangeability of places and attachments as much as their distinctiveness—a sign of the artist's itinerancy as much as his rootedness.

Heap of Birds explains that the *Neuf* paintings can be made anywhere. Only the first was painted en plein air—on-site. The rest have been painted from memory in the studio, drawn from the first. In a sense, we might see them as portable homelands, a sign for the artist's identity and embodied perception wherever he might be.

Interestingly, Heap of Birds is willing to have the forms read differently for varying audiences—as trees, leaves, clouds, or other forms. After a 1994 artist-residency project in Australia, during which time he snorkeled on the Great Barrier Reef, Heap of Birds began comparing the forms to the bodies of brightly colored tropical fish. The forms are mobile and adaptable. They have also appeared, translated and reimagined, on new surfaces and objects. In 1992, with the Fabric Workshop in Philadelphia, Heap of Birds produced a suite of printed silk scarves featuring the *Neuf* shapes. For a 2007 glass project in Murano, coordinated with his appearance at the Venice Biennale, Heap of Birds reinterpreted the *Neuf* shape as a human figure—the bodies of Native performers who died while traveling in Europe with Buffalo Bill's Wild West show. These translations are also significant in that they transform the *Neuf* shapes into tactile experiences—scarves that can be worn, vases that can be handled. A visual experience becomes physical. Heap of Birds's own embodied perception of the landscape can, in some fashion, become entangled with our own. Notably, Heap of Birds considers the shape to be an optimistic and life-affirming symbol. As he explained, "These . . . painted works seek to project the understanding that the world, as witnessed from the sage, cedar, and red canyon, is a lively and replenishing place."[28] Thus, if the *Neuf* landscapes are an expression of being in, with, and of nature, it makes sense that the shapes can also become tropical fish, among which one swims, and with whom one shares an ocean and an environment. They are optimistic and life affirming, even as they become human bodies in the Venice glassworks, fallen, returning to the earth. They are figures for an idea that self, other, and nature might be mutable, interchangeable, and relational, or even share an identity at some deep level.

Heap of Birds's best-known works have been site specific, engaged with specific places and their histories. The *Neuf* landscape forms respond to new locations, even as they remain the same. The strategy employed in *Native Hosts*, Heap of Birds's ongoing series, is similar. The interventions conform to a standard format, even as he travels to new locations to cre-

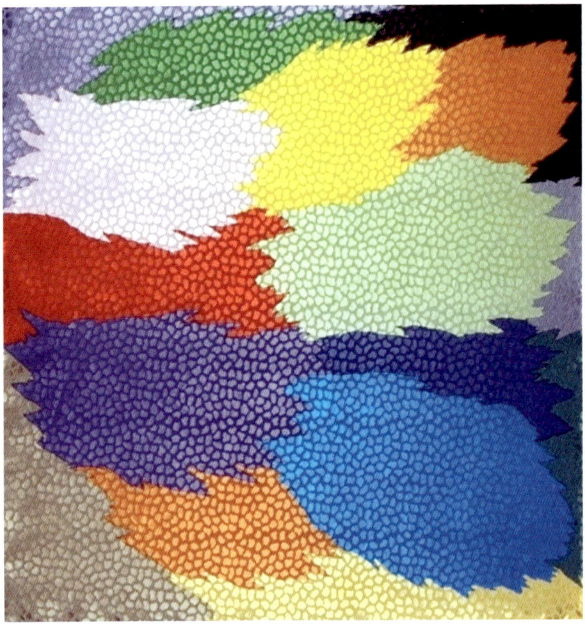

1.8 Edgar Heap of Birds, *Neuf* series scarf, 1992. Acid dyes on silk jacquard, 40 × 40 inches. Artwork © Edgar Heap of Birds.

1.9 Edgar Heap of Birds, *Most Serene Republics, Native Bodies of Remembrance Murano Glass Vases*, 2007. Glass, metal, and organic material, each approximately 31 inches tall. Artwork © Edgar Heap of Birds.

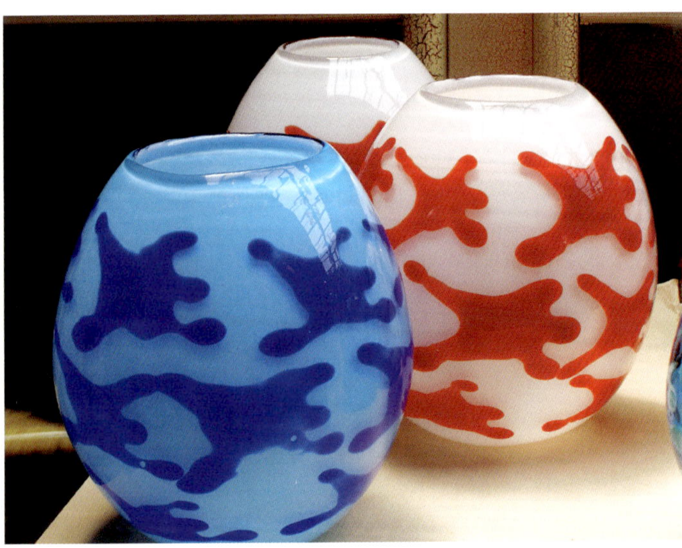

ate new works. In New York City in 1988, commissioned by the Public Art Fund, Heap of Birds installed the first *Native Hosts* project, a suite of six panels for City Hall Park in lower Manhattan (each commercially printed on aluminum in a standard size, as in numerous later works). Droll yet pointed interventions in the public park, the panels announced "NEW YORK [in reversed text] / TODAY YOUR HOST IS Seneca," or one of five other tribes with traditional ties to the land that is now the greater New York area: Shinnecock, Cayuga, Montauk, Mohawk, and Oneida.[29] Since 1988, versions of the work tailored to the local history have been installed in Vancouver (1991 and 2007); Buffalo (1996–98); Norman, Oklahoma (2000); Portland, Oregon (2002); Champaign-Urbana, Illinois (2009); Lansing, Michigan (2009); St. Croix, U.S. Virgin Islands (2011); Claremont, California (2013); and other locations. In each installation, Heap of Birds works with local communities, enlisting them as coauthors of the work, choosing the words for how they should be represented. "I let them talk, or have them help me talk about what they have there," he explained. "I try to respond to what is around me, wherever I go. Although I don't like to speak for another tribe, or handle their issues, often no one asks them to talk. That door needs to be opened."[30]

Interpretations of the *Native Hosts* series have focused primarily on Heap of Birds's use of language. As critic Jean Fisher writes, the series "lays bare the problem of language: the vehicle through which the history and culture of his people were disavowed and redefined. . . . If the law dispossessed the people of their homelands, language continues to disinherit the Native American from the right to speak in her or his own name. Language most clearly demonstrates the unbridgeable distance that exists between Anglo and Indian perceptions of the world."[31] But as Fisher notes, the panels bring together in one space dominant and Native languages. This tactic forces "a confrontation between what are essentially mutually unintelligible words."[32] Also significant, the colonial names of familiar places are reversed. In doing so, Heap-of-Birds's public installations defamiliarize the local setting and inform viewers of the nations that once held aboriginal sovereignty over these lands. As critic Robert Pincus writes, text reversal is "a tidy visual metaphor for the great divide between American Indian history and general American history. Hold the sign up to a mirror and New York would read correctly and everything else would be backward. It's as if Heap of Birds is using English while reminding us it never fully defines his world."[33] Thus, the reversal of place names signals a historical perspective—a looking back—as well as a metaphor for embodied knowledges at mutually incomprehensible cross-purposes. Importantly, Native names are never reversed, and always appear in an insistent and declarative present-tense sentence: "TODAY YOUR HOST IS . . ."

The series also engages with specific places and histories and in this regard might be seen as further evidence of Heap of Birds's affinity with an archival impulse, in that the artworks make available histories that have been obscured or repressed. Moreover, locations and the names of tribal hosts are chosen in collaboration with local stakeholders and Native communities, as are the names used to address non-Native viewers ("New York" in City Hall Park; "Fighting Illini" at the University of Illinois). The basis of each installation design—Heap of Birds's research into local history and work with local collaborators—locates the series in a history of site-specific artworks, as well as with a drive to foreground alternative knowledge and countermemory. In New York, *Native Hosts* was placed near and in dialogue with a monument to Horace Greeley, the founder of the *New York Tribune* and author of the famous slogan of U.S. territorial expansionism and Manifest Destiny: "Go West."

Native Hosts operates by revealing hidden histories of displacement, of ongoing claims to territory, of sovereignty lost, stolen, reclaimed, and regained, and to the traumatic relationship of Native peoples to land in North America. However, what has remained unremarked is that these works have also modeled an ethics—a protocol, a form of diplomacy, and an appropriate way of being a visitor in a foreign territory. They represent an indigenous perspective, in which relations between peoples are relations between sovereign equals—whether as allies or enemies—by acknowledging those with a claim to a particular place in their language, and in the name they give themselves.

Indigenizing Urban Spaces

In addition to creating his ongoing series recognizing and reclaiming Native lands, Heap of Birds has also created public artworks that foreground the historical experience of displacement and homelands lost by Native peoples. In 1989, *Apartheid Oklahoma* marked the one-hundred-year anniversary of the 1889 Oklahoma Land Run, which opened the territory

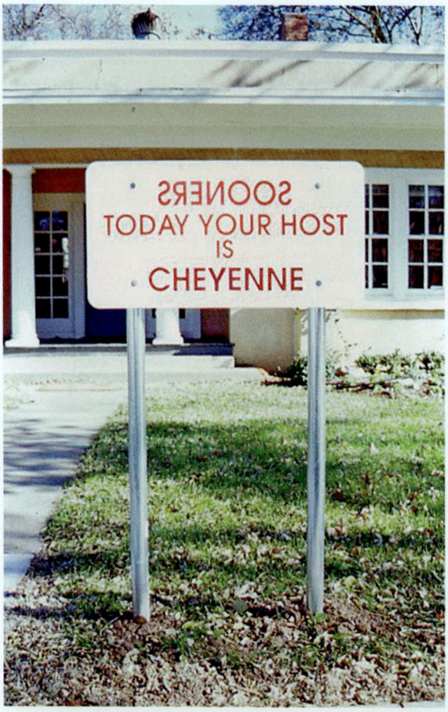

1.10 Edgar Heap of Birds, *Native Hosts* series, 2000. Steel panel, 24 × 36 inches. Artwork © Edgar Heap of Birds. *Native Hosts* installed in Norman, Oklahoma.

1.11 Edgar Heap of Birds, *Native Hosts* series, 2011. Steel panel, 24 × 36 inches. Artwork © Edgar Heap of Birds. Patricia Swan, faculty at the Good Hope School, poses next to Heap of Birds's artwork in St. Croix, U.S. Virgin Islands.

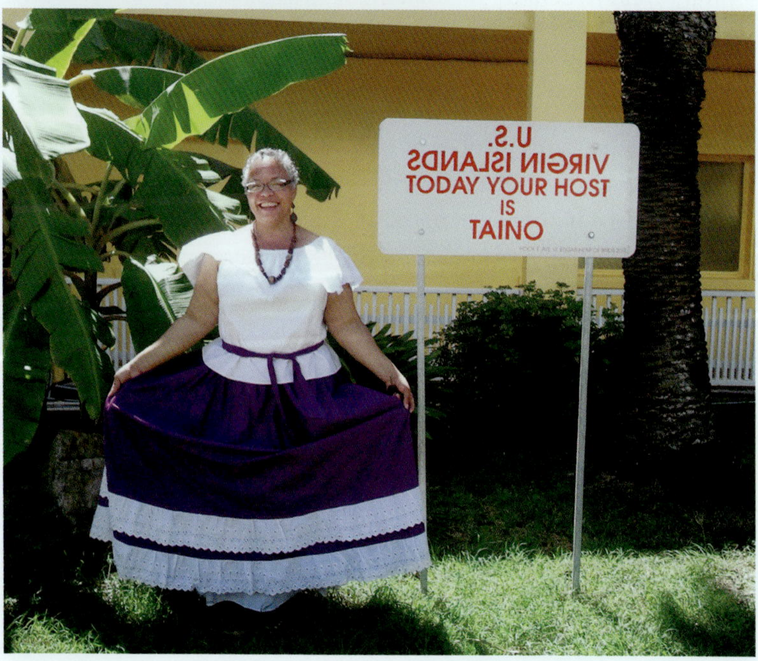

to white settlement on prime lands ceded to the U.S. government by the Creek (Muscogee) and Seminole Nations—lands onto which these displaced Southeastern tribes had been relocated by the Indian Removal Act just five decades earlier in 1830. Heap of Birds's artwork consisted of five billboards installed throughout Norman and Oklahoma City, Oklahoma, in solidarity with a protest march by Native American activists and supporters, staged in opposition to official celebrations of the centennial. The billboards, in red text on a white background, read:

> SOONERS [printed backward, as in *Native Hosts*]
> RUN OVER
> INDIAN NATIONS
> APARTHEID OKLAHOMA

In his description of the work in the *Claim Your Color* exhibition catalog, Heap of Birds wrote:

> The non-Indian citizens of Oklahoma commemorate the land-run by celebrating the beginning of the seizure of over 30 Indian reservations in 1889, from what was mandated by the U.S. congress as *Indian Territory*.
>
> From this celebration, now promoted as the birth of the white state, we can truly understand the festivities as a blatantly offensive act on the part of the so-called "Sooners" and their insensitive pioneer spirit.

Noting that the Native nations of Oklahoma had been "forced to Indian territory as refugees," Heap of Birds argued, "To recall those grave days in the form of a statewide joyous observance, i.e., picnics, parades, carnivals and playground programs for school-age students, is a disgrace. . . . The exercises in racism and cover-ups of true 'American' history must be answered."[34] *Apartheid Oklahoma* did just that; the billboards were an act of guerrilla public history. In his essay "Insurgent Messages for America" (1986), he wrote, "As in today's South Africa, the United States of America jointly dominated their Native hosts by establishing reserves and relocating the indigenous people for the profits and pleasures of the dominant white culture."[35] Heap of Birds's project linked the creation of the modern state of Oklahoma out of what had earlier been created by federal policy as Indian Territory, the mandated new home of the displaced Native nations of the Southeast and Great Plains, to the white minority apartheid regime

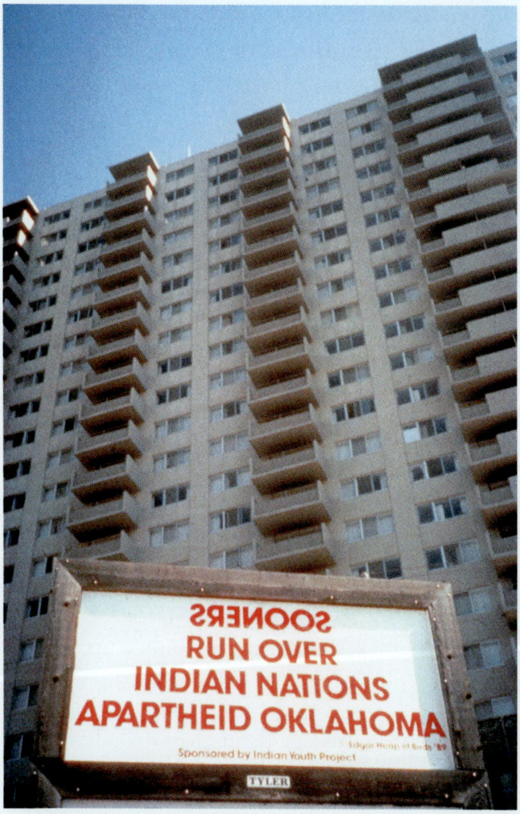

1.12 Edgar Heap of Birds, *Apartheid Oklahoma*, 1989. Five billboards, each 5 × 9 feet. Installed throughout Norman and Oklahoma City, Oklahoma. Artwork © Edgar Heap of Birds.

of South Africa (still clinging to power when Heap of Birds designed and installed his billboards).

Day/Night, installed in Pioneer Square, Seattle, memorialized Chief Seattle (Sealth, Seathl, or See-ahth, c. 1786–1866), a leader of the Suquamish and Duwamish Native American tribes in present-day Washington State. Heap of Birds told an interviewer that when he received the commission, he knew immediately that he "wanted to do something for the chief."[36] The artwork, however, also commemorates the displaced Native peoples who have lived and died in urban ghettos such as Seattle, a destination for many Native people who left their poverty-stricken reservations in the decades after World War II in search of a better life in the cities of the Midwest and West. Flanking an existing bronze portrait bust of Chief Seattle—made by artist James Wehn and erected by city leaders in 1909—Heap of Birds placed two porcelain-glazed steel panels, with text in English and Lushootseed, a local, indigenous language. Heap of Birds's text, "FAR AWAY BROTHERS AND SISTERS WE STILL REMEMBER YOU / CHIEF SEATTLE NOW THE STREETS ARE OUR HOME," floating in a disorienting field of dollar signs and Christian crosses, or surrounded by abstract forms from the *Neuf* paintings, speaks to the deep and powerful connections to traditional communities and indigenous senses of place still felt by contemporary urban Indians, for whom the streets are home. Heap of Birds wanted to bring attention to the living Native people who were all but invisible to the tourists who regularly visited Pioneer Square to be photographed next to the Chief Seattle statue.[37]

Heap of Birds's artwork was originally commissioned as part of *In Public*, a festival of new genre public art in 1991. Funded by local percent for art provisions (which stipulated a percentage of the total construction budget for large civic projects be set aside to fund public artworks), the Seattle Art Museum, Seattle City Light, and grants from the Virginia Wright Fund and the National Endowment for the Arts, *In Public* was to include twenty-five projects, including works by Barbara Kruger, Daniel Joseph Martinez, Jonathan Borofsky, General Idea, Martha Rosler, Gary Hill, Buster Simpson, and others. A number of works by local and international artists including Chris Burden, Ilya Kabakov, Choi Jae-Eun, Tatsu Miyama, Louise Lawler, Cildo Meireles, Lorna Simpson, and David Hammons were rejected or canceled, owing to public controversy—or rather, worry about public controversy—as a number of works did address social and political issues in strident tones. Martinez installed a series of seventy-nine black-and-white banners on light posts throughout central Seattle asking provocative questions—"Did you attend private school? Was it Ivy League?"; "Do you know anyone who can't read or write?"; "Are you healthy?"; "Are your teeth straight?"; and "Are you too poor to see a doctor?"—sparking a public conversation about economic inequality in the gentrifying urban core. Other works, including David Hammons's proposed "piss shields," deployed to protect city sites from urination, and a photo lightbox by Jeff Wall depicting teenagers and graffiti, proved too provocative for festival sponsors and organizers. In response to the rash of canceled projects, the

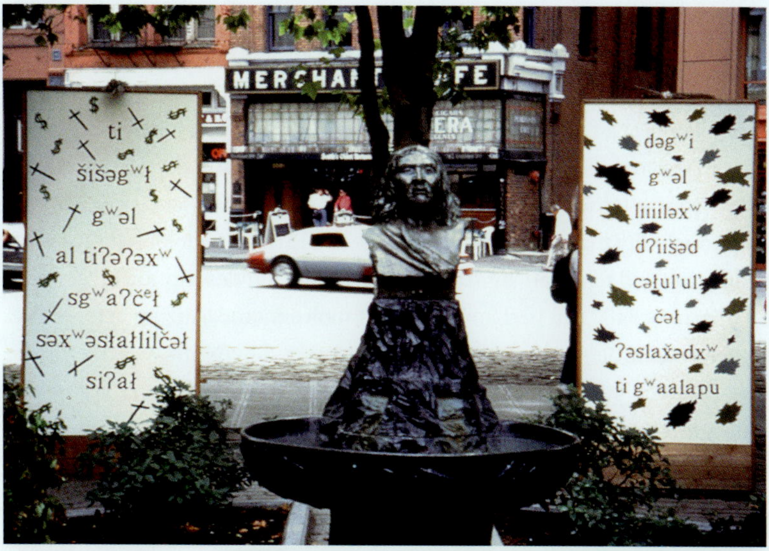

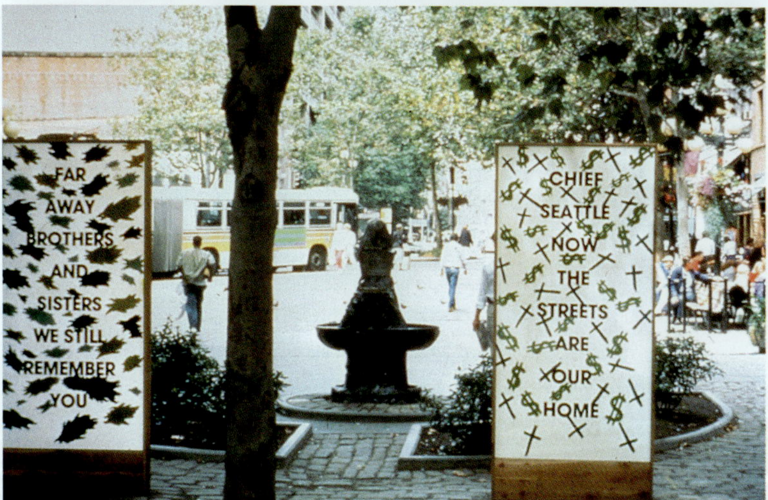

1.13 Edgar Heap of Birds, *Day/Night*, 1991. Seattle, Washington. Front view. Artwork © Edgar Heap of Birds. *Day/Night* took its title from Chief Seattle's famous (and probably apocryphal) Treaty Oration of 1854, which contained the line "Day and night cannot dwell together. The Red Man has ever fled the approach of the White Man, as the morning mist flees before the morning sun."

1.14 Edgar Heap of Birds, *Day/Night*, 1991. Seattle, Washington. Back view. Artwork © Edgar Heap of Birds.

artists' collective Group Material published a series of public service announcements in the *Seattle Post-Intelligencer*, addressing issues such as censorship, obscenity, and art.[38]

Speaking at a 1991 symposium at the University of Washington on public art and the artist's role in society, Heap of Birds explained that his artwork drew from a legacy of making art to address pressing social concerns—a responsibility that he argued tribal artists had always shouldered. "Art is for protection and renewal," he said, echoing his earlier description of artworks as "sharp rocks."[39] But perhaps because it took a memorializing perspective, rather than a blatantly confrontational stance, *Day/Night* was one of the best-received artworks in the festival. *Seattle Post-Intelligencer* columnist David Horsey had worried that political statements in and of themselves might not constitute great art. "I expected not to like this one," Horsey wrote of *Day/Night*. "Amid the human wreckage congregating around the Pioneer Square pergola, it seemed that it would be redundant to point out the tragic circumstances of some of Chief Seattle's tribal descendants. But, instead, the panels stand like exclamation points amid the living proof of their indictment."[40] The work was met by an audience ready to accept its message. Unlike most of the other projects created for *In Public*, *Day/Night* remained in place. Heap of Birds's intended temporary intervention—designed to briefly provide a new critical context for Wehn's statue—was embraced by the city. Local homeless vowed to protect the panels from harm. In 1998, the Seattle Arts Commission voted to purchase the installation, making Heap of Birds's powerful and popular work permanent.

In the context of the other works created for *In Public*, Heap of Birds's project spoke to contemporary urban poverty and issues of uneven development. But references to the historical Chief Seattle and histories of displaced nations, as well as the use of a text in Lushootseed, links *Day/Night* to his other text-based and public history projects. As in *Native Hosts*, *Day/Night* reinserts an indigenous presence in contemporary urban spaces—reminding passersby that the cities of North America were built on Native lands. As such, *Native Hosts*, *Apartheid Oklahoma*, *Day/Night*, and other public projects are works that seek to bring history into focus—in spaces where the experience of indigenous people has been repressed, where the historical fact of the conquest and colonization of the Americas has been forgotten, even as the descendants of Chief Seattle and other tribal nations persevere in a changed landscape.

Landscape's Obligations

Heap of Birds's works have also brought an environmental focus to bear on the topic of land in the Americas and the aftermath of colonialism. *In Memory of Rainforest*, a series of text prints published in the literary journal *Caliban* in 1990, shares with the *Neuf* paintings a sense of the landscape as an interconnected community in which ambitions and desires that play out in the developed North have hemispheric ramifications. Like *Apartheid Oklahoma*, *In Memory of Rainforest* uses telegraphic series of four-line statements that link the local to the global—and human actions to their effects on nonhuman nature:

BURNING
DEBT
BURNING
BURGERS

FOOD
FOR THE
BRICK
PRICK

THE
LIZARD
FEEDS
U.S.

Heap of Birds's parable-like artist statement described "towering penises built of stone and brick" that inhabited "larger communities called cities." Heap of Birds continued, "Housed within the male-organs were men with suits and ties and women in skirts and blouses with business bows." To "satisfy the pricks" required a steady stream of resources, so the silo-like pricks tilted their heads toward the south—toward the "continent located on the still fertile underside of the earth" where "animals that had always been residents of this southern world sought to share the foods of the environment with the indigenous tribes and a few visitors that were newly present." The lizard (a recurrent character in Heap of Birds's work—a stand-in for indigeneity and a key personage in the Cheyenne Earth Renewal ceremony) has already endured "trials of land, sea, and sky."

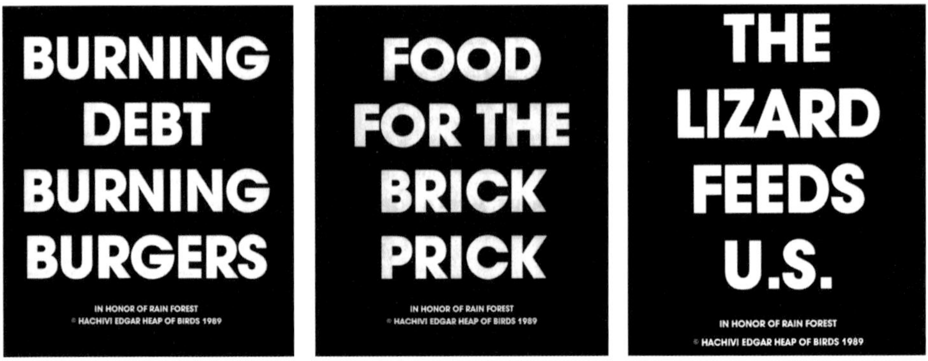

1.15 Edgar Heap of Birds, *In Memory of Rainforest*, 1989. Three serigraph prints, each 36 × 40 inches. Artwork © Edgar Heap of Birds.

Here, the lizard is a figure for the global South. As Heap of Birds explained, "The southern world strains to live through the most brutal challenge of all—a northern demand for more dollars." He concluded that it is an "outrage" to allow the "hungry heads to devour the flesh of the world, its rain forests."[41] W. Jackson Rushing III has written, "Engaged viewers or readers are obliged to unravel the complex web of political and economic relationships that make consumers throughout the world part of the problem of, and therefore part of the solution to, the ever-growing ecological disaster in the Amazon."[42] Burgers are a metaphor for banal desires, but they are also a very real factor in a world system that depends on geographically uneven economic development; complacent consumers are complicit with the "pricks" responsible for the expropriation of resources, deforestation, and other environmental disasters.

These are all landscapes, but in a broader sense than that generally suggested by the term—a conventional view into perspectival space that offers, as Andrews wrote, a combination of "information and invitation." Heap of Birds's landscapes offer information and invitation of another sort; they express a depth of attachment and affinity to specific places, and also offer insights into the complicated experience, history, and memory of places—landscape not as a stock of resources over which one claims dominion, but as actor and agent to which one recognizes certain obligations. In these works Heap of Birds models a kind of ethics, such as that invoked by philosopher Kwame Anthony Appiah's attempt to revitalize a notion of cosmopolitanism, which he defines as an "ethics in a world of strangers."

Appiah avers that this ideal demands that we recognize "obligations to others [that] stretch beyond those to whom we are related by ties of kith and kin, or even the more formal ties of a shared citizenship."[43] But we might ask, prompted by Heap of Birds's art, if our notion of ethics should be extended to the landscape itself and its inhabitants—to the lizard that "feeds U.S."—to those nonhuman agents that ecological writer Timothy Morton has termed "strange strangers."[44] Heap of Birds's art expresses an ethics of landscape, of which the human community is part. Moreover, an ethics of landscape—landscape as a set of reciprocities and relations—resonates with indigenous notions of sovereignty, place, and identity—landscape as a vital collective. Heap of Birds's art has explored and given form to these ideas for over three decades.

In *Please the Waters*, Heap of Birds narrated a history of the Hudson River valley in the four hundred years since Henry Hudson, in the employ of the Dutch East India Company, navigated the waterway in search of the fabled Northwest Passage to the Far East.[45] *Please the Waters*, comprising eight twenty-four-by-thirty-six-inch commercially printed steel panels (as well as a suite of preparatory text drawings) was part of the exhibition *The Muhheakantuck in Focus*, installed in 2009 at Wave Hill, a contemporary art center and public garden on twenty-eight acres overlooking the Hudson River with picturesque views of the New Jersey Palisades. The organizers cast the exhibition as concerned principally with the significance of the river for Native peoples. Collectively, as curator Jennifer McGregor wrote, the artworks in the exhibition "explore[d] the significance of the waterway to Indigenous peoples before and after Hudson's arrival." The river, McGregor wrote, "provided both a connective route for the Indigenous people and a conduit for launching European trade and expansion beyond the region, ultimately impacting the entire continent."[46] The exhibition took its title from the word for the waterway used by the Lenape (or Delaware Indians) who traditionally occupied lands between the Delaware River and the lower Hudson River—encompassing present-day New Jersey, eastern Pennsylvania, northern Delaware, and southeastern New York State before their displacement by Iroquoian rivals and encroaching white settlers in the nineteenth century. In Lenape, the Muhheakantuck is the "river that flows two ways," as the Hudson is in fact a salty, tidal estuary, in which currents move north as far as the city of Troy, New York, and south toward New York Bay and the open waters of the Atlantic. Each panel, in shades of blue and bordered by an iconic pattern of animal, chemical, technological, and financial symbols, begins with the phrase "MUHHEAKANTUCK KNOWS," followed by a terse three-line phrase relating a human and natural history of the lower Hudson. A panel reading "MUHHEAKANTUCK KNOWS / SALT TIDES / WINDS / SEA" is dated "CIRCA 4000 BC," suggesting a primeval blank slate when the region and the waterway were formed by the watershed and the moon's gravitational influence on the waters of the Atlantic.

Heap of Birds explained that the watershed has also been home to a changing and often conflictual community of human and nonhuman denizens. Following chronologically, viewers read that "CIRCA 800," the lower Hudson hosts a dense population of fauna: "MUHHEAKANTUCK KNOWS / BEAR HAWK HERON / BEAVER EEL DEER / TURTLE SNIPE WOLF." By "CIRCA 2005," the region's population of animal inhabitants includes "HUDSON SHAD OSPREY / STRIPED BASS / BALD EAGLE / ATLANTIC STURGEON." Humans and cultural conflict mark the region by "CIRCA 1609," the year of Hudson's first voyage. Representing this juncture, Heap of Birds created two panels: "MUHHEAKANTUCK KNOWS / DUTCH / EAST INDIA / COMPANY" and "MUHHEAKANTUCK KNOWS / ENGLISHMAN / JOHN COLEMAN / ARROW IN THROAT," narrating the killing of a Hudson's Bay Company captain. Human habitation has debased the watershed by "CIRCA 1960," as toxic chemical compounds released into the ecosystem by industry turned the region into a federal Superfund site: "MUHHEAKANTUCK KNOWS / DIOXIN / POLYCHLORINATED BIPHENYL"; "MUHHEAKANTUCK KNOWS / FURANS / POLYCYLIC / AROMATIC HYDROCARBONS."

However, by "CIRCA 2009," as the exhibition opened in the quadricentennial year of Hudson's first voyage, the river was witnessing the beginnings of an ongoing restoration, as well as an event that Heap of Birds interprets as the natural world asserting its power over human technology—"MUHHEAKANTUCK KNOWS / LGA AIRBUS A-320 / USAIR / 1549"—a reference to the well-known story of a passenger jetliner en route from New York's La Guardia Airport to Charlotte, North Carolina, that was struck by a flock of Canada geese minutes after takeoff and that ditched in the river near Midtown Manhattan on January 15, 2009. Heap of Birds has described the incident as "the birds asking the plane to land"; the plane, due to calm waters, was brought down safely.[47]

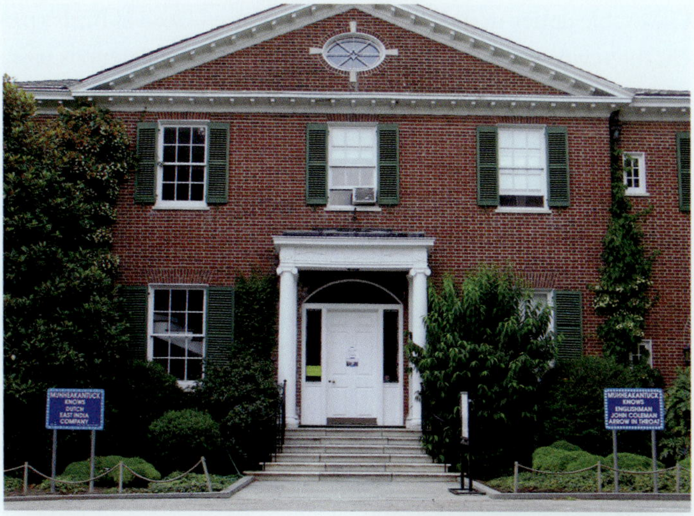

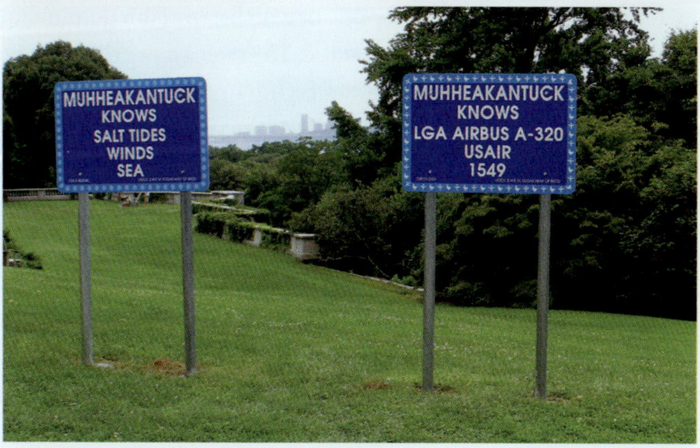

1.16 Edgar Heap of Birds, *Please the Waters*, 2009. Eight steel panels, each 24 × 36 inches. Wave Hill, Bronx, New York. Artwork © Edgar Heap of Birds. The borders of each panel included images of biological mutation, currency symbols ($ ƒ), eagle and fish forms, abstract images of waves, a bear claw, a gas mask/respirator, arrowheads, a bird, and an airplane. Heap of Birds explained that the choice of the color blue (his customary color for public signage has been red) was a tribute to his youngest son, Wougim—whose Cheyenne name is the word for the blue sky.

1.17 Edgar Heap of Birds, *Please the Waters*, Wave Hill, Bronx, New York, 2009. Artwork © Edgar Heap of Birds.

A favorable notice in the *New York Times* praised Heap of Birds's panels, which, the reviewer wrote, "remind us of a vanished indigenous past, but also that the Hudson River is an ecosystem that required constant stewardship and care."[48] But such characterizations largely miss the point of *Please the Waters*. First, rather than focusing on a vanished past, Heap of Birds's panels, like all of the artist's text-based work, make use exclusively of the present tense. Moreover, only one of eight panels makes explicit reference to the Native human inhabitants of the region—the Lenape—who might be credited with shooting an arrow into the throat of an English interloper in 1609. Second, the notion of the lower Hudson as an "ecosystem that required constant stewardship and care," in addition to recycling stereotypes of Native peoples as natural environmentalists—"stewards"—fails to recognize what Muhheakantuck knows: that the region is a vital network of human and nonhuman, organic and inorganic actors, any of which may at one moment be ascendant, but none of which can claim dominion. The river knows that an ecosystem is not static. The river knows that the Lenape and their Dutch partners depleted the region's population of beaver and other fur-bearing mammals by the middle of the seventeenth century. The river knows the destruction wrought by manufacturing in the nineteenth and twentieth centuries. If Heap of Birds took Wave Hill's brief—that his artwork place "in focus" the significance of the river for its Native human neighbors across four turbulent centuries—he also expanded that brief to describe a landscape dense with human and nonhuman histories. *Please the Waters* was concerned not only with the region's native peoples but also with the landscape itself, before and after the catastrophe of discovery and colonization.

The river also knows that birds can bring down planes. The technical term for the incident that befell US Airways Flight 1549 is a "bird strike"—a phrase that would seem to assign agency to the birds rather than the more powerful and deadly aircraft with which they have become mixed up, but which nevertheless they have brought down in a postmodern media event. The animals (and chemical compounds) listed on Heap of Birds's panels are forces with agency in their own right. The bear, hawk, heron, beaver, eel, deer, turtle, snipe, wolf, Hudson shad, osprey, striped bass, bald eagle, Atlantic sturgeon, and sundry industrial by-products might be seen to have shaped the region as much as the human actors and corporate protagonists that figure on just two panels. Heap of Birds refers to his animal actors as clan mothers of the Lenape, citing a powerful linkage to human identities as well. The panels document the intertwined histories of the human and nonhuman—and organic and inorganic—agentic forces in the landscape. But Muhheakantuck itself "knows." The river, in Heap of Birds's telegraphic narrative, is possessed of awareness—attention and intention—a mind.

The environmental perspective voiced in his prints for *Caliban* and in *Please the Waters* suggests that the focus on tribal sovereignty in much of his work is part of an indigenous epistemology that understands the human community in relation to an extended field of human and nonhuman relations. A version of *Native Hosts* created in 2013 in Claremont, California, took Heap of Birds's ongoing series in a new direction, in a sense closing the gap between his projects recognizing sovereign indigenous nations and those addressing obligations to the landscape. The Southern California installation honored the Tongva (or Gabrielino, so named for Mission San Gabriel Arcángel, the historic Spanish mission in the Los Angeles basin), the indigenous peoples who consider the Los Angeles region their traditional homelands. Heap of Birds created this public installation in dialogue with local tribal elders, from whom he learned the names of villages and sacred sites. Heap of Birds has had an interest in visiting local indigenous sacred sites for many years. "When I travel," he said, "my process is to go back in time to ceremonial sites."[49] These names—traditional places of human habitation as well as landmarks such as the principal rivers and mountains that define the Tongva lands—are featured on twenty sign panels installed throughout the Pitzer College campus, built on the flatlands of the great alluvial fan of San Antonio Creek, at the base of the San Gabriel Mountains. The place names—including Torojoatn'gna, the village of Claremont; Joat, nearby Mount Baldy; and Tototingah, the San Gabriel River—are in the Tongva language.

As in earlier installations of *Native Hosts*, *Day/Night*, and other works, the confrontation between English and Tongva is jarring—mutual incomprehensibilities that have the effect of making settled and familiar places feel strange. The names that Heap of Birds has generally used in *Native Hosts* are those names that Deloria and Lytle translate as "the people." They are the names of human communities that find their place and their home within a field of human and nonhuman interaction—the names that Native communities traditionally used to define themselves within and

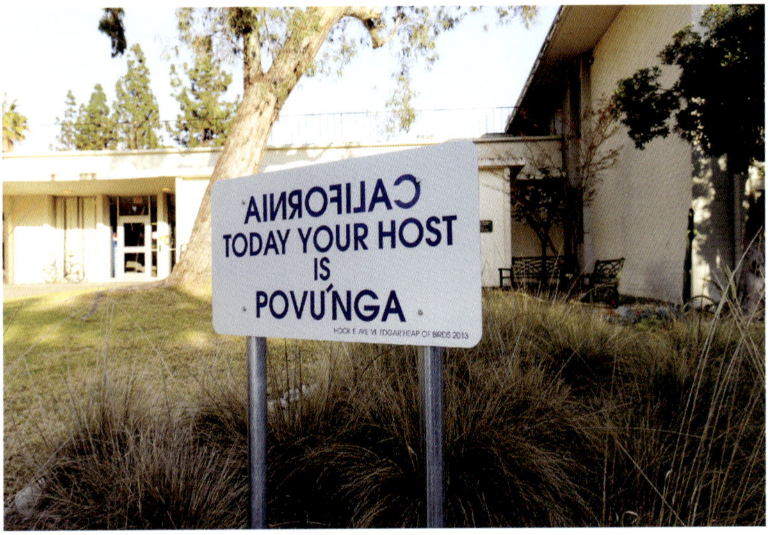

1.18 Edgar Heap of Birds, *Native Hosts* series, 2013. Twenty steel panels, each 24 × 36 inches. Pitzer College campus, Claremont, California. Photo: Scott Phillips. Artwork © Edgar Heap of Birds. Heap of Birds created a *Native Hosts* installation recognizing sites and landmarks in the Los Angeles basin in the Tongva language. *Povu'nga* is the Tongva word for Long Beach, fifty miles southwest of Claremont, suggesting the scope of the Tongva people's traditional lands.

against a vital environment, and which gave form to their relationship with the natural and supernatural worlds. In California—where the Tongva and many other tribes no longer hold title to their ancestral lands and are thus hosts in a different sense than other Native nations—passersby are hailed by places and sites of spiritual significance, rather than by entities with legal and political standing in the strictest sense. The landscape itself is host, with all the reciprocal obligations incurred by that hospitality: "TODAY YOUR HOST IS AKVANGNA" (Mount San Jacinto). As "CALIFORNIA"—in reversed type—becomes strange, a word for this place in another language comes into focus. Another embodied perception, another sense of place and time, is made visible, if not accessible. Translations are not supplied to the viewer; as in previous *Native Hosts* and other works by Heap of Birds, the onus is on the viewer to complete the circle, to become entangled in another view, to recognize the host.

Like the earlier iterations of *Native Hosts*, this is not merely an illustration of a prior understanding of landscape but embodies a position vis-à-vis place and its histories—bringing viewers into awareness and criticality, or at least presenting the opportunity for such. In his landscapes, Heap of Birds's art suggests a way of thinking about land and being in place—and about sovereignty—that is not limited by the Eurocentric legal and political tradition. With these works, Heap of Birds looks back to what Rickard termed a shared ancient imaginary. Heap of Birds addresses this point: "I have always remarked that we should not always focus only upon the more trivial relationship of Indians against some figure like President Bush or Custer. While this violence has been deadly, the dominant culture actually wishes it that way, keeping them in the picture, making the argument about them, from their power position. To open the discussion up to include the Milky Way Galaxy is much more real to our Native understanding."[50]

The California installation features place names in the Tongva language, which the Tongva are currently laboring to reconstruct and revive, even as they lack status as a federally recognized tribe. The Tongva language was lost in the aftermath of the Spanish settlement of California, as far-flung villages were relocated to live near the Franciscan missions, communities were torn apart and remade, and Native nations disappeared into the Spanish-speaking majority. Dispossessing the Tongva and other Native peoples of their language was an expedient to liquidating their claims to traditional territories—language being so foundational in encoding a sense of making and inhabiting place. Indeed, even as the *Neuf* paintings are abstract—wordless—much of Heap of Birds's landscape practice has depended on language; or rather languages, words in conflict or in play, embodying different epistemologies of landscape, brought into dialogue, face-to-face, as it were, through Heap of Birds's distinctive typographic reversals. Language has been wielded as a weapon, to be sure, in the past. It is also a tool for reshaping perceptions.

2

WORDS

Insurgent Messages

As much as serial painting functions as a grounding process for Heap of Birds's artistic practice, words have been his primary media. In *Public Enemy Care for Youth*, a sequence of three serigraph prints produced in 1993, short sequences of words are brief enough to remember. They reward reading out loud and are handsomely composed, clear, and bold. As they stick in the mind they raise questions: How did beautiful children become mad dogs? Whose enemy? Whose youth? Heap of Birds presents terse phrases that do not so much connote blunt violence (although he certainly does so in other artworks) as speak to history's legacies—"beautiful children" raised to be "mad dogs." If America has failed to care for youth, that responsibility has fallen to—or been assigned to—enemies. Is the "Public Enemy" the welfare state, demonized by neoconservative politicians in the 1980s and 1990s? Or perhaps Heap of Birds is calling out to the influential and outspoken hip-hop group, whose members included at one time the community activist Sister Souljah, lambasted by presidential candidate Bill Clinton for her comments in the wake of the 1992 Los Angeles riots blaming violence in black communities on the brutal history of white racism in America. In Heap of Birds's artwork, America is not merely alleged to be brutal, but is named as "brutality," as if no other adjective could temper its

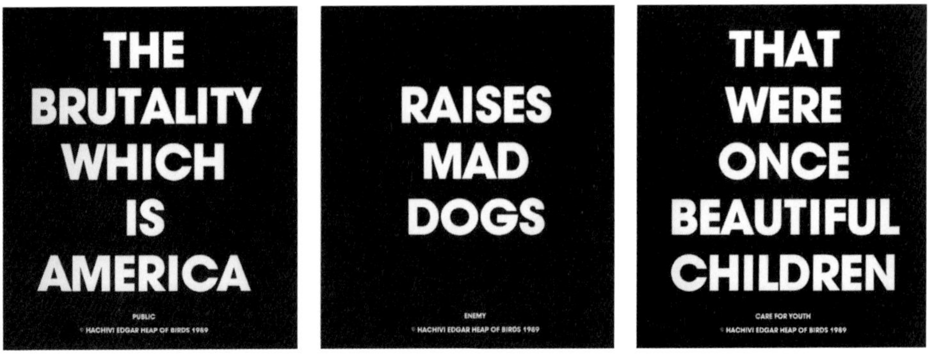

2.1 Edgar Heap of Birds, *Public Enemy Care for Youth*, 1993. Serigraph, 33½ × 40 inches. Artwork © Edgar Heap of Birds.

true, selfsame nature. His words grab. They compel repeating and turning over in one's mind, teasing out the numerous possible meanings, opening up new perspectives on unexamined histories, places, and ideas. These are words that ask questions, or make us ask them—words that work.

In his *Native Hosts* series, Heap of Birds's choice of words is specific, even as it plays on ambiguity. The English word "host" can be seen to have two ancient roots. In its modern usage it denotes receiving and entertaining guests. This meaning of the word derives from the Latin *hospes*, which refers to one who receives and welcomes strangers as well as one who is a stranger seeking recognition, and evokes the many complexities of reciprocal obligations. The English word "hospitality" comes from this root. Alternatively, it can also refer to a large group or a multitude, as in a group of soldiers or angels. When we use the word "host" in this sense, the meaning is derived from the Latin *hostis*, or enemy. The English word "hostile" derives from this root.[1] Heap of Birds chooses words that will lodge themselves in consciousness, in memory, in perspective, and proceed to remake them.

Historically, language was a powerful weapon wielded by the imperial nations of Europe and their colonial proxies against indigenous peoples in the Americas. From the earliest contact, Native nations were manipulated and terrorized by the colonizers' language. Hundreds of distinct peoples speaking unique languages were misrecognized as "Indians." Individual nations were misidentified, often with the epithets used by traditional rivals. As Heap of Birds explains, "Cheyenne" is in fact an erroneous name for his people. "The word Cheyenne is inaccurate in describing my tribe," he writes, "as it is a mistaken form of a Lakota word meaning 'Unintelligible Speech.' The correct word is Tsistsistas, which means ourselves."[2] Colonial place names from New England to Venezuela (literally: "Little Venice") were superimposed over a landscape occupied for generations by indigenous communities. Later, indigenous names and identities were Anglicized or Hispanicized and redeployed as the settlers sought to claim autochthonous authority over people and places—"going native" even as the Natives were disappeared. Eventually, indigenous peoples were subjected to forced education in the languages of their oppressors and faced severe punishment for speaking their ancestral languages. The colonizers' language continues to undermine and denigrate indigenous memory. It matters whether we call a tragic historical event a "massacre" or a "battle," or if we call a work of architecture a "mound." When Heap of Birds calls out "THE BRUTALITY WHICH IS AMERICA," the violence of naming is turned around against the aggressor, much as colonial place names are reversed in *Native Hosts*.

As art historian Kate Morris writes, Heap of Birds's language-based artworks "make an eloquent case for the part that words themselves play in the battle over representation."[3] Fittingly, Heap of Birds has compared his art to the arrow points—"sharp rocks"—fashioned by his Cheyenne ancestors: "In touching these weapons I have found clues as to the useful current day defensive and preservation tactics that can serve living Native Americans."[4] He has learned to sharpen his words into effective tools.

As Heap of Birds explained to an interviewer early in his career, "My ideas are really political and representational, but I'm not a representational painter, so I just started using photographs and words. Then the words themselves became their own kind of medium. I got comfortable using them like I use paint and they got abstract also."[5] Heap of Birds's description of using words "like paint"—as visual and physical formal elements—resonates with theorist and artist Johanna Drucker's observation that words are characterized by a duality: they are simultaneously verbal—or symbolic—and visual.[6] Over the course of his career, Heap of Birds has produced language-based works in multiple modes exploiting the dual nature of visible language. A number of his early gallery installations were created with machine-made, die-cut letters, painted and temporarily attached to the walls of the exhibition space. He has employed commercial printers for outdoor signage and other interventions. Heap of Birds also uses commercial printers for projects on giveaway shopping bags and T-shirts, as other artists seeking to infiltrate public spaces have done, such as Jenny Holzer. Heap of Birds's extensive body of work in traditional fine art media—language-based works in pastel or marker that are hand drawn or produced with master printers—contrasts with the projects using commercial and mechanical means. His hand-drawn and handmade works explore more private emotions and experiences. These seek to address more select audiences, at a smaller scale and in more intimate surroundings, but pack no less punch.

Heap of Birds's carefully composed and designed language-based artworks have antecedents in a number of twentieth-century art movements, including concrete poetry and cubism, which incorporated text—such as headlines clipped from the newspaper. For these movements, typography served as a formal device—a language and material for two-dimensional composition, as well as effecting the modernists' goal of dismantling the illusion of three dimensions—asserting the truthfulness of the flat surface of the picture. Undermining the conventions of art that had held since the Renaissance was linked to broader goals. For the Dadaists, futurists, and other subversive modernist movements, the use of mechanical type to idiosyncratic, often illegible effect was an attack on language—indeed on the notion of rational discourse—aimed at overthrowing the stagnant conventions and beliefs of bourgeois culture. Blurring the distinction between visual and verbal communication has a radical pedigree.

A more immediate influence on Heap of Birds's use of language is the conceptual and postmodernist art that emerged in the late 1960s. In his 1969 essay "Situation Aesthetics," Victor Burgin, an artist and theorist associated with conceptual art's radical political wing, noted a tendency toward the "placing of art entirely within the linguistic infrastructure, which previously served merely to support art."[7] In her book *Words to Be Looked At: Language Art in the 1960s*, art historian Liz Kotz notes that language has always surrounded works of art—as captions or as criticism and explanation. The notion that art and text—the visual and the verbal—were separate and mutually unintelligible discourses is actually an artifact of a narrow historical period. Mid-twentieth-century art theory, most famously that espoused by the archmodernist Clement Greenberg, sought to keep competing expressive modes such as literature and visual arts separate to ensure the purity of the arts. Each artistic medium was to discover its unique métier and excel within its specific limits. However, by the 1960s "snippets of language decisively reentered the picture plane . . . as Pop painters drew on advertising and poster designs, the use of language as a graphic emblem or visual sign was commonplace."[8]

Moreover, language itself became the form in which artworks were created, from the "scores" of composers such as John Cage and the performance artists associated with the Fluxus movement to "the wide-ranging adoption of language as an instruction, schema, or template for works constructed in all types of media."[9] Artworks that existed first and foremost as text exemplified what critics Lucy Lippard and Seth Siegelaub termed "dematerialization." In 1968 Sol Lewitt began formulating proposals for dematerialized artworks that were to be executed by assistants or curators according to his instructions, drawn directly on the wall. As Lewitt wrote in his groundbreaking essay "Paragraphs on Conceptual Art," "In conceptual art the idea or concept is the most important aspect of the work. When an artist uses a conceptual form of art, it means that all of the planning and decisions are made beforehand and the execution is a perfunctory affair. The idea becomes a machine that makes the art."[10] Even when a particular instantiation of one of Lewitt's wall drawings is intentionally destroyed at the end of an exhibition, the "machine that makes the art"—the ideas, as immaterial information—survives.

Lawrence Weiner's text works—phrases that may be applied to a wall or another surface—are precursors to Heap of Birds's deployment of texts in multiple media and in various contexts in and out of the gallery. But whereas Weiner's playful punning often thematizes the experience of looking at art—calling attention to the physical situation of the work in the exhibition space—Heap of Birds's insurgent messages look beyond the walls of the institution and seek to further a critical and political project as much as an aesthetic one. As such, Heap of Birds's work resonates with an important radical strain within conceptual art in the 1960s, which expressed the political ideals of the New Left. Like that of their early twentieth-century forebears, the art of conceptual art's radical innovators—Burgin, in addition to Hans Haacke, Joseph Kosuth, Adrian Piper, and Yoko Ono, as well as collectives such as Art and Language—was in theory anticapitalist, antiracist, antisexist, and antiwar, even if in practice much of the work produced seemed concerned primarily with linguistic and philosophical propositions. (Weiner, Michael Asher, and others explored the physical

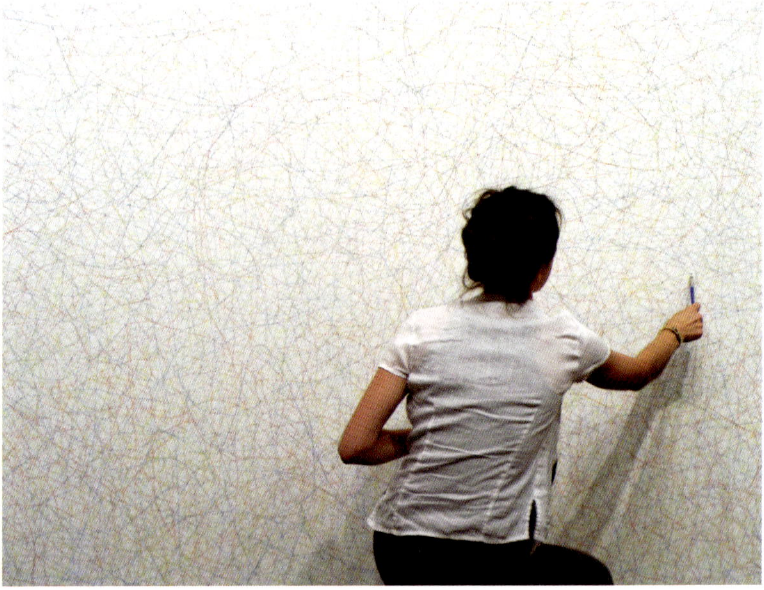

2.2 Sol Lewitt, *Wall Drawing #65, Lines not short, not straight, crossing and touching, drawn at random using four colors, uniformly dispersed with maximum density, covering the entire surface of the wall*, 1971. Dorothy and Herbert Vogel Collection, National Gallery of Art, Washington, DC. Artwork © Sol Lewitt / Artists Rights Society (ARS), New York. Photo courtesy National Gallery of Art, Washington, DC, Gallery Archives. Assistant executing Lewitt's artwork for exhibition at the National Gallery of Art East Building in May 2004.

and sociological dimensions of art exhibition in their work, as a means of "institutional critique" aimed at denaturalizing and ultimately transforming notions of the aesthetic as a privileged realm, aloof from the mundane world of politics and commerce.) Moreover, the dematerialization of the artwork—its distillation to pure idea, pure experience—was a radical goal, aimed at the total remaking of society and echoing the antibourgeois politics of the futurists and other earlier avant-gardes, and very much in keeping with the anticapitalist mood of the 1960s counterculture. As Lippard wrote in 1969, "Art intended as pure experience doesn't exist until someone experiences it, defying ownership, reproduction, sameness. Intangible art could break down the artificial imposition of 'culture' and provide a broader audience for a tangible, object art."[11]

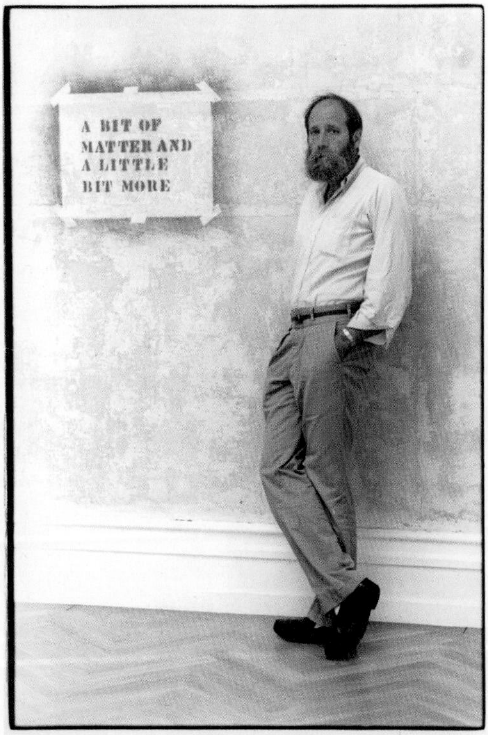

2.3 Lawrence Weiner, *A BIT OF MATTER AND A LITTLE BIT MORE*, 1976. Artwork © Lawrence Weiner / Artists Rights Society (ARS), New York. Weiner photographed with his work at the Kunsthalle Bern, Switzerland, in 1983.

Radical artists transformed their practice into a kind of activism or muckraking investigative journalism that exposed the connections of museums such as New York's Guggenheim and Museum of Modern Art (MoMA) to networks of economic and political power. In 1969, the Art Workers' Coalition called for a Moratorium of Art to End the War in Vietnam, closing MoMA, the Jewish Museum, and the Whitney Museum for a day. In 1970s, Haacke—a member of the Art Workers' Coalition—presented an artwork in *Information*, an early exhibition of conceptual art at MoMA, in which museumgoers were asked, "Would the fact that Governor Rockefeller has not denounced President Nixon's Indochina Policy be a reason for your not voting for him in November?" Visitors were instructed to deposit their answers into transparent Plexiglas ballot boxes. In addition

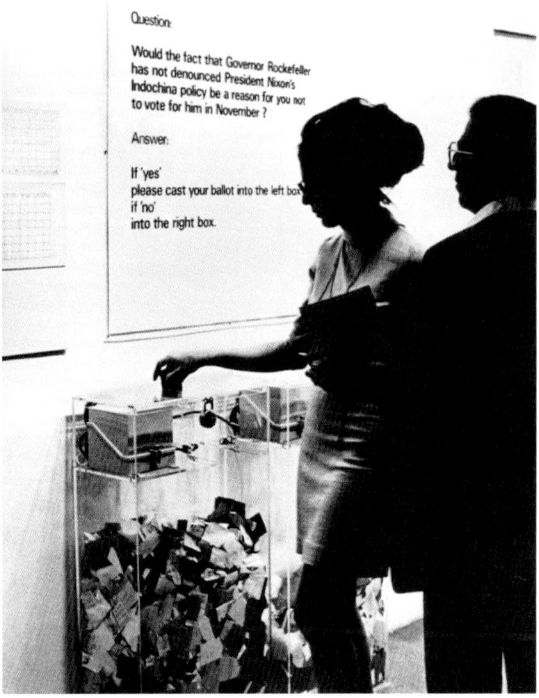

2.4 Hans Haacke, *MoMA Poll*, 1970. Two transparent acrylic boxes, photoelectric counting devices, paper ballots, 101.5 × 51 × 25.5 cm each. Artwork © Hans Haacke / Artists Rights Society (ARS), New York. Courtesy of Hans Haacke and Paula Cooper Gallery, New York.

to demonstrating that MoMA patrons opposed further military escalation in Vietnam by a two-to-one margin, Haacke's artwork implicated New York governor Nelson Rockefeller—a museum board member and major donor—and thus the institution and the art world in American foreign policy. Art—as algorithm or information-making machine—was taking on the machine of late capitalist state power.

But if conceptualism succeeded in dematerializing the art object, the hoped-for transformation of society failed to materialize. A wall drawing by Lewitt could still be bought and sold—what changed hands was a legal contract. As Lippard would write in 1973, "I think the art world is probably going to be able to absorb conceptual art as another 'movement' and not pay much attention to it. The art establishment depends so greatly on objects which can be bought and sold that I don't expect it to do much about an art that is opposed to the prevailing systems."[12] While the initial radical, anticapitalist goals of conceptualism remained unrealized, the movement did provide a powerful set of critical tools for artists. Conceptualism is the most influential development in the art world since the 1960s, and it predominates in the global art world in the early twenty-first century. Conceptual art's "post-medium condition"—in art historian Rosalind Krauss's terminology—is ascendant, much as Greenberg's modernist purism had been at midcentury.[13] In the "poststudio" art world, ideas overshadow craft.

Moreover, the turn by conceptual artists to language-based art forms in the 1960s was part of a broader "linguistic turn" in philosophy and the humanities generally. Informed by the structuralism of linguist Ferdinand de Saussure and his later interlocutors, words were analyzed as one-half of a linguistic structure known as the "sign"—a pair made up of a signified (a thing represented) and an arbitrary signifier. Exploring the arbitrary nature of language—recognizing that words did not naturally and transparently represent reality but were in fact units in historically determined and ideologically ordered cultural systems—scholars and artists undermined the notion of language as a passive and transparent vessel, a neutral means of conveying ideas and information. The linguistic turn and conceptual art opened the door to critiques of the political functions and mystifications of language and deconstructions of regimes of what the influential social theorist Michel Foucault termed "power/knowledge."[14]

The work of conceptual artists and other critical postmodernists sought to puncture the seamless surface of power/knowledge, of language and representation, to create a semiotic rupture or *tort*, as described by philosopher Jacques Rancière. As Rancière reminds us, what is taken for granted ("common sense") and what is visible are profoundly political. The "distribution of the sensible," in Rancière's terms, is in fact the terrain of politics—a politics of representation with very real ramifications.[15] Recall that Heap of Birds described his artworks as "sharp rocks" (weapons for community protection), that his text-based works labor to bring suppressed and neglected information and voices silenced by the historical record into the present—what Hal Foster describes as an "archival impulse"—to open up new perspectives and ways of seeing, and new ways of relating to place and history.

Heap of Birds came of age as an artist in a postconceptual generation.

The work of feminist, black, and queer artists since the 1970s has interrogated the power, biases, and violence of language and practiced a politics of representation, appropriating the aesthetic and critical sensibilities of their conceptualist predecessors and, as in the agitprop of the AIDS crisis–era artist-activist collective Gran Fury, infusing the forms with the urgency of identity politics in the aftermath of the unfinished civil rights movement. Significantly, Heap of Birds was part of a cohort of Native American artists working in postconceptual modes who emerged during this period, incorporating writing, performance, and new media alongside painting and sculpture to explore and make visible the legacies of colonialism. Bob Haozous, Hulleah Tsinhnahjinnie, Jimmie Durham, George Longfish, James Luna, Jaune Quick-to-See Smith, Shelly Niro, and others, exhibited alongside other radical postconceptualists, although their critical work—concerned with the struggle over representation and exemplary of the culture wars of the 1980s and 1990s—has been underrecognized by critics and historians.[16]

Public Speaking

Many of Heap of Birds's artworks appear in public places, and as his works occupy shared space they invite dialogue about the nature and meaning of those spaces—introducing new information and perspectives about historical and ongoing claims to territory, as in *Native Hosts*, or about deeper human and nonhuman histories, as in *Please the Waters*, or raising questions about who speaks in and for the public, what stories are told, and what is known and taken for granted. Heap of Birds's first public artwork, in 1982, was an animated message that appeared on the Spectacolor billboard in New York City's Times Square, sponsored by the Public Art Fund, in a curated selection of works by twelve artists, who each worked with a programmer to develop brief segments that played across the massive screen—cutting-edge digital technology at the time. The participating artists—including Hans Haacke, Howardena Pindell, Keith Haring, and Jenny Holzer—were selected by Jane Dickson, a member of the radical artists' collective Collaborative Projects (or Colab).[17] Dickson's selection was significant—a cross section of socially engaged artists from diverse racial and ethnic backgrounds, embodying the politically charged and multicultural makeup of the artist-run spaces and new genre public art movement of the era.

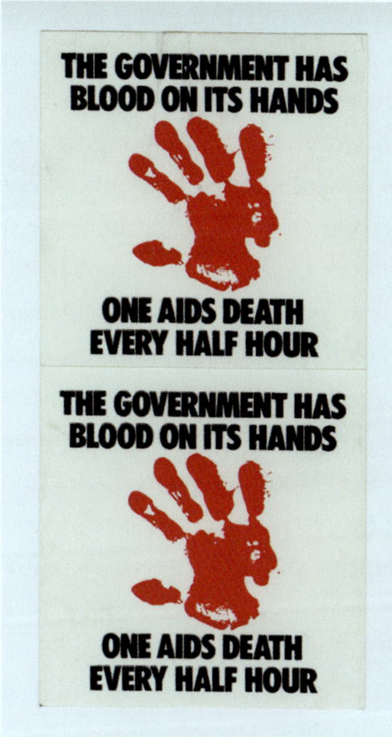

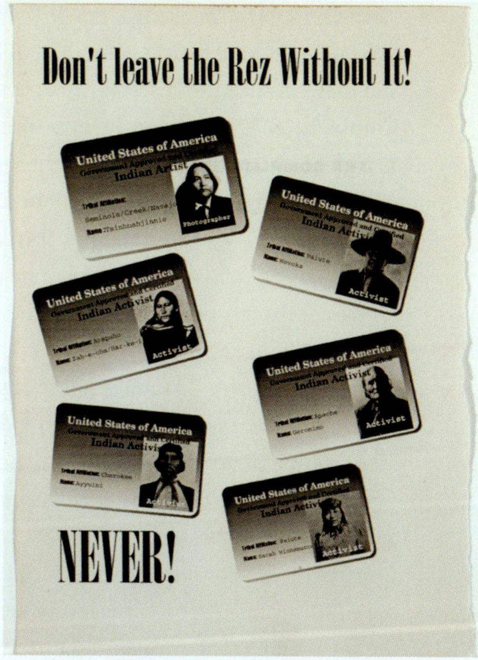

2.5 Gran Fury, *The Government Has Blood on Its Hands [One AIDS Death Every Half Hour]*, 1989. Sticker, 3 × 3 inches. Gran Fury Collection, Manuscripts and Archives Division, New York Public Library, Astor, Lenox and Tilden Foundations. The artist collective Gran Fury was founded in 1988 as the unofficial "information ministry" within the activist organization ACT UP (AIDS Coalition to Unleash Power), using the techniques of advertising and mass communications to spread awareness of the AIDS epidemic. In 1987, ACT UP developed the "Silence = Death" campaign, plastering New York and other cities with posters featuring the slogan and the pink triangle, first used to mark homosexual prisoners in Nazi concentration camps during World War II.

2.6 Hulleah J. Tsinhnahjinnie (Tuskegee/Diné), *Don't Leave the Rez Without It!* From *Photographic Memoirs of an Aboriginal Savant*, 1994. Unique digital print on aged book stock, 14 × 11 inches. Artwork © Hulleah J. Tsinhnahjinnie.

In Our Language exemplifies the tricky maneuver that Heap of Birds's language-based artworks effect. He uses words to unearth, make visible, and memorialize lost histories and perspectives that have been repressed.[18] In this, he might seem to be appealing to an understanding of language as a clear channel of communication—a type of documentary or activist realism. And yet, the very nature of language—especially in the context of the colonial histories Heap of Birds's work explores—is complicated, compromised, and anything but transparent as a medium of information exchange. In the same operation, then, Heap of Birds must also critique dominant languages and systems of representation, which have denied agency and power to indigenous people. He must upset and undermine language as he resorts to words to lodge his critique, even as names and other words were weapons used against Native peoples in the relentless campaign for assimilation, which supplanted an earlier genocidal campaign of extermination.

Initial plans for an elaborate sequence in which an abstract image receded to reveal a written text were scrapped as Heap of Birds discovered the limitations of the still-rudimentary technology. He opted instead for a rhythmic sequence of short phrases, similar to the wall installations he was also developing at that time. For his part, Heap of Birds rejected the label of conceptual art for the piece, choosing instead to emphasize the aesthetic experience and the formal properties of the new digital medium—light, color, and time. And while the content of the work is paramount, he approached the unique abilities of the animated billboard as an opportunity to explore the rhythm of repeating strings of words in English and Cheyenne. "It's not conceptual art," he later told an interviewer. "It's painting. It deals with size, weight, color. . . . I worked with the rhythm of the words."[19] Curtis King, the programmer who collaborated with the artists in realizing their projects, concurred: "I thought his words had a nice ring to them."[20]

Nevertheless, the very fact of speaking in the Cheyenne language in North America—where indigenous languages had been pushed to the brink of extinction—had political implications. Similarly, the artist-activists of ACT UP and Gran Fury recognized the power of representing the facts of the AIDS crisis in the face of a political establishment that preferred to keep them invisible ("Silence = Death" proclaimed a particularly powerful ACT UP slogan), as well as feminists and other activists representing marginalized groups and communities demonized by neoconservative

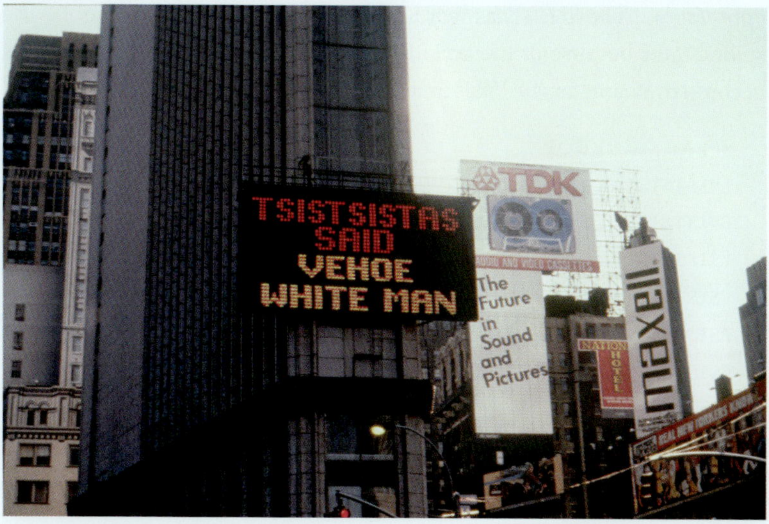

2.7 Edgar Heap of Birds, *In Our Language*, 1982. Digital animation for Spectacolor billboard. Times Square, New York. Artwork © Edgar Heap of Birds.

politics in the 1980s, who would take up the Quaker phrase "speaking truth to power." Beyond the aesthetic of appeal of its poetic rhythms, *In Our Language* takes as its topic the power of language and naming. Offering a lesson in Cheyenne to passersby is a strategy in a battle of representations, much as the English education forced on Heap of Birds's Cheyenne and Arapaho ancestors and other Native people was as effective as any weapon in the conquest of North America. Heap of Birds used the rhythm of the words—sequenced in nine phrases that flashed across the Spectacolor screen—to reclaim the power to name himself and his people. The first two phrases displayed on the screen read, "IN OUR LANGUAGE; TSISTSISTAS 'CHEYENNE.'" "The Tsistsistas (Cheyenne in English) have been given a chance to define themselves and the whiteman in their own language," he wrote, noting that the name "Cheyenne" is in fact a historical misnomer.[21] Heap of Birds's insistence on using his own language to name himself would resonate with his practice in *Native Hosts*, in which local tribal communities are consulted in selecting the appropriate names to identify and honor themselves, and other public works that make use of indigenous languages and words in combination with English or other majority languages. Heap of Birds also claimed the privilege to name his oppressors: "The Tsistsistas word VEHOE has been used to describe the spider, later because of the actions of the dominant culture, VEHOE has become the name of the Whiteman."[22]

SPEAK OF VEHOE
TSISTSISTAS SAID VEHOE WRAPPED UP
TSISTSISTAS SAID VEHOE FENCED IN
TSISTSISTAS SAID VEHOE CATCH YOU
TSISTSISTAS SAID VEHOE TRAP YOU
TSISTSISTAS SAID VEHOE SPIDER
TSISTSISTAS SAID VEHOE WHITE MAN

Imperial Canada, a temporary public intervention from 1988, also focused on the performative power of language and naming. The project was mounted as part of the exhibition *Revisions* at the Banff Center, in Alberta, Canada, alongside work by Native artists including Canadian Anishnaabe Rebecca Belmore, in support of Lubicon Cree, who were protesting an exhibition of Native artifacts titled *The Spirit Sings*, which had been organized by the Glenbow Museum in conjunction with the 1988 Winter Olympics in Calgary. Lubicon activists noted that one of the exhibition's sponsors, the Shell Oil Corporation, was currently drilling on land from which the Lubicon had been evicted. Pointing to the hypocrisy of the multinational petroleum giant burnishing its public image by sponsoring the most expensive museum exhibition ever mounted in Canada, Lubicon Cree activists argued that the exhibition organizers were "decimating its culture" and called for an international boycott of the exhibition, imploring museums to renege on loan agreements to the Glenbow.[23] Heap of Birds joined with other Native artists and activists in support of the boycott, which became a national debate on the status of indigenous people in Canada and on Canada's Indian Act, the legal framework that grants the Canadian government broad authority over indigenous people. He contributed a billboard reading:

IMPERIAL CANADA
DOESN'T MAKE INDIANS
NATIVE
PEOPLE
RECOGNIZE
THEMSELVES

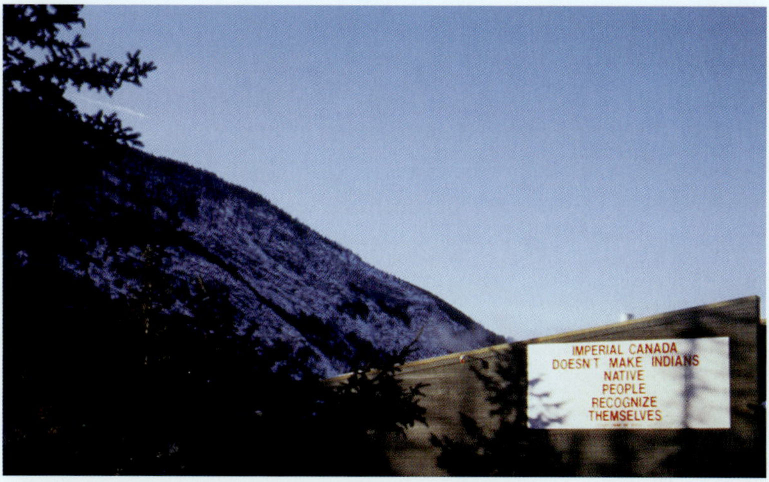

2.8 Edgar Heap of Birds, *Imperial Canada*, 1988. Billboard, Banff Center, Alberta, Canada. Artwork © Edgar Heap of Birds.

Heap of Birds wrote, "It is a racist-imperial nation that takes upon itself the outrageous privilege to determine who shall be considered Native in a land where the national lawmakers are immigrants."[24]

As it was for most Native Americans born in the twentieth century, English was Heap of Birds's first language. His ancestors were subjected to a compulsory English education as they suffered military imprisonment, physical internment, and government boarding schools. As an adult, he worked to rebuild a relationship with his ancestral language. He wrote:

> I heard it spoken mainly by my Grand Mother Lightning Woman, Alice Heap of Birds. I spent a lot of time with my father's folks as a child. Early in my childhood I would hang out with my Grand Pa Guy Heap of Birds, Alice's husband. He taught me Cheyenne songs and words although I did not retain much from those early days.
>
> In my life today my Cheyenne language knowledge comes mainly from the Earth Renewal ceremony. As you know I have been active in these ways since the early 1980s. This is where I pick up most of my words and language concepts. I do research to find words and also my Father Many Magpies, Charles Heap of Birds is a Cheyenne speaker and can help me too.[25]

As Jean Fisher writes, "Like many colonized peoples, Native Americans quickly learned that language was a weapon to be used against them. However, in Heap of Birds's work the blade has turned around. He cuts, dismembers, or reverses the English language; he invades it with his own. . . . He infuses its interstices with a disturbing and alien identity."[26] This resonates with the riposte made by the character Caliban in the *Tempest*, in Shakespeare's time a figure for the New World of the Americas and a key figure for contemporary artists and others who struggle against settler colonialism: "You taught me language, and my profit on't is, I know how to curse. The red plague rid you for learning me your language!"[27]

In manipulating words visually—adopting different styles for various contexts and purposes—Heap of Birds reminds us that language is never merely a transparent and neutral vessel for the transmission of information. Language is always already ideological; the simplest utterance is a politically situated and constructed act, historically located, and demanding careful unpacking and deconstructing. Heap of Birds's words are a call for critical reading, and for guerrilla interpretation.

As Heap of Birds says of his words: "They got abstract also."[28] In Heap of Birds's art, words are hard and supple, blunt and elastic. Words can be brutal. They can convey information that might otherwise be too difficult to witness, which may actually be unrepresentable. But words also engage in a slippery play of punning and trickster humor. This is what makes them so powerful.

"My Work Became Politicized"

Heap of Birds began incorporating text into his art during graduate school. He initially attempted to express an indigenous point of view through abstract artworks, in which modernist, geometric shapes clashed with patterns drawn from Plains beadwork—for example, the moccasins worn by his grandmother Lightning Woman—and other traditional arts. But he found that his teachers, who were trained as abstract artists in an era when the most advanced art was believed to be nonrepresentational and politically aloof, would respond to his works in purely formal terms. His teachers read what he intended as a culturally specific and critical statement about the vitality of Native people and traditions only in rarefied aesthetic terms—as autonomous arrangements of color, line, and shape. "My work

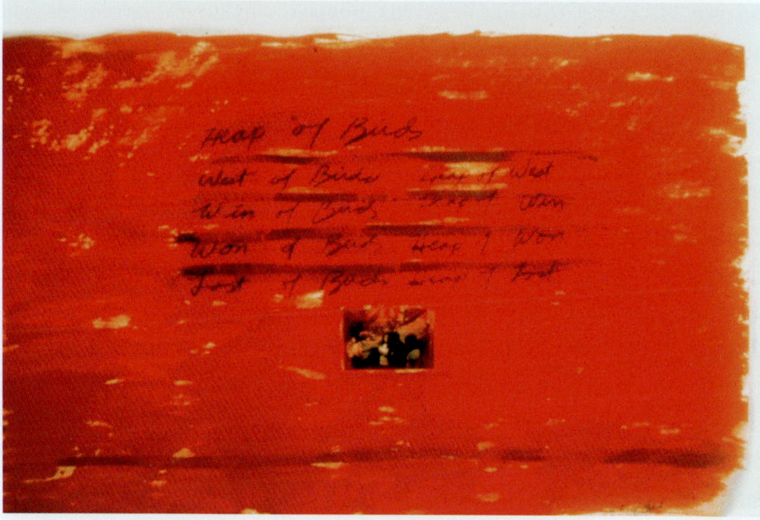

2.9 Edgar Heap of Birds, *Win of Birds*, 1978. Mixed media on paper, 24 × 36 inches. Artwork © Edgar Heap of Birds.

became politicized," he explains. To counter their misreading, he began introducing language into his abstract works, ultimately eliminating everything but the words to force a confrontation with his message.[29]

Win of Birds, from 1978, is an early example—five lines of handwritten text and a snapshot photograph layered over an abstract field of monochrome red. Heap of Birds combined the idea of the history of the West in terms of winners and losers (recalling but not quoting directly the phrase "How the West was won") with his own name, creating a rhythm of three-word phrases: West of Birds, Heap of West, Win of Birds, Heap of Win, Won of Birds, Heap of Won, Lost of Birds, Heap of Lost. This pattern of three-word phrases foreshadows his use of text in later wall lyrics, marker drawings, and prints.

By the end of his graduate studies, Heap of Birds had separated words and abstract painting into distinct practices. (He returned to abstract painting—devoid of language—in his series of *Neuf* paintings begun in the early 1980s, shortly after he returned to Oklahoma.) Created after completing his graduate work in 1979, *Fort Marion Lizards*, as W. Jackson Rushing III has noted, is a "key early work in terms of establishing the primacy of words in [Heap of Birds's] artistic arsenal."[30] Turning to words without images, Heap of Birds sharpened his message—made it unavoidable. He also succeeded in transforming his art into a weapon of his own, much like the "sharp rocks" fashioned by his ancestors, a tool of self-defense that also preserves the memory of the Cheyenne's historical struggles and remarkable perseverance.

Fort Marion Lizards memorializes the imprisonment of Southern Plains combatants at Fort Marion in Florida in the aftermath of the Red River War of 1874–75. Upon their surrender, some six dozen Cheyenne and Kiowa warriors and other detainees were transported to a military prison established within the walls of Fort Marion (Castillo de San Marcos), a Spanish colonial-era structure overlooking the Atlantic Ocean near Saint Augustine, Florida.[31] The work consists of two four-by-eight-foot sheets of wallboard, oriented vertically, and hung side by side, as if they were the open leaves of a book (and recalling the bound ledgers in which many prisoners kept visual records of their experiences). The words FLORIDA, ENGLISH, WORDS, BOYS, PRISONERS, INDIAN have been created with raised, die-cut letters of the type Heap of Birds would use in the later works *Don't Want Indians*, *Death from the Top*, and *Possible Lives* (from 1982, 1983, and 1986, respectively) before he stopped using mechanical type in his wall installations, but prefiguring his later use of commercially produced panels, such as his *Native Hosts* series. The words in die-cut letters overlap, but are also partially camouflaged by, a much more aggravated palimpsest of repeated, hand-scrawled words—ENGLISH, WORDS, INDIAN, PRISONERS—and, written just once, ST AUGUSTINE.

Among the handwritten words, Heap of Birds lists the names of the prisoners of war. These names are included in the manner of a roll call or war memorial to honor the men. "I always try to honor them as I work," Heap of Birds explains.[32] The roster of names also illustrates the role of the colonizers' language in the war that was waged against Native peoples. A handful of the names are rendered phonetically in Cheyenne: MAH NIMIC, MOCOMISTA, COME UH SEE VAH, MOCHIE. But the majority of the names are in English, including LITTLE CHIEF, transliterated from Hachivi (or Hock E Aye Vi), the nephew of Chief Heap of Birds. Heap of Birds was named after his uncle, Edgar Heap of Birds, who was in turn named after the Fort Marion prisoner. Hock E Aye Vi was translated by the U.S. military, first to "Many Magpies," then to "Heap O Birds," and later to "Heap of Birds." In the overall cacophony of words, the most prominent

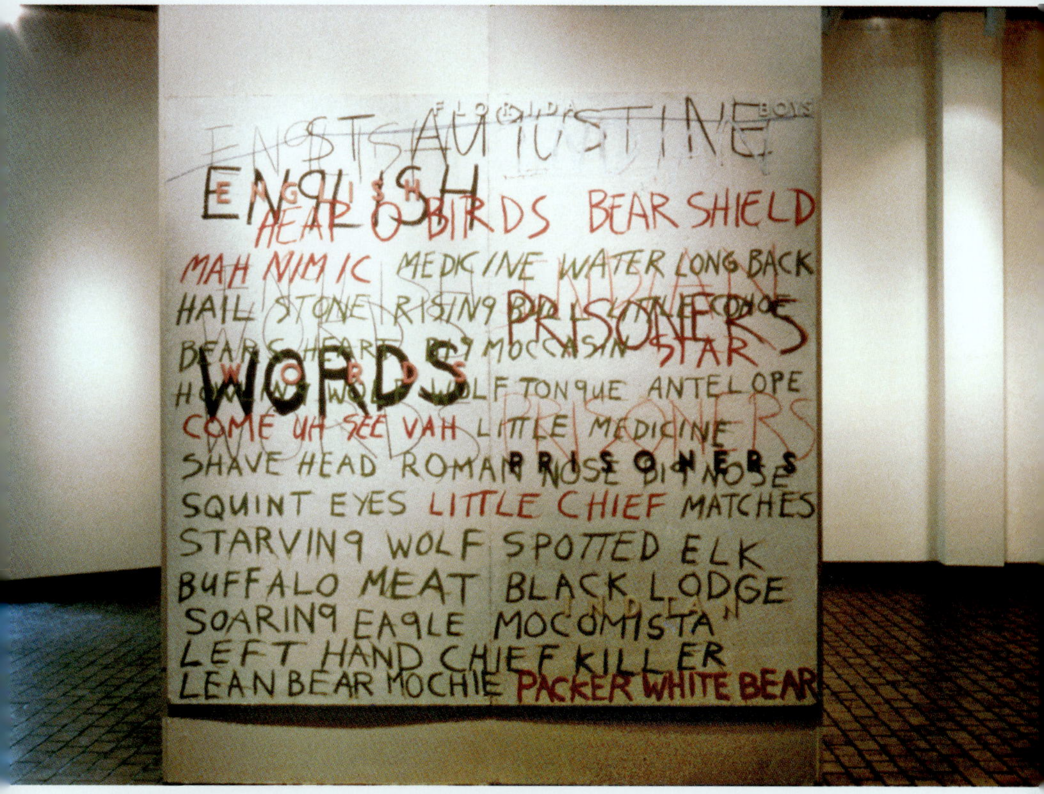

2.10 Edgar Heap of Birds, *Fort Marion Lizards*, 1979. Acrylic on wallboard, 8 × 8 feet. Artwork © Edgar Heap of Birds.

are ENGLISH, WORDS, INDIAN, and PRISONERS, suggesting, as Heap of Birds explained, the Plains men "were not only imprisoned by walls of the stockade; they were in a more emphatic sense captives of the English language that was used to ineptly alter their names."[33]

The new battlefield faced by the imprisoned warriors (and their families and communities likewise imprisoned in the newly established reservations on the Plains) was semiotic and cultural, unlike the more conventional armed struggles between the Native peoples of the Plains and the expansionist settler state, but no less urgent. Significantly, the warriors imprisoned at Fort Marion were also, like Heap of Birds, artists, in keeping with time-honored Plains tradition. In the prison at Fort Marion, Plains men lived under the wardenship of Richard Henry Pratt, who had com-

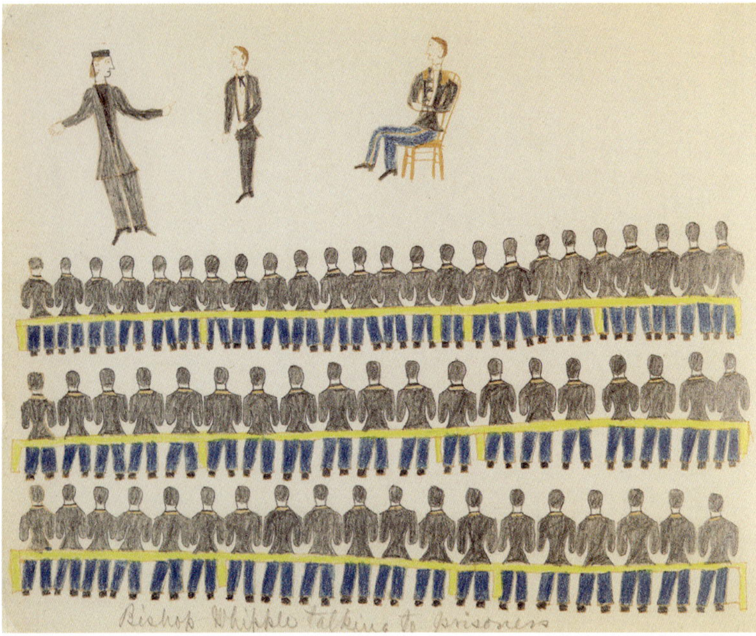

2.11 Bear's Heart, *Bishop Whipple Talking to Prisoners*, 1876. National Museum of the American Indian, Smithsonian Institution, 20/6231. Bear's Heart's drawing shows Henry Benjamin Whipple, the Episcopal bishop of Minnesota, who commissioned many books of drawings from the warrior artists, which he was fond of giving as gifts, and as evidence of the success of education and proselytizing as solutions to the "Indian Problem." Also shown are Lieutenant Richard Henry Pratt and George Fox, an interpreter.

manded the Buffalo Soldiers—African American freedmen and recently freed slaves at Fort Sill, Oklahoma—and who had served in a number of key conflicts of the Indian Wars on the Southern Plains, including the Battle of Washita of 1868–69 (in which Black Kettle was killed) and, most recently, the Red River campaign. At Fort Marion, Pratt pioneered a peculiar marriage of military imprisonment with an educational curriculum. Pratt crafted an experimental curriculum for his charges, designed to, as he famously declared, "Kill the Indian and save the man." Under Pratt, former combatants were treated to lessons in Christianity, English, and arts and crafts. They were given haircuts and military uniforms and trained to serve as their own guards. (After the close of the Indian Wars, Pratt's model became the curriculum of the Carlisle Indian School, of which he was a founder and long-serving superintendent, and would later become the model followed by government and church-run Indian schools into the twentieth century.) At Fort Marion, encouraged by Pratt and other patrons, Plains men including the Southern Cheyenne warrior Bear's Heart continued the tradition of keeping visual records, but in the new environment there was a shift from documenting personal exploits in battle (traditionally recorded on hide and, later, on ledger books acquired from traders and military men) to recording their experience of capture, rendition, imprisonment, and forced assimilation. Their remarkable body of work today comprises an important counterhistory of America's war on Native people.

But why *Lizards*? Heap of Birds's provocative title comes from multiple sources. The lizard is an esteemed totem animal in the Cheyenne Earth Renewal. In 1979, as a young man finding his voice as an artist and his footing in Cheyenne tradition, Heap of Birds admired the lizard dancers, who vowed to undertake the exhausting ceremony for the sake of the community. The lizard was the first "paint" that Heap of Birds earned upon completing his first cycle of four annual Earth Renewal ceremonies. But on a more personal level, the lizard is also Heap of Birds's metaphor for the Indian as an outsider, a figure that appears in other works of his. As an art student in London and Philadelphia, or in other places where there were not many Native people, Heap of Birds explains, "you would get stopped and asked weird questions. It was almost like you were a lizard running around town, like we were reptiles that were out of place."[34] Heap of Birds sees these men—prisoners and "lizards"—as his forebears; he identifies with them as chroniclers and defenders of Cheyenne culture. He at once offers a critique of the power of language and naming—the U.S. campaign for "peace" by means of assimilation that supplanted the earlier campaigns of isolation and extermination—and simultaneously honors the warriors and artists.

Combating (Mis)representations

Don't Want Indians is a wall-sized installation from 1982. Heap of Birds again turned his attention to the power of language in the dispossession of Native people, lodging a critique of mainstream, European appropriation and representation of Native cultures. In this piece and in others Heap of Birds tackled the legacy of primitivism and its impact on contemporary Native people. Primitivism's celebration of Indians as "children of nature" is a seemingly positive estimation, but one that effectively strands living indigenous people and cultures in an edenic past, cut off from the mainstream of history and progress, which is understood to favor European civilization and the settler states of the colonized Americas. As nature's primitives, Indians might be admirable—they might serve as a role model for moderns who feel the woes of too much civilization, and play a handy role as figures of environmental consciousness. They might serve as romantic reminders of bygone times in the names of cities and real estate developments. But ultimately, the idea of the natural Indian serves to paper over the excesses of an expansionist, capitalist society—drafted into service in advertising campaigns and sports team mascots. ("Smile for Racism," Heap of Birds suggested in *American Leagues*, an acidic billboard parodying the Cleveland Indians in 1995.) In all these guises, as Heap of Birds reminds us, the "possible lives" of "living people" are made to disappear, even as Indians become projection screens for white fantasies.

Representations of Native people were also the subject of Heap of Birds's installation created with die-cut letters for the exhibition *Sharp Rocks* at CEPA Gallery, in Buffalo in 1985. Here, representations are a "folkloric distraction" (written in reverse) altogether "unlike possible lives" of Native people. Heap of Birds appeared to leave unanswered the question of whether such distractions foreclosed the possibility of authentic lives, or whether these lives remained an unfulfilled possibility.

In the heady days of postmodernism, Heap of Birds's trenchant text-based interventions claimed a terrain similar to that of artist-activists Gran Fury, and feminists such as Jenny Holzer and Barbara Kruger, who applied the techniques of 1960s conceptualism to contemporary social issues. They addressed audiences and readers in galleries and public spaces with slogan-like statements designed to call attention to the power of language and representation—the "forest of signs" described by theorists of an emerging postmodern culture or "society of the spectacle"—in creating a shared reality. Like that of many artists who had cut their teeth in the mass media, Kruger's art spoke the language of advertising, drawing from her experience working as a layout artist for Condé Nast magazines, to reveal the role of representations—image and text—in maintaining a patriarchal society, and suggested that her generation of feminists would tolerate the status quo no longer. Kruger's photo-text collage of 1983, *We Won't Play Nature to Your Culture*, implied a clear distinction between a speaker—a politicized, collec-

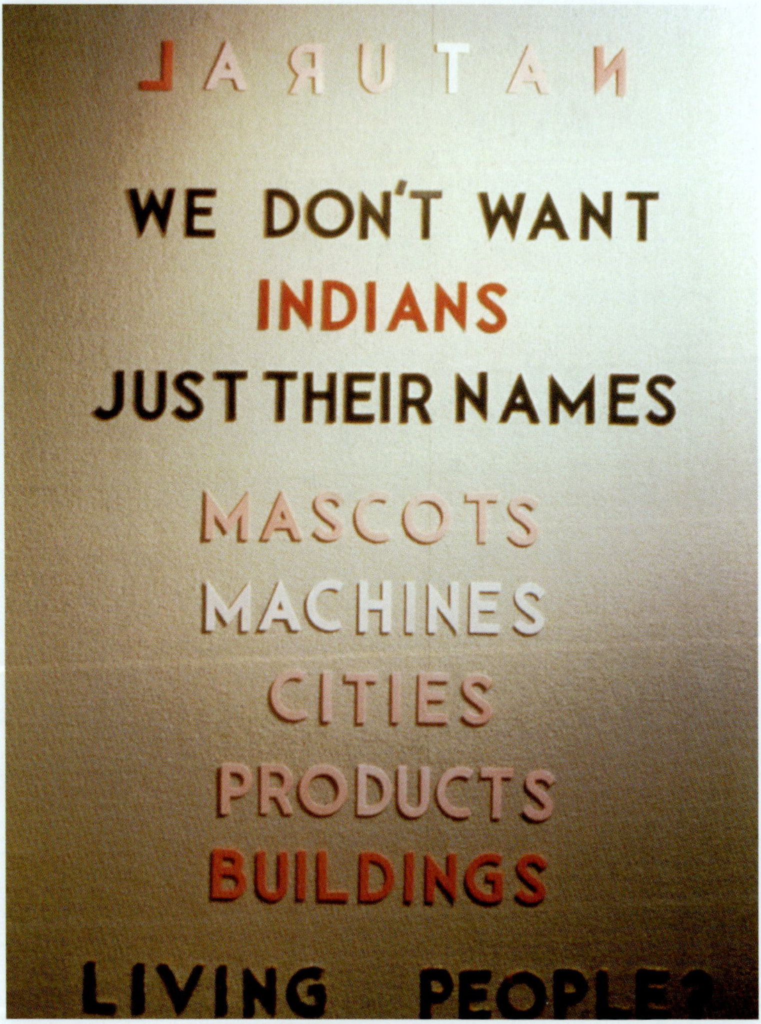

2.12 Edgar Heap of Birds, *Don't Want Indians*, 1982. Painted die-cut text installation, 5 × 8 feet. Artwork © Edgar Heap of Birds. The wall installation *Don't Want Indians* was also shown with the radical art collective Group Material in the 1985 Whitney Biennial, and in 1989 the text was reprised as a screenprint, *Telling Many Magpies, Telling Black Wolf, Telling Hachivi*, that also incorporated Heap of Birds's distinctive *Neuf* forms.

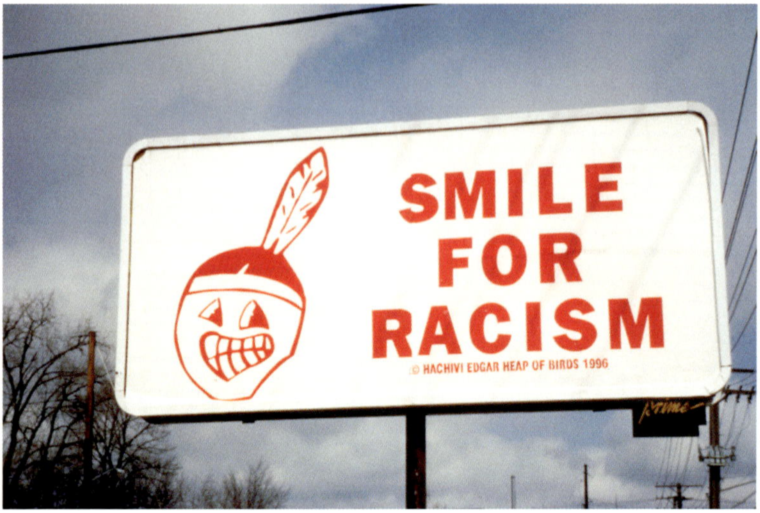

2.13 Edgar Heap of Birds, *American Leagues*, 1995. Billboard, 6 × 12 feet. Cleveland, Ohio. Artwork © Edgar Heap of Birds.

tive "we" rendered as no longer passive by the act of speaking out—and an audience, rendered passive and disempowered by the logic and force of the work's critique. Kruger's phrase—concise, incisive, and razor sharp—calls out a complacent culture in which binary oppositions (female and male, black and white) isometrically reinforce others (nature and culture, powerless and powerful) undergirding a systemic inequality. But for Kruger (as for Holzer and other artists) the pronouns "we" and "your" remain unidentified, leaving the reader to come to her own conclusions about the artist's message. For his part, Heap of Birds was critical of his postmodernist cohort: "they raise questions," he told an interviewer, "but do not answer them."[35]

If Heap of Birds was reproachful of the ambivalence of some of his peers, his own work aimed for terse concision. If his phrases were multivalent ("hosts" or "enemies"?), he did not want audiences puzzling over the identity of ambiguous pronouns. When in 1982 Heap of Birds (like Kruger a year later) addressed the coding of a population as "natural," he was clear about the target of his critique. In *Don't Want Indians*, he bracketed the phrase "WE DON'T WANT INDIANS / JUST THEIR NAMES / MASCOTS / MACHINES / CITIES / PRODUCTS / BUILDINGS" (in pink die-cut letters) with the word "NATURAL" (in backward type) at the top, and with the phrase "LIVING PEOPLE?" (in yellow-green) at the bottom. Heap of

Birds explains, "Even as these grave hardships exist for the living Indian people, a mockery is made of us by reducing our tribal names and images to the level of insulting sports team mascots, brand name automobiles, camping equipment, city and state names, and various other commercial products produced by the dominant culture. . . . This strange and insensitive custom is particularly insulting when one considers the great lack of attention given to real Indian concerns."[36] To make his point, Heap of Birds deployed color and typography symbolically: the pink lettering for the words MASCOTS, MACHINES, CITIES, PRODUCTS, and BUILDINGS links them to "the true color of the Anglo American," while the yellow-green of the phrase "LIVING PEOPLE?" references "the living, vital, and *growing* American Indian."[37] The different colors and orientations suggest different voices and varying critical readings of key words. In much of the critical

2.14 Edgar Heap of Birds, *Possible Lives*, 1985. Painted die-cut text installation. CEPA Gallery, Buffalo, New York. Artwork © Edgar Heap of Birds. Heap of Birds posing with his grandmother, Lightning Woman, whose beadwork moccasins were referenced in an early abstract artwork.

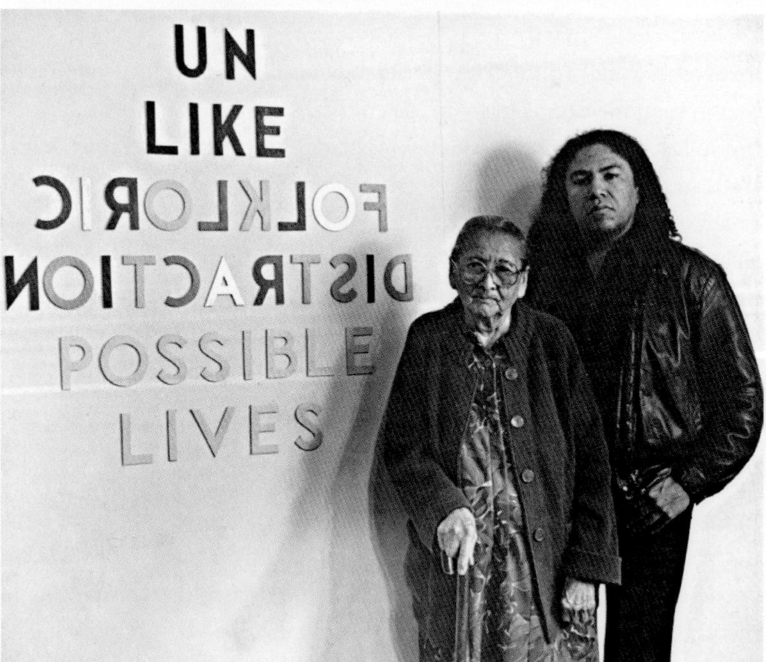

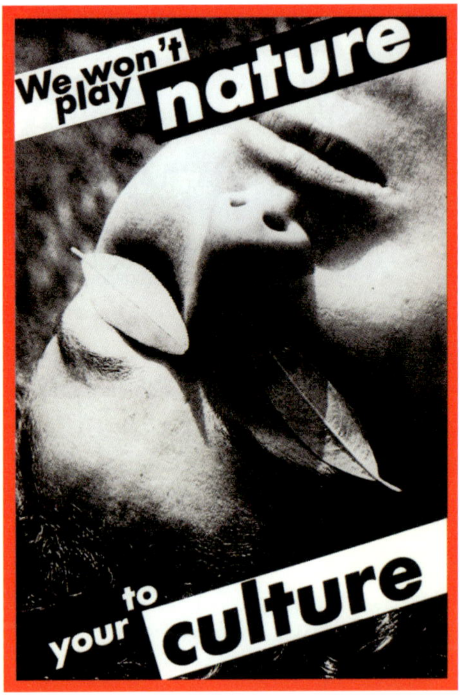

2.15 Barbara Kruger, *Untitled (We Won't Play Nature to Your Culture)*, 1983. Photograph, 73 × 49 inches. Artwork © Barbara Kruger. Courtesy of Mary Boone Gallery, New York.

text-based work of the 1980s, artists took on different voices, suggesting that in semiotic campaigns—in the cultural struggles that were taking on the stakes of conventional politics—personas were mutable, roles might shift, and identities were not essential. Heap of Birds addressed his readers as among the "WE" who "DON'T WANT INDIANS." But if Heap of Birds shared a sense of the mutability of identities with his postmodernist peers, however, his work drew clear lines between history's winners and losers, visitors and hosts. The installation was also Heap of Birds's first use of reversed type—an effect that has become the artist's signature.

Narrating Countermemory

In the 1983 installation *Death from the Top*, Heap of Birds took as his topic the Washita Massacre of November 27, 1868. The massacre is also known as the Battle of Washita. Heap of Birds is attentive to the power of naming for historical memory. "If white people died," he says, "it was called a massacre. If Indians died, it was a battle."[38] To be sure, the word "battle" conjures an image of evenly matched protagonists. Washita was certainly a massacre—a defeat—for the Southern Cheyenne, by then living in western Oklahoma, for whom the event is a formative historical moment.

To recount the events at Washita, Heap of Birds created a text installation in capitalized die-cut letters arranged in three columns, suggesting a grid. Recalling *Win of Birds*, he created groups of two- to three-line phrases—clusters that suggest images. Moving left to right, the top row reads, WESTERN, LIVING (reversed), HEMISPHERE; bracketed along the bottom row, from right to left (as is suggested by the reversed text): "DOMINATE RELOCATE DESTROY" and "MOVING AGAINST EARTH." Sandwiched between these two rows are two- and three-line phrases: "WASHITA RIVER / NOV 27, 1868"; "DEATH / FROM THE / TOP"; "FORGET / FORGOT"; "SLEEPING / CHILDREN"; "RUNNING CHILDREN"; "MURDERED / IN THE / WATER"; "FIND / MY PEOPLE"; "KILL / MY PEOPLE"; "PROUD / BRAVE / BRUTALITY." The text can of course be read in any particular order, but a narrative and a commentary emerge nonetheless.

In addition to being an early work that made use exclusively of text, *Death from the Top* was Heap of Birds's first use of a recovered historical voice; he authored his text in dialogue with the description of the massacre as recalled by Moving Behind, a Cheyenne girl who was fourteen years old when General George Custer's troops murdered and mutilated the bodies of Cheyenne in Black Kettle's camp. Moving Behind remembered:

> Many Tsistsistas (Cheyenne) were killed during the fight. The air was full of smoke from gunfire, and it was almost impossible to flee, because bullets were flying everywhere. However, somehow we ran and kept running to find a hiding place. As we ran, we could see the red fire of shots. We got near a hill, and there we saw a steep path where an old road used to be. There was red grass along the path, and although the ponies had eaten some of it, it was still high enough for us to hide.
>
> In this grass we lay flat, our hearts beating fast; and we were afraid to move. It was now broad daylight. It frightened us to listen to the noise and cries of the wounded. When the noise seemed to quiet down and we believed the battle was about to end, we raised our heads high enough to see what was going on. We saw a dark figure lying near a hill, and later we learned it was the body of a Tsistsistas woman and child. The woman's body had been cut open by the soldiers.[39]

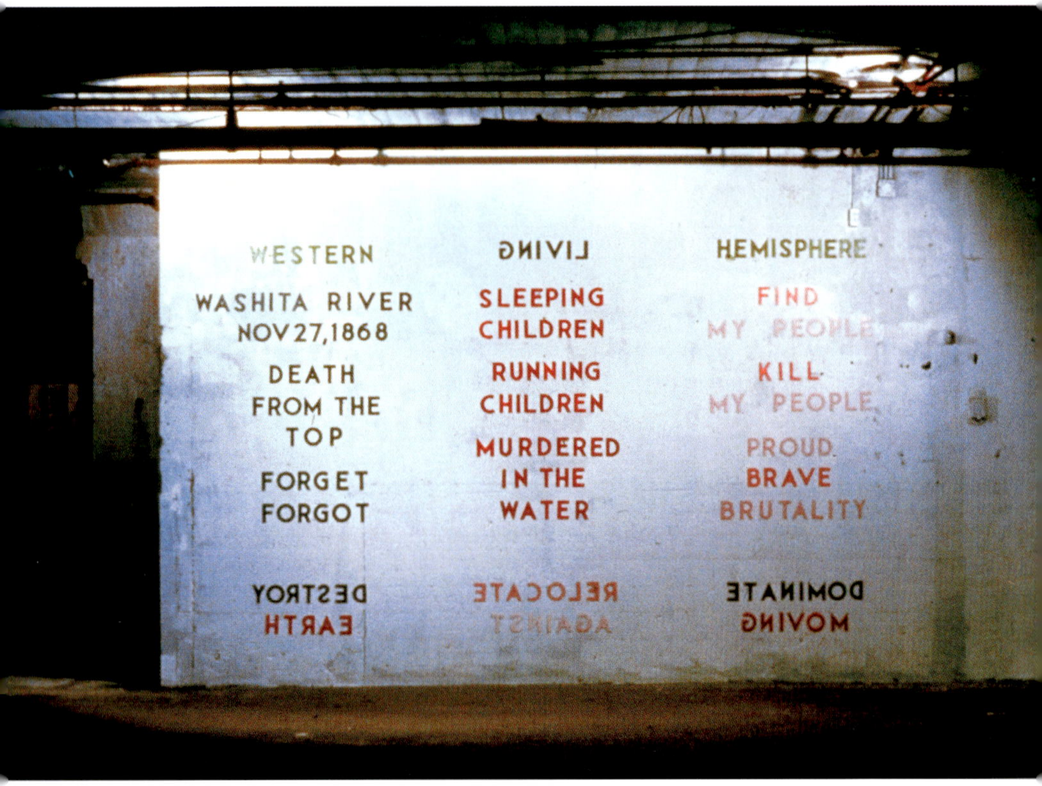

2.16 Edgar Heap of Birds, *Death from the Top*, 1983. Painted die-cut text installation, 8 × 20 feet. Artwork © Edgar Heap of Birds. From the exhibition *Preparing for War, Terminal New York* at the Brooklyn Military Terminal, 1983. In 1985, *Death from the Top*, in a slightly altered, smaller form (8 × 12 feet), was included in the exhibition *Image/Word: The Art of Reading*, organized by poet Barret Watten at New Langton Arts in San Francisco, featuring artists working in a conceptual text-based mode, including Vito Acconci, Mitchell Syrop, Allan Ruppersburg, Gary Hill, and others. Heap of Birds describes his participation in the *Preparing for War* exhibition as transformative, because he exhibited with Acconci, who had made an impression when he visited and spoke at the Tyler School of Art when Heap of Birds was a student.

Heap of Birds doesn't quote from Moving Behind's testimony in *Death from the Top*. He reacts to it. His text establishes a setting and links the historical tragedy that Moving Behind witnessed to the larger project of U.S. expansionism. In an essay in 1989, Heap of Birds argued that American society is organized hierarchically: "White America certainly considers that the best in life is theirs for the enjoyment, and that they alone occupy the 'Top.' Furthermore, a sharing of the whiteman's accumulated or stolen privileges is not forthcoming towards Native Americans."[40] Death came from the top in the new society that was violently coming into being in North America in the nineteenth century. White rule and white privilege, Heap of Birds argues, are constructed on a foundation of murder. But while the language is graphic—speaking of sleeping children murdered (drowned?) and Cheyenne hunted down and killed like prey—the execution in mechanical type has the effect of silencing the gunshots and clamor of the massacre scene. Rushing describes *Death from the Top* as a "soundless précis of murderous rage and lamentation."[41]

Silence might be interpreted as a metaphor for experiences lost to history—voices that have not become part of a shared cultural inheritance because they challenge the simplistic story of the winning of the West (the very phrase Heap of Birds disassembled and jumbled in *Win of Birds*). Heap of Birds has explained that he never learned about the massacre, despite its importance, until he was an adult: "No one ever talked about it," he said.[42] Moving Behind's is an exemplary countermemory of the Native experience of American Manifest Destiny, but her damning testimony remains mostly forgotten, locked in the archive—silent. Heap of Birds included her statement in his *Sharp Rocks* artist's book as an act of archival remembering and reactivation. Moved and "sickened" by the story of Cheyenne murdered in cold blood, Heap of Birds has refused to produce "syrupy narrative paintings" about Indians as history's victims.[43] Instead, making Moving Behind's account of the Washita Massacre the basis for a contemporary artwork—and reprinting an excerpt from it—Heap of Birds critiques America's historical amnesia. The nation founded on theft and murder is still unable to reckon with its violent past. *Death from the Top* in many ways represents unfinished business. Powerful phrases from this work—"DEATH FROM THE TOP"; "RELOCATE DESTROY"—reappear in later artworks, their memory work an unfinished, ongoing responsibility.

The Artist's Voice: Wall Lyrics

By the mid-1980s, Heap of Birds had developed a new style of hand-drawn lettering. Accumulations of multicolored pastel marks read alternately as shaggy or engulfed in flames. Heap of Birds first made the pastel drawings as sketches for his die-cut text installations. However, after showing the sketches in a window exhibition in Seattle, he decided that he preferred the raw and expressive quality of the pastel drawings and stopped making die-cuts.[44] He also began to separate his work into two distinct modes: works produced by commercial typesetters and printers, intended as interventions in public spaces; and handmade drawings (as well as studio print editions). In general, the handmade works were destined for the more intimate spaces of the gallery. With their agitated marks, they explored personal themes and experiences in a more diaristic tone. Heap of Birds termed these new artworks "wall lyrics," underscoring their links to music and their improvisational, rhythmic nature. And like song lyrics often are, the language of the hand-drawn works—including the later marker drawings and painterly monoprints—is coded, stylized, and abstracted. In these works, Heap of Birds delights in word play and ambiguity. One critic described them as "pointed and austere, elliptical and full of poetry."[45] (As critic Shanna Ketchum notes, Heap of Birds maintained the distinction between more intimate, handmade works and industrially produced public works until 2005, when the two modes were merged in *Wheel*, an outdoor public work installed at the Denver Art Museum, discussed in chapter 3.)[46]

Heap of Birds began work on *Heh No Wah Maun Stun He Dun (What Makes a Man)* in 1986, after completing his first four-year cycle of the Earth Renewal and taking on a leadership role in the ceremonial life of his reservation community. He was in his early thirties and coming to terms with his own identity and responsibilities as a Cheyenne, husband, father, and artist. Dealing now with deeply personal feelings, Heap of Birds developed a new technique for rendering the words in pastel, imparting a confessional urgency to the series. Rushing writes, "The group of pastels that constitutes 'What Makes a Man' is courageously candid, sharing with feminist art a willingness to speak/sing the self in terms of nature, gender, family and society (or tribe)."[47] In addressing what he termed "the personal politics of manhood," Heap of Birds sought to make more complex notions of Native identity and experience. "To open Native artistic endeavors to the issue of sexual energy," he wrote, "will bring about public recognition that Natives in America are *Individuals*."[48] As with his die-cut type installations, the layout does not dictate a sequence in which the individual drawings should be read, but taken together the drawings, according to Heap of Birds, "portray love, hate, dominance, nurturing, growth, death, questioning, loneliness, leadership, responsibility, sexuality, and many other emotions."[49]

The series—completed between 1986 and 1987—comprises four large, composite drawings, each in turn comprising a grid of fifteen individual pastel drawings on twenty-two-by-thirty-inch rag paper. Each individual sheet of paper contains a phrase of two, three, or four words. As critic Jean Fisher has noted, Heap of Birds grouped his drawings "according to the primary categories of a man's life"—*Self*, *Sexual*, *Tribal Warrior*, and *Boy, Woman, Family*.[50] The groupings *Self* and *Sexual* are arranged vertically, echoing the proportion of a full-body portrait (five high and three across), embodying their exploration of individual identity. *Boy, Woman, Family* and *Tribal Warrior* are arranged horizontally, five across by three high, and express roles and responsibilities of the individual within the family and the community—the "tribal responsibilities of a traditional headsman of the Cheyenne (Tsistsistas) Elk warrior society," Heap of Birds explains.[51]

The groupings are productively studied in pairs. The vertical orientation of *Self* suggests a portrait, appropriate to the group's meditation on the artist as individual—"IN LIMBO ALONE." Several panels refer to intense states and personal processes of emotional growth: "ENTER DARK POOLS, STATE OF RAGE, BOY INTENSE, FIXING THE NEED, PUSH YOUR LUCK, KNOW ROUND SHADOW." The phrase "NO TIME JUST SEASONS" seems to find an accommodation with the cyclical, ritual calendar of the Cheyenne, based around the rhythm of the seasons and beginning with the summer solstice and the Earth Renewal. Some panels seem to indicate a negotiation—if angrily—with Native identity: "NATIVE IS PAIN"; "PISS ON RED EARTH." Others hint at emerging relationships: "ENTER LOVE FLAMES"; "WISHING TO TRUST"; "ASK NOTHING SHE." The individualistic pursuit of fulfillment in *Self* contrasts with the horizontally arranged *Tribal Warrior*. Here the landscape format seems to suggest the broader milieu in which the individual faces responsibilities to find meaning in the collective, in which individual desires are subordinated to the group. Heap of Birds's participation in the Earth Renewal is key to reading the piece: the

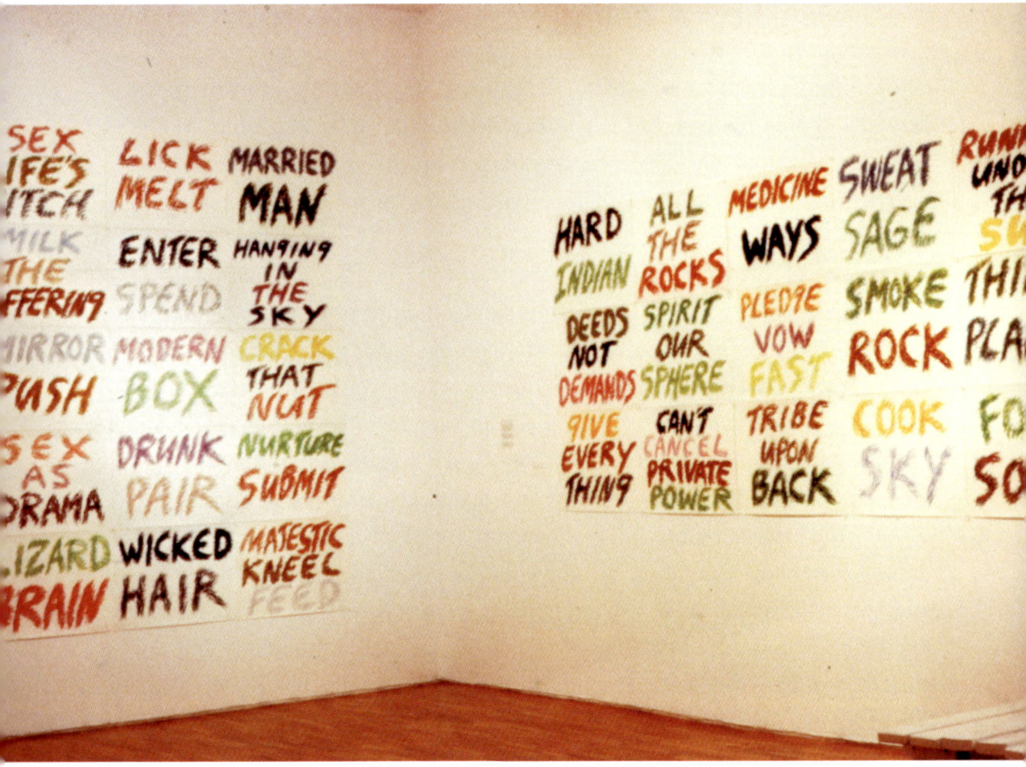

2.17 Edgar Heap of Birds, *Heh No Wah Maun Stun He Dun (What Makes a Man)*, 1986–87. Pastel on rag paper, sixty drawings, each 22 × 30 inches. Two groupings 110 × 90 inches; two groupings 66 × 150 inches. Artwork © Edgar Heap of Birds. Detail of installation with *Sexual* (left) and *Tribal Warrior* (right).

"HARD INDIAN . . . CAN'T CANCEL PRIVATE POWER." The artist as warrior must "GIVE EVERYTHING"; perform "DEEDS NOT DEMANDS," and carry the "TRIBE UPON BACK," for whom he has committed to "PLEDGE, VOW, FAST." Several words refer specifically to the experience of the ceremony: "MEDICINE WAYS"; "SWEAT SAGE"; "RUNNING UNDER THE SUN"; "COOK SKY"; "FOUR SONGS"; "SPIRIT OUR SPHERE." The panel "THIRD PLANET" recalls Heap of Birds's description of the Earth Renewal lodge as a type of "space craft."

The grouping *Sexual* is oriented vertically—presented like *Self* as a portrait. It includes phrases that connote passion and the primal nature of sex: "LIZARD BRAIN," "SEX AS DRAMA," "NURTURE SUBMIT," "ENTER

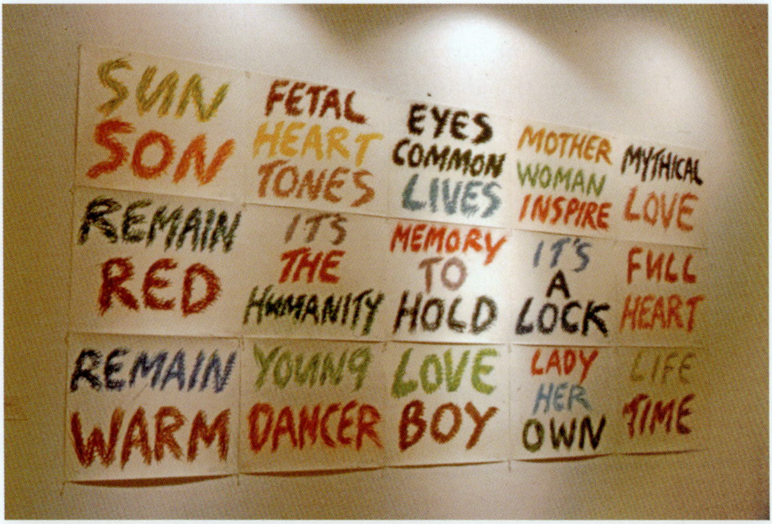

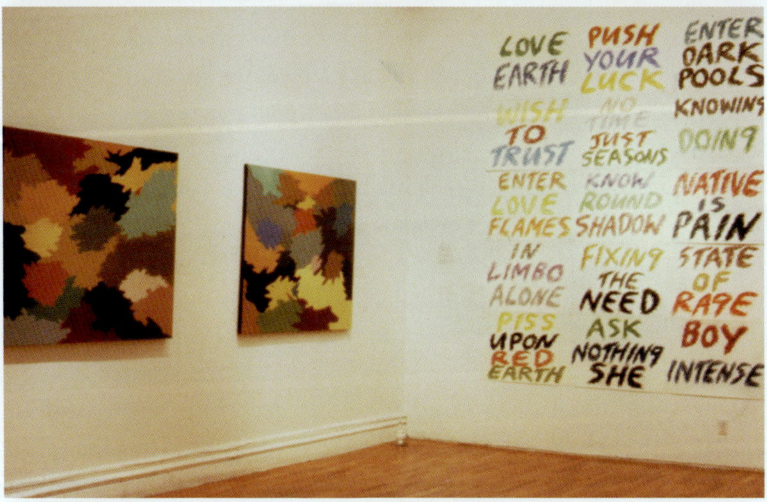

2.18 Edgar Heap of Birds, *Heh No Wah Maun Stun He Dun (What Makes a Man)*, 1986–87. Pastel on rag paper, sixty drawings, each 22 × 30 inches. Two groupings 110 × 90 inches; two groupings 66 × 150 inches. Artwork © Edgar Heap of Birds. Detail of installation with *Boy, Woman, Family*.

2.19 Edgar Heap of Birds, *Heh No Wah Maun Stun He Dun (What Makes a Man)*, 1986–87. Pastel on rag paper, sixty drawings, each 22 × 30 inches. Two groupings 110 × 90 inches; two groupings 66 × 150 inches. Artwork © Edgar Heap of Birds. Detail of installation with *Neuf* series paintings (left) and *Self* (right).

SPEND," while "MARRIED MAN" hints at the tensions between individual sexual fulfillment and life in a partnership and family unit, which is the subject of *Boy, Woman, Family*—oriented, like *Tribal Warrior*, horizontally. This grouping expresses the larger landscape of commitment and the idea of the family as the engine of community renewal: "REMAIN RED," "EYES COMMON LIVES," "MOTHER WOMAN INSPIRE," "LIFE TIME," even as individual members remain individuals: "LADY HER OWN."

When *What Makes a Man* was included in a traveling exhibition, the series of sixty drawings was shown, hung in the four groups, alongside four *Neuf* paintings. Exhibiting the wall lyrics with his abstract landscapes, Heap of Birds effectively grounded—emplaced—the series in the specific home place of the Cheyenne-Arapaho reservation in Oklahoma, from which Heap of Birds spoke. The titles of the four *Neuf* paintings, *Sweat Lodge Fire—Lava Rock*; *They Built a Fire in Summer*; *The Circle Was Hot*; and *Old Man Sat Calm Near the Heat* (all 1987), refer to the sweat lodge, the ceremony of personal and communal purification that is widely practiced by Native peoples. As Heap of Birds explained, the paintings "form[ed] the backdrop for the psychological and personal issues presented in the wall lyrics."[52]

For *American Policy*, a series of wall lyrics begun in 1986, Heap of Birds's hand-drawn words lend themselves to a critique of the costs of expansionist military and economic agendas in a personal, stream-of-consciousness mode. If in *Death from the Top* Heap of Birds began with a text by a survivor of the Washita Massacre, in *American Policy* Heap of Birds's own voice is foregrounded. Key phrases from *Death from the Top* are repeated from the die-cut letter installation—"DEATH FROM THE TOP" (which does not appear in the earlier work), "RELOCATE DESTROY"—linking the earlier installation to the later series. His essay "Living upon a Grave: American Policy / Native Hosts" (1989) makes clear this intended connection (and also established linkages with *Native Hosts*). In quoting *Death from the Top*, *American Policy* returns to the Washita Massacre but also invokes the memory of the November 29, 1864, massacre of Cheyenne and Arapaho encamped with Black Kettle (who would die four years later at Washita) under a U.S. flag at Sand Creek.

The phrase UTERINE HATS is among the most graphic that Heap of Birds has authored—fully in the tradition of Goya's famous *Disasters of War*, which recounted in horrific detail the atrocities of Napoleonic France's

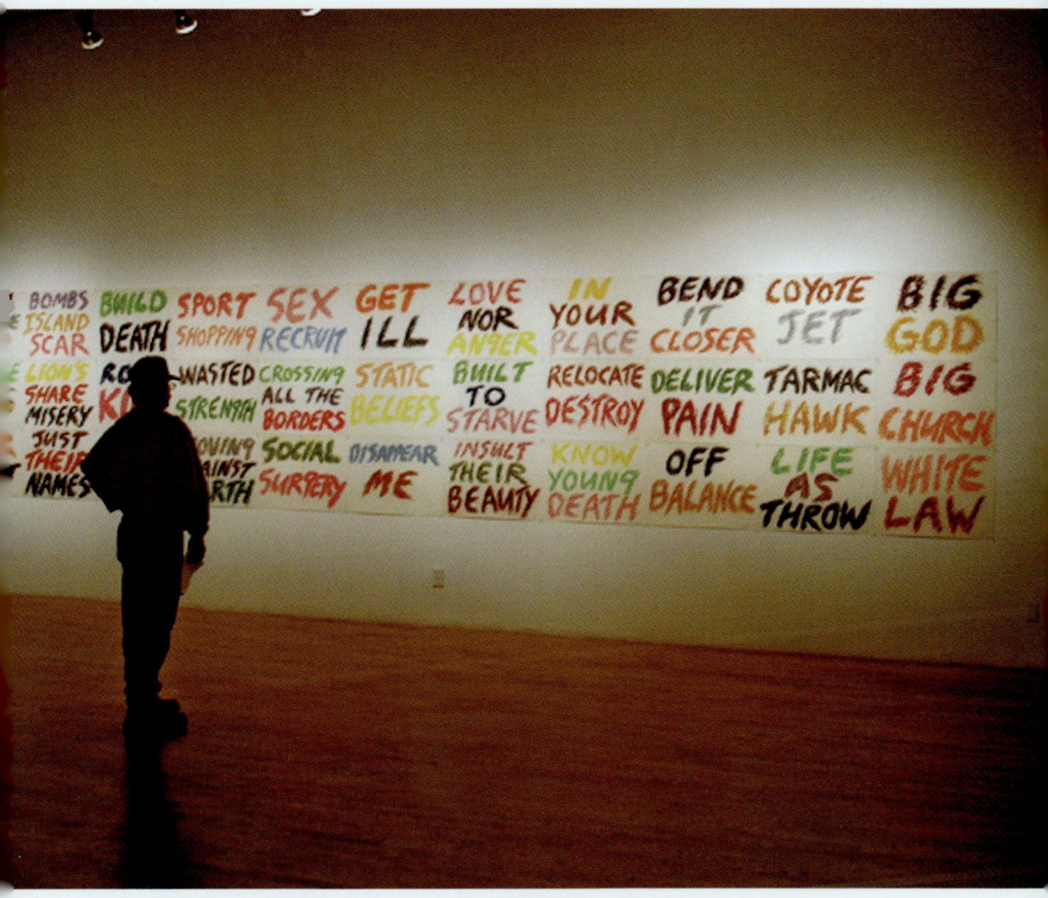

2.20 Edgar Heap of Birds, *American Policy*, 1988. Pastel on rag paper, twenty-four drawings, each 30 × 22 inches. Artwork © Edgar Heap of Birds.

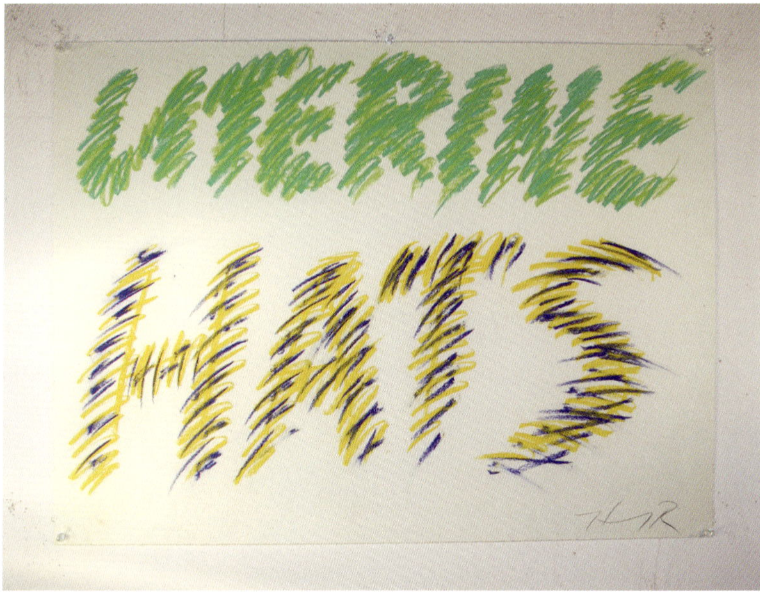

2.21 Edgar Heap of Birds, *American Policy*, 1988. Pastel on rag paper, twenty-four drawings, each 30 × 22 inches. Artwork © Edgar Heap of Birds. Detail: *Uterine Hats.*

wars of empire. As Heap of Birds explains the gruesome phrase, based on his research into the history of the massacre: "After the killing was complete, America's monstrous soldiers found sport in cutting open the bodies of dead Tsistsistas [Cheyenne] women. These soldiers feverishly sought to destroy the Native womb. They were intent upon ripping away the uterus of the Cheyenne, taking away the once loving home of our future infant. After seizing the wombs from the silent bodies, the soldiers paraded each uterus upon a stick and then fashioned the female organs into ornaments for their hats."[53]

Graphic references to America's bloody Indian wars share space with phrases that suggest military adventures on a world scale ("CROSSING ALL THE BORDERS," "ISLAND SCAR," "COYOTE JET") and a legacy of violence at home ("KNOW YOUNG DEATH," "ROAD KILL"). *Death from the Top* and *American Policy* contributed to a developing body of critical works in several media comparing the global reach of the U.S. military to the history of domestic repression and violence against Native peoples, implicating the development and wealth of the settler state with the policies that dispossessed and still disadvantage indigenous communities in North America, and placing U.S.-Indian relations in a broader, global context that Heap of Birds would continue to develop in later works.

Heap of Birds stopped making pastel drawings for many years as the marker drawings he had made as studies for the wall lyrics took on a life of their own in 1994, during a residency in Australia, and as the process of producing the pastel drawings became too physically grueling to sustain. The marker drawings began as plans for pastel drawings, which he grouped in page-like arrangements on his studio walls. He then moved on to large sheets of rag paper, which better accommodated the large motions of drawing freehand with marker.[54] The effect of the marker drawings is similar in some respect to the interlocking-patterned fields of the *Neuf* paintings, distinguishing them from the regularized grid of the pastel wall lyrics, when they are hung in rectangular groupings. Their surfaces are thickets—sometimes dense, at other times more sparse—of marks showing the artist at work; indexes of a psychological and physical process that unfolds over many days, weeks, and months. In his studio, Heap of Birds works on the drawings on large sheets of paper tacked to the wall, gradually covering the entire surface with a free-form accretion of phrases that skew across the surface, often cutting across earlier words and strings of words. Art historian Jo Ortel describes the marker drawings with a geological metaphor, likening them to "so many fissures in a rock face" that develop over long periods.[55]

They also share characteristics with the personal palimpsest of a well-used notebook or scratch pad, to which they are in fact close relatives. "My Marker Drawings served as kind of a diary log-in platform. Each piece was made over maybe one year of time," Heap of Birds explains. "The words are mostly personal reflections in a coded language."[56] An example is the marker drawing that Heap of Birds exhibited in 2002 as part of the exhibition *Eagles Speak*—a collection of three-letter international airport codes, a remembered itinerary of Heap of Birds's career as an artist. Others, such as the marker drawings that were part of the preparatory process for works such as *Ocmulgee* (2005), *Wheel* (2005), or *Please the Waters* (2009), allow a view into the creative process. In other instances, such as *Thursdays* (2005), created with students at the Bandung Institute of Technology, Java, Indonesia, in 2005, the marker drawings became a kind of collaborative word game that was exhibited as an artwork in its own right. Some drawings—

such as VACANT, WANT, or OTTAWA—are anchored by a single word, drawn at large scale and built up from numerous agitated marks. The labored feeling of these central words compares to the pastel words in the wall lyrics, but the marker drawings are executed solely in black on white. Curator Susan Snodgrass noted that the black-and-white palette of the drawings is a clue to their origin as a private, diaristic, and generative process, not initially intended for public display—contrasting with the vibrant color of the more considered and composed pastel wall lyrics.[57]

The word MONETISH (1994) appears as a reference to Claude Monet, to whose work Heap of Birds's abstract *Neuf* paintings might be compared; their lack of a horizon line echoes the impressionist painter's late landscapes and waterscapes, themselves antecedents of abstract expressionism—another art historical precedent for Heap of Birds's landscape paintings. Monet's late landscapes immerse the viewer in a boundless field that extends beyond the edge of the canvas. The marker drawings also conjure such a visual experience. (Heap of Birds also notes that the term "Monetish" can refer to something that appears good from a distance but up close looks "jacked up."[58] Or perhaps, with a shift in orientation and perspective, or accumulated strata and geological processes, as Ortel suggests, it could be a meditation on place and history in the most expansive sense.) Moreover, both artists based their serial paintings in their immediate and intimate environment: Monet's gardens at Giverny and Heap of Birds's reservation home place. A reference to Monet, of course, locates Heap of Birds in a world history of art—something to which any artist might aspire. But the coined word MONETISH also suggests other words—"Monetary," "Money," "Remuneration"—suggesting possible thoughts that might run through a working artist's mind in the studio. Other strings of words and phrases—at different scales—woven throughout the composition might also be read in this light: "SELLING YOUR ASS," "TASTE THE BLOCK," "DESPERATE PUPPETS."

But in general the subject of each marker drawing is private. *Tell Your Self*, the title of an early exhibition of marker drawings at the Art Gallery of New South Wales in 1994, reinforces the idea that the drawings are personal and exploratory, as well as an index of the artistic process, linking Heap of Birds to Surrealism and the technique of automatic writing, which influenced him. As opposed to the edited and refined wall lyrics, or the mechanical text of the public messages, the marker drawings remain private and obscure. Heap of Birds has been critical of the national penchant

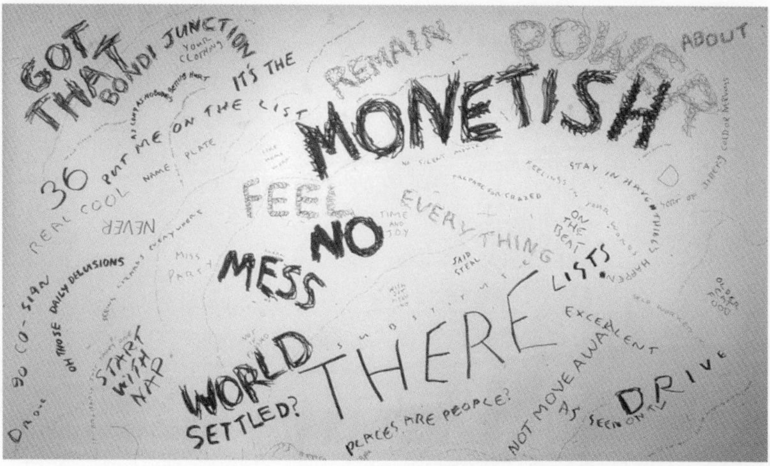

2.22 Edgar Heap of Birds, *Monetish*, 1994. Marker on rag paper, 6½ × 13 feet. Artwork © Edgar Heap of Birds.

for placing Native Americans on perpetual display—public property, as it were, projection screens for white fantasies but silenced on their own account. If in some works—most notably *What Makes a Man*—Heap of Birds is confessional and revelatory, in the marker drawings the thought process is coded; the artist is present, but he remains unreadable, unknown.

In 2009, Heap of Birds returned to his pastel technique for *Crosses for Diné/Tepoztlan*. His previous pastel drawings had been exhibited in a grid format—a default format dictated as much by the rectangular shape of the rag paper as by anything deliberately chosen. But the grid carried connotations that were not altogether amenable to Heap of Birds's intended message—the grid inevitably invokes ideal geometrical forms associated with rationalized mapping and the checkerboard pattern of privatization, settlement, and enclosure, which was overlaid onto the North American landscape regardless of topography and which aided in the dispossession of Indian lands, which were held in common and across which movement was uninhibited. For all the emotional complexity and anti-imperialist critique of the pastel drawings *What Makes a Man* and *American Policy*, the grid remained the unexamined framework. When he returned to the pastels, Heap of Birds felt he needed to find a more intentional arrangement. He arrived at the form of the cross for his first pastel drawings in several years, which were exhibited in 2009.

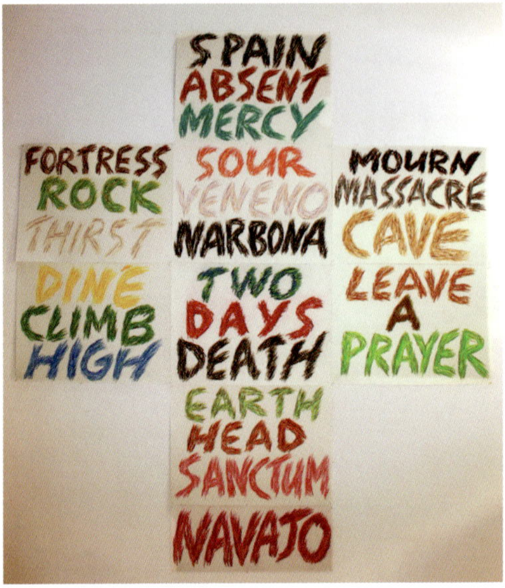

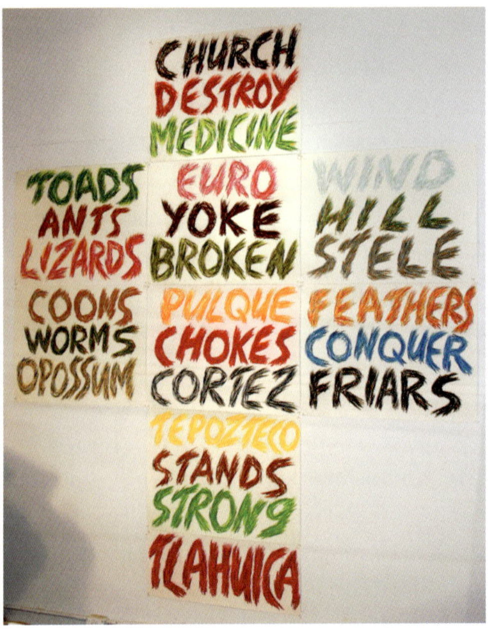

2.23 Edgar Heap of Birds, *Cross for Diné*, 2009. Pastel on rag paper, each sheet 30 × 22 inches. Artwork © Edgar Heap of Birds. When *Cross for Diné* and *Cross for Tepoztlan* were installed at the Kresge Art Museum at Michigan State University, the exhibition was accompanied by a temporary outdoor installation of the site-specific *Native Hosts* series.

2.24 Edgar Heap of Birds, *Cross for Tepoztlan*, 2009. Pastel on rag paper, each sheet 30 × 22 inches. Artwork © Edgar Heap of Birds.

For *Crosses for Diné/Tepoztlan*, Heap of Birds arranged his pastel drawings on nine sheets of paper, approximating a Latin cross, in reference to the symbol carried by the first Spaniards in the Americas—conquerors and missionaries. The new format added a layer of meaning to Heap of Birds's critical engagement with the history of European imperialism. He produced two crosses, dedicated to "our Native peoples lost in Tepoztlan and Canyon de Chelly"—the Tlahuica Nation, from Tepoztlan in present-day Morelos, Mexico, and the Navajo or Diné from Canyon de Chelly in present-day Arizona. In his signature three-word phrases, Heap of Birds recounted and reclaimed these histories of conquest. As Heap of Birds writes, although "indigenous spirits suffered due to violence perpetrated by the Spanish crown, army and church," both peoples endured despite the onslaught. The Tlahuica suffered "the burning of their city by Hernan Cortez and the sacking of the ceremonial pyramid temple, Tepozteco, by the friars, 1521." And yet, as the *Cross for Tepoztlan* proclaims: "PULQUE CHOKES CORTEZ," "FEATHERS CONQUER FRIARS," and "TEPOZTECO [the destroyed pyramid] STANDS STRONG," as "TOADS ANTS LIZARDS," and "COONS WORMS OPPOSUM" also persevere (echoing the enduring Hudson River ecosystem Heap of Birds celebrated in *Please the Waters*). Heap of Birds writes that three centuries later the Diné "survived the Spanish bullets at Massacre Cave, as over one hundred and twenty-five Navajo/Dine were killed by the 'Norbona Expedition' 1805."[59] The *Cross for Diné* urges viewers to "MOURN MASSACRE CAVE" and "LEAVE A PRAYER." The installations are ambivalent memorials, taking the form of the cross as do many such shrines but also critiquing, implicitly, the deadly power of the symbol as it was wielded by would-be conquerors throughout history.

Monoprint Series: A Public Journal of Process

In 2004, Heap of Birds began to create series of monoprints—unique, noneditioned prints, which are produced from a painting made on a plate run through a press, creating a mirror image of the original composition. For the first works, produced in Santa Fe, New Mexico, Heap of Birds developed a process in which he would generate evocative three- or four-word phrases that represented a single thought—collected on three-by-five-inch index cards in his studio, over the course of days and weeks—in much the same way that his marker drawings had evolved, creating an

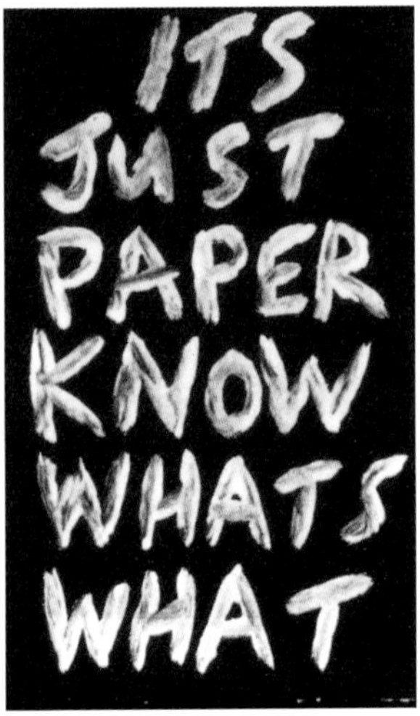

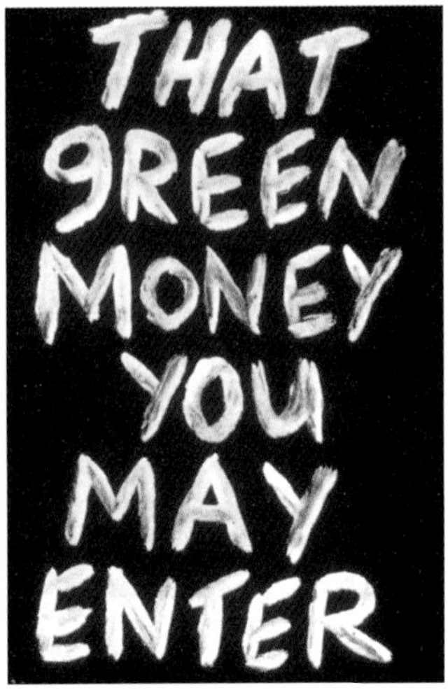

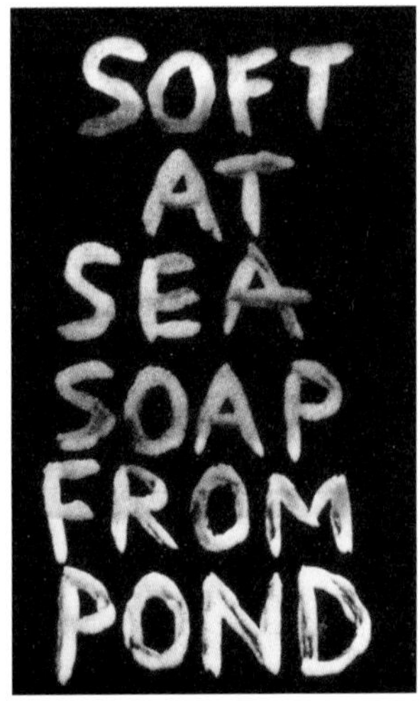

2.25 Edgar Heap of Birds, *Its Just Paper Know Whats What*, 2004. Monoprint on rag paper, 15 × 22 inches. Artwork © Edgar Heap of Birds.

2.26 Edgar Heap of Birds, *That Green Money You May Enter*, 2004. Monoprint on rag paper, 15 × 22 inches. Artwork © Edgar Heap of Birds.

2.27 Edgar Heap of Birds, *Soft at Sea Soap from Pond*, 2004. Monoprint on rag paper, 15 × 22 inches. Artwork © Edgar Heap of Birds.

index of his thoughts and working process, which, nonetheless, remained a coded and opaque record of the artist's experiences. The three-word phrases were then joined into groupings of six words, in the manner of a surrealist exquisite corpse.

In the monoprints, phrases from earlier works reappear—in particular, phrases that reference the history of Native American genocide and images of horrific violence. As in *Death from the Top* and the wall lyrics, Heap of Birds responds to the historical record in personal terms—fixating on key strings of words that resonate as poetic images: "CRY FOR WHITE CROW BASHED BABY"; "BULLETS ARE RAPID FLESH IS SOFT"; "FIND PEOPLE KILL PEOPLE WASHITA RIVER"; "MAKE UTERINE HATS YOUR SPORT." Other prints in the series mark the still ever-present specter of death for contemporary Native people: "INDIO ROAD KILL AGAIN AND AGAIN"; "DEAD INDIAN RUN OVER BY CARS"; "BODY BAG IN BACK DINÉ TRUCK." Other repeating phrases, such as the one authored shortly after it was revealed that the U.S. military used the name of the Chiricahua

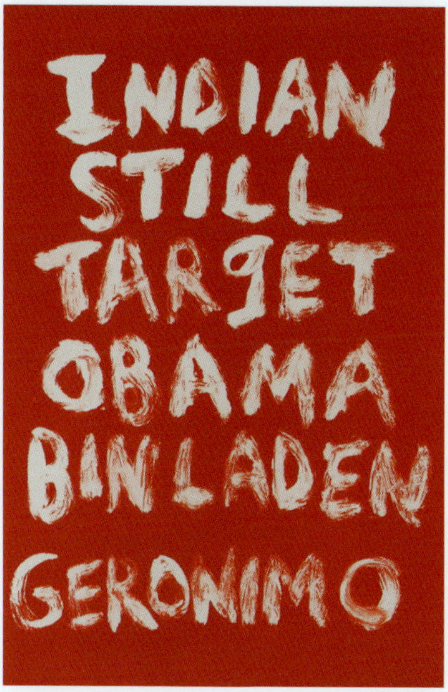

2.28 Edgar Heap of Birds, *Indian Still Target Obama Bin Laden Geronimo*, 2011. Monoprint on rag paper, 15 × 22 inches. Artwork © Edgar Heap of Birds.

Apache warrior Geronimo as the code for the fugitive leader of Al Qaeda, suggested that the image of the Indian as enemy combatant still haunts the American national imaginary as a figure for the violent and feared other: "INDIAN STILL TARGET OBAMA BIN LADEN GERONIMO."

The series constitutes a virtual catalog of the themes Heap of Birds has explored in his text-based works, as well as a public journal of new ideas and directions that are developed in other aspects of the artist's ongoing practice—the series is generative as well as reflective. Several phrases reference Heap of Birds's role in the Earth Renewal ceremony and Cheyenne traditional life, linking back to panels from *What Makes a Man*: "TRIBE UPON BACK CARRY WITH PRIDE"; "RENEW FOR EVERYONE DANCE WATER"; "ACROSS OUR SKY THE HOLY PEOPLE"; "NUANCE OF SKY HONOR OUR WAYS." Some phrases suggest issues of environment, individual and collective responsibility—"SOFT AT SEA SOAP FROM POND"—that would reappear in later works, such as *Please the Waters*. Others feature and obscure poetic observations: "TRYING TO BE LARGE SOFT BUSY"; "DELICATE FINGERS TRAVEL ACROSS YOUR VIEW"; "TRY HIDE SPOTS KITTY SAID MEOW." Other phrases are unique to the places Heap of Birds was when he produced each print series, referencing the lo-

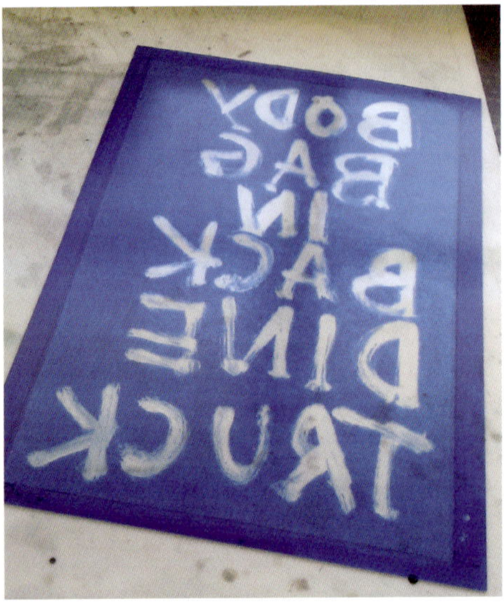

2.29 Edgar Heap of Birds, plate from monoprint series *Secrets in Life and Death*. Josephine Press, Santa Monica, California, 2012. Artwork © Edgar Heap of Birds.

cal context and studio experience in New Mexico, Minnesota, New York, or California.

Working with a master printer, Heap of Birds paints each phrase in reverse on a printer's plate and pulls a single monochrome image from each original. The process recalls in some ways Heap of Birds's signature use of backward text. In the monoprints the reversed text—reading right to left—creates an impression that reads left to right. The two incommensurable viewpoints are now resolved into one. The backward-reading original is destroyed in the process. Only the version that points forward remains.

For the first series in Santa Fe, Heap of Birds also created a large digital gicleé print that collected all the three-word phrases onto one composition and functioned like a compendium of the studio process. Taken together, the Santa Fe set reveals the thoughts and materials of a working artist, delighting in stream-of-consciousness word play but also engaged in the realities of the artist's life inside and outside the studio, the realities of the art market, and the uprooted life of the professional traveler, similar to the themes pursued in *Monetish* (1994) and his 2002 marker drawing of airport codes.

The monoprint series *Words, Trees, Chiapas* (2009) drew from Heap of Birds's travels to the state of Chiapas, in Mexico, where he visited the ancient Maya temples of Palenque and learned about the contemporary

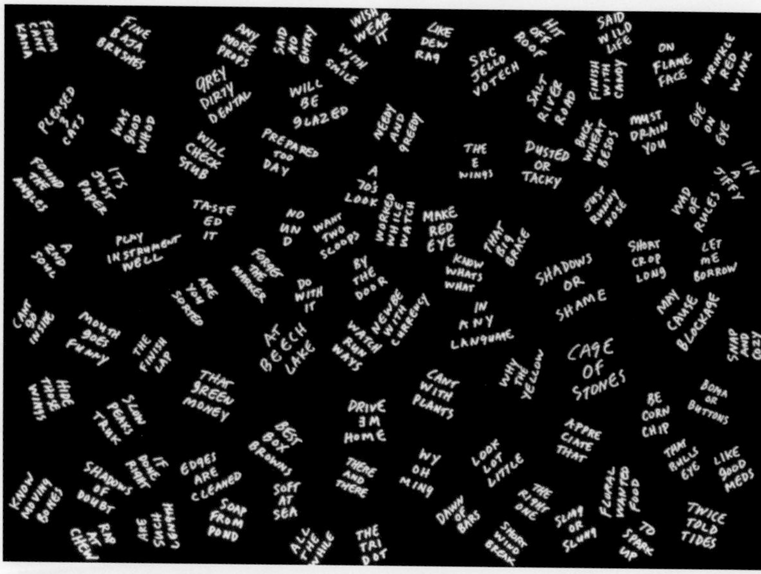

2.30 Edgar Heap of Birds, untitled gicleé print, 2004.
Artwork © Edgar Heap of Birds.

indigenous resistance movement spearheaded by the Zapatista Army of National Liberation (EZLN). He sought to make links between indigenous communities across the Americas: "My desire was to honor the spirit of the tree and our indigenous communities throughout the Americas, both past and present, south to north."[60] For the exhibition, monoprints hung alongside photographs documenting Heap of Birds's travels, depicting him standing near an ancient and impressive ceiba—esteemed by the Maya as the Tree of Life, which anchored the center of the universe and connected earthly and spiritual realms. Other photographs depicted the famous sarcophagus of Pacal, the ruler of the Maya city of Palenque in the late classic period. The monoprints make numerous references to Maya cosmology. "BLUE FACE TOMB READY FOR WATER" refers to Pacal's death mask, carved in blue-green jade, a powerful symbolic material that linked the deceased ruler to the watery underworld. The series also referenced Heap of Birds's own orientation as a northerner and a visitor in Central America: "HEAD TO NORTH FEET TO SOUTH." "INDIO COME SEE ON FREE DAY" refers to the one day per week that the site was opened to local indigenous people. In this print, Heap of Birds comments on the disconnection

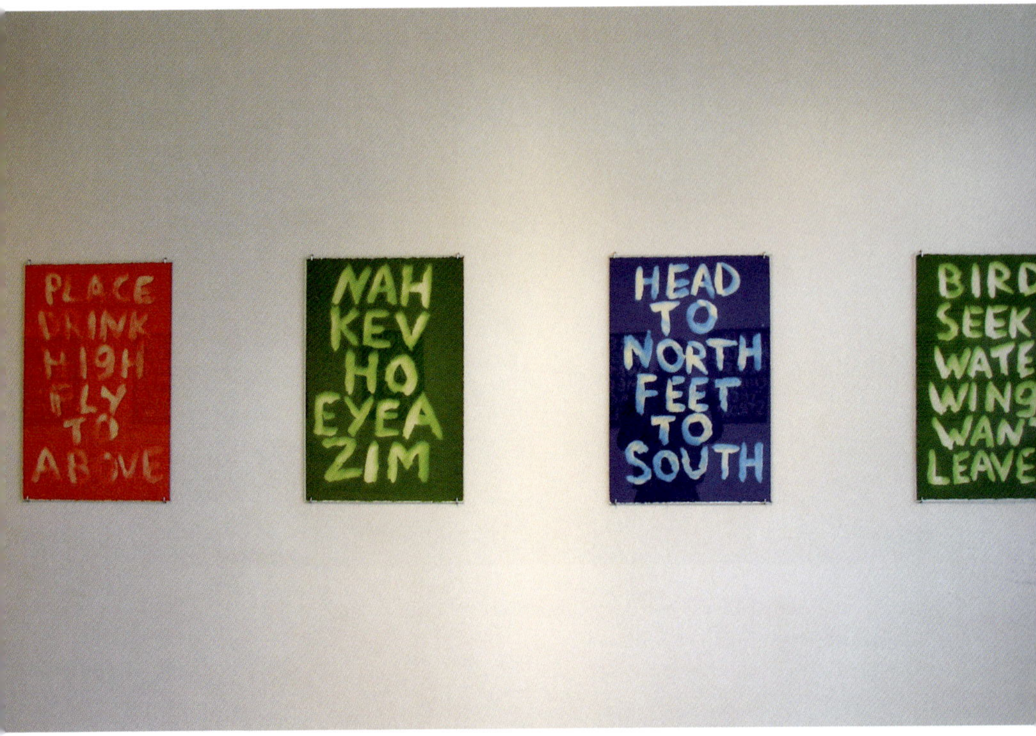

2.31 Edgar Heap of Birds, installation of four prints from *Words, Trees, Chiapas*, 2009. Monoprint series, each 15 × 22 inches. Artwork © Edgar Heap of Birds. Heap of Birds wrote that the series *Words, Trees, Chiapas*, printed in Minnesota and created to be shown at the Grunt Gallery in Vancouver, was linked conceptually to two public artworks and a gallery installation mounted elsewhere in the city, creating a four-part project he called Public Art of the Americas. The project included *Insurgent Messages for Canada*, ten commercially printed posters installed in bus shelters throughout the city in 2006; a new installation of *Native Hosts*, in which twelve tribal name panels were deployed around the campus of the University of British Columbia in 2007; and an installation of the graphic overlays used to fabricate his public artwork, *Wheel* (Denver 2005), exhibited at the Museum of Anthropology at the University of British Columbia.

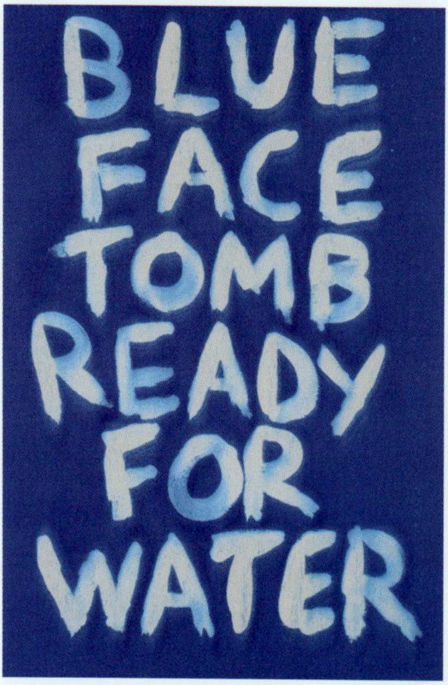

2.32 Edgar Heap of Birds, *Blue Face Tomb Ready for Water*, from *Words, Trees, Chiapas*, 2009. Monoprint on rag paper, 15 × 22 inches. Artwork © Edgar Heap of Birds.

between the indigenous past—often an object or commodity of a tourist economy or a matter of academic interest—and the present. Several panels speak to the Zapatista struggle for indigenous autonomy, linking the contemporary campaign to the Maya past: "EZLN FREE CHIAPAS MEX HONOR INDIO"; "ZAPA MARCOS RESIST CHIAPAS TREE STRONG."

Water Desert Words, created in 2010, grew from Heap of Birds's research among the Diné in Arizona and the Tuscarora in the Buffalo, New York, region, where the prints were published. Heap of Birds notes that both Diné and Tuscarora are matrilineal cultures, based in cultivation of corn/maize, and profoundly affected not only by Euro-American expansionism but by the economies of tourism. New markets grew around the commodification of art forms traditionally produced by women for local community use. Tuscarora beadwork and Diné woolen textiles were produced in large quantities for eager white audiences beginning in the nineteenth century as the Great Lakes region and the Southwest became popular destinations for travelers. Coincidentally, both art forms began to incorporate English as they accommodated new markets and responded to a changing world. As Heap of Birds writes, "Often the choice of text elements can be read as playful and ironic, sometimes bordering on an

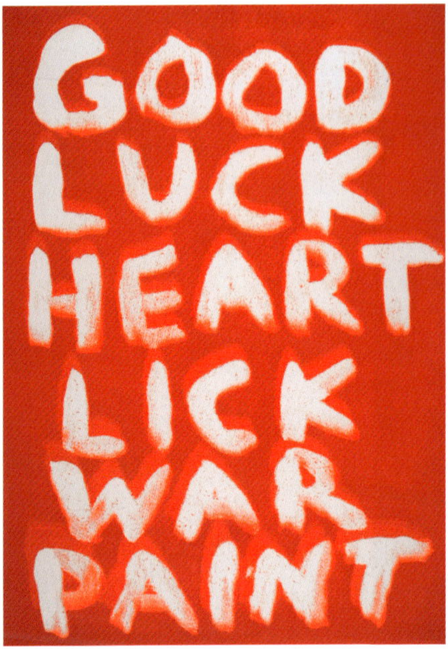

2.33 Edgar Heap of Birds, *Good Luck Heart Lick War Paint*, from *Water Desert Words*, 2010. Monoprint on rag paper, 15 × 22 inches. Artwork © Edgar Heap of Birds. Printed in New York and exhibited at CEPA Gallery, Buffalo, New York. Many of the works in *Water Desert Words* reference Tuscarora "whimsies" and Navajo text weavings and the influence of tourism and collecting on traditional Native American women's arts.

indigenous ridicule of the tourist's desire or expectation."[61] The use of language makes them uncanny ancestors to pop and conceptual art, and to Heap of Birds's own practice.

For each print in the series, Heap of Birds paired three words found in works by Diné and Tuscarora women with three words culled from his own generative process. "GOOD LUCK HEART LICK WAR PAINT" seems to poke fun at the ravenous hunger for all things Native in the marketplace. Perhaps the female Tuscarora maker of the beaded whimsy, shaped like a cheap and sentimental Valentine's Day card, shared Heap of Birds's bemusement at her customers' undiscriminating acquisitiveness. "WAS SO HAPPY LIKE BLUE BIRD" refers to the words "Blue Birds Flour" translated into a Diné blanket by an unknown weaver, who borrowed the words from a package of the popular trading post staple—a reservation Warhol generations before pop; an indigenous appropriationist. Heap of Birds writes that he "enjoy[s] openness in language and culture," taking pleasure in the fact of Native women's irreverent resourcefulness: "Given a broadminded vantage point, one may also appreciate the monoprints as representing an ongoing interpretation and creation of the former and forthcoming unexplained wit, spirit and freedom of indigena."[62]

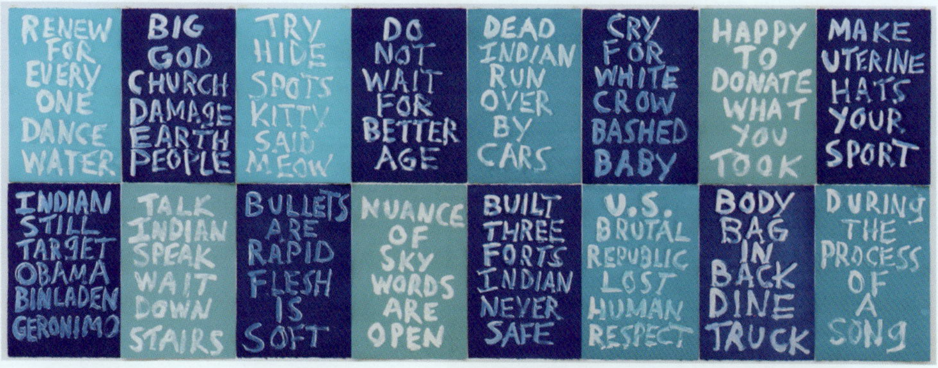

2.34 Edgar Heap of Birds, selections from monoprint series *Secrets in Life and Death*, 2012. Monoprint on rag paper, each 15 × 22 inches. Artwork © Edgar Heap of Birds.

For *Secrets in Life and Death*, created in 2012, Heap of Birds worked in shades of blue and in multiples of four to produce four arrangements of sixteen prints. The series was shown as part of the exhibition *Nuance of Sky: Edgar Heap of Birds Invites Spirit Objects to Join His Art Practice* (2013), alongside four new *Neuf* Paintings, a selection of four Murano glass works (*Most Serene Republics: Native Bodies of Remembrance*, 2007), and a selection of historic Native American artworks, all of which prominently featured shades of blue. The prints interacted visually as well as conceptually with the traditional artworks on view in the gallery. One print featured a wry commentary on the provenance of Native artworks in the museum collection: "HAPPY TO DONATE WHAT YOU TOOK."

If the monoprint series as a group is no less angry—no less acidic—than many of his other artworks, there is room for optimism. There is dark humor, but Heap of Birds also allows himself moments of poetic reverie, and he takes pleasure in the inventiveness of Native artists in times past. The series, an ongoing journal of past projects and new ideas to explore, journeys taken, and moments of creative inspiration, is a compendium of Heap of Birds's own history of art making and life as an artist, as well as an extended meditation on the ramifications of history and its legacies in the present. Indeed, these works, which begin in reverse—facing backward—end up looking forward as well as back.

A 2004 print in intense red references another archival voice, that of Captain John Mason, commander of the Massachusetts Bay Militia, and a

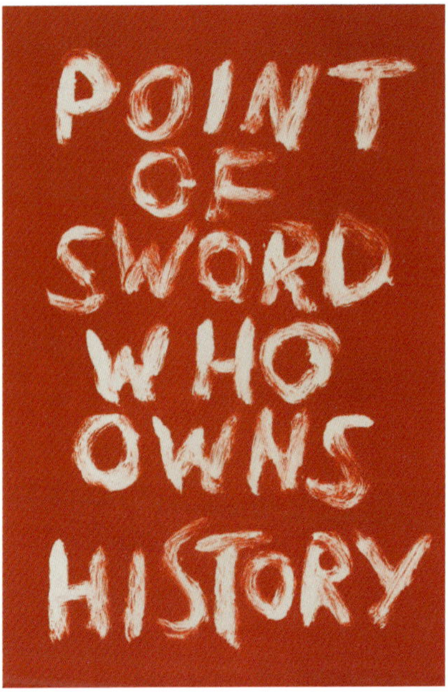

2.35 Edgar Heap of Birds, *Point of Sword Who Owns History*, 2004. Monoprint on rag paper, 15 × 22 inches. Artwork © Edgar Heap of Birds.

ringleader in the massacre of more than six hundred Pequot men, women, and children on the banks of the Mystic River in the Connecticut Colony in 1637. For a public artwork in Hartford, Connecticut, in 1996, Heap of Birds excerpted Mason's words recounting the burning of men, women, and children—the survivors were "received and entertained . . . with the point of the sword." Here, Heap of Birds returned to Mason's words—one of few first-person accounts of the massacre—pairing the phrase "POINT OF SWORD" with "WHO OWNS HISTORY." Heap of Birds sometimes poses the phrase as a question: "Who Owns History?" Here, it appears as a statement, an assertion. The point of the sword owns history. Like language, history is often a weapon wielded by the conqueror. Like all of Heap of Birds's text-based work, the monoprint series invites a conversation about power—about the ownership of language and the right to speak and be heard—and the performative power of language to sharpen and define experience, but also the legitimacy of competing claims to memory and history, which define the nature of community in the present and future.

3

HISTORIES

Who Owns History?

Heap of Birds created *Who Owns History* in 1992 for the Three Rivers Arts Festival in Pittsburgh, Pennsylvania, an annual event held in Point State Park, an urban park at the confluence of the Allegheny and Monongahela Rivers—the headwaters of the Ohio River. Adjacent to Pittsburgh's central business district, the park was reclaimed during the city's post–World War II renaissance from a derelict commercial district. The present-day park, a vast green lawn dominated by a fountain overlooking the confluence of the rivers, comprises the remains of historic Fort Duquesne and Fort Pitt, eighteenth-century structures built by the French and English, respectively. The forts were significant sites in the French and Indian War, the name used in the United States describing the North American theater of the Seven Years' War, fought among the major European colonial powers, giving North America to the British and eliminating France as an ally to many Native American nations and a hedge against further British expansion. Later, the site served as the gateway for the white settlement of the Ohio Valley. In 1778, signatories of the first U.S.-Indian treaty, with the Delaware Nation, gathered at Fort Pitt to pledge "perpetual peace and friendship" and allegiance to the new nation in their war of independence from Great Britain.

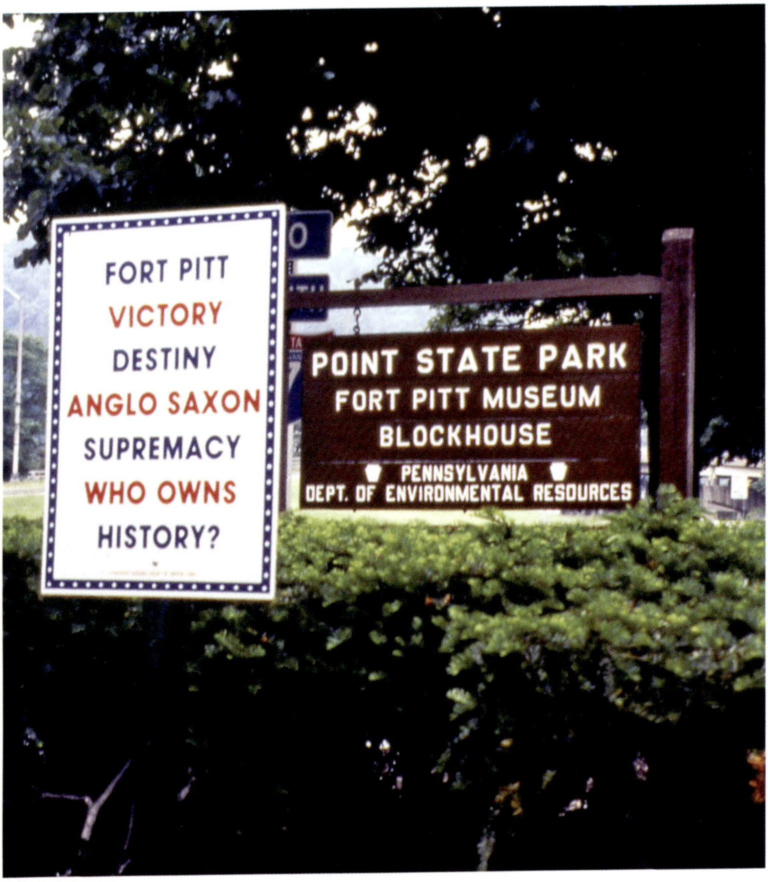

3.1 Edgar Heap of Birds, *Who Owns History*, 1992. Twenty-five steel panels, each 12 × 18 inches. Installed at Point State Park, Pittsburgh, Pennsylvania. Artwork © Edgar Heap of Birds. Heap of Birds had planned to place two markers on either side of the 1930 monument originally installed by the Pennsylvania Historical Commission and the Daughters of the American Revolution. He was informed that he was prohibited from placing panels within forty feet of the original. To address the fact that viewers would see his work without context, Heap of Birds added stickers to each panel reading, "These Words Come from a Historic Plaque Near the Fort Pitt Museum in Point State Park." Looking into the incident, a reporter for the *Allegheny Bulletin* found that there had been a breakdown in communication between the Fort Pitt Museum, Bureau of State Parks, and the Historic and Museum Commission. Ultimately, Heap of Birds was allowed to install his panels where he had originally intended.

For Heap of Birds, the location was rich in history—and irony. Near the Fort Pitt Museum, he was struck by a historic marker placed there by the Pennsylvania Historical Commission and the Daughters of the American Revolution (DAR) in 1930 in tribute to the victory of General John Forbes over the French and their Indian allies in 1758. The 1930 plaque reads in part:

> FORT DUQUESNE
> END OF FORBES ROAD
> OCCUPIED BY GENERAL FORBES
> NOVEMBER 25, 1758 AND BY HIM NAMED PITTSBURGH
> HIS VICTORY DETERMINED THE DESTINY OF THE
> GREAT WEST AND ESTABLISHED ANGLO-SAXON
> SUPREMACY IN THE UNITED STATES
>
> HIS NAME FOR AGES TO COME WILL BE DEAR TO AMERICANS
> AND APPEAR WITH LUSTRE AMONG CONTEMPORARY WORTHIES
> IN THE BRITISH ANNALS

Heap of Birds's project for the festival was an intervention into the historical narrative propounded by the marker. He created twenty-five signs—commercially printed on machine-made aluminum panels and mounted on steel posts of the type used to install No Parking and other traffic signs. Isolating key words from the 1930 plaque, his new panels read, "FORT PITT / VICTORY / DESTINY / ANGLO-SAXON / SUPREMACY." He added his own final phrase, a question: "WHO OWNS / HISTORY?"

If by 1992 the patinaed bronze marker had passed from public notice, disappearing into the green space of a park that was a destination more for lunch-hour joggers from nearby downtown office towers than for history buffs, Heap of Birds's intervention sought to render the old monument once again visible, opening it to new scrutiny. As in *Death from the Top*, his 1983 installation based on the 1868 Washita Massacre, Heap of Birds initiated a dialogue with a historical voice, in this case the creators of the state historical monument who were seeking to bolster their version of history. In 1930, the plaque's sponsors conflated British hegemony in North America—the outcome of the French and Indian War—with "Anglo-Saxon supremacy in the United States." Heap of Birds described the marker as "just as much a white supremacy statement as anything made today . . .

incredibly presumptuous. . . . I'm sure the bulk of the people of Pittsburgh aren't Anglo-Saxon."[1] As Heap of Birds rightly noted, the DAR and the Pennsylvania Historical Commission were alarmed at the changing demographics of industrializing Pittsburgh and thus created a monumental "statement about exclusivity" in a city with a predominantly immigrant population.[2] The fact that Point State Park was also a site of significance for Native American history—a history erased by the 1930 marker—is also telling.

The question "Who owns history?" is especially pertinent in settler societies, founded as colonial outposts. While modern settler nations such as Australia, Canada, New Zealand, South Africa, and the United States have long been established as independent states, the relationship of the descendants of the first European arrivals and their original indigenous inhabitants remains unfinished business. Art historian Annie E. Coombes writes, "The colonisers' dealings with indigenous peoples—through resistance, containment, appropriation, assimilation, miscegenation or attempted destruction—is the historical factor which has ultimately shaped the culture and political character of the new nations, mediating in highly significant ways their shared colonial roots/routes."[3] Moreover, settler societies are beset with a dual tension, between colonials (in particular the group that Benedict Anderson described as creole elites—those of European ancestry born in the colonies) and the metropolitan center, and between colonials and creole elites and the indigenous population.[4] This dual tension was characterized by a deep ambivalence; colonials and creole elites often felt themselves to be peripheral and subordinate to the imperial center, but identified with the center in their relations with local indigenous communities. The situation of settler societies differs fundamentally from former external colonies, as art historian Ruth Phillips writes, because "for internally colonized peoples there have been no definitive acts of political liberation, and no formal closure to the colonial era." In the absence of a decisive moment of decolonization, Phillips writes, there is an urgent "need to recover and restore indigenous accounts of the past to the national history." Further, she argues, "the lack of a formal closure on a political level has given special prominence to activist projects within the sphere of the visual arts."[5] Heap of Birds's public artworks certainly fit within this context, inquiring into the politics of history and its contemporary relevance. Of the marker placed in Pittsburgh's Point State Park by the DAR in 1930, we might ask: is it a violent act to memorialize? Surely national memorials and other state-sponsored acts of memorializing enact a kind of violence, as official memorials can preclude the recounting of other memories, other namings. As Jean Fisher writes, Heap of Birds's public works are "sited at interfaces of difference: places of real or symbolic exchange or of conflict between alternative usages and meanings of public space, and between Indian and non-Indian historical interpretations."[6] In locating these works in charged locations outside the gallery, Heap of Birds stages interventions in the public sphere, opening to critical scrutiny the stories by which communities define themselves, by calling attention to the violence upon which they are based.

As such, Heap of Birds's public artworks confront historical traumas in an effort to come to terms with the ramifications of history—forgotten in an amnesiac culture, or actively repressed—for the present. What is forgotten or repressed may be horrific—as in the dispossession and genocide that accompanied the conquest and colonization of the Americas—or it may be the way in which other experiences have been lost—an insidious, psychological dispossession—and other perspectives foreclosed. Heap of Birds's public projects undertake to reinscribe in the public sphere those countermemories. These works do not seek reconciliation and healing—or at least not only that—but a more important reckoning with the past. As Hal Foster notes of the archival impulse, "Artists are often drawn to unfulfilled beginnings or incomplete projects . . . that might offer points of departure again."[7] Renewal, Heap of Birds suggests in his public projects, can begin only once a clear-eyed accounting has taken place. His artworks represent an act of willful and activist remembering, in hopes of creating a shared history, in which the past can be held to account.

Raising difficult questions about the stories that communities tell about themselves—and how those representations define community—Heap of Birds's public artworks reveal conflicts about the nature of the public itself, of community. His artworks reveal conflicts that structure the public sphere. Heap of Birds seeks to scrutinize the antagonisms that are erased by conventional historical monuments. The political moment that motivated the DAR's statement of Anglo-Saxon supremacy has passed, and the marker itself is largely ignored today—echoing Robert Musil's famous pronouncement: "There is nothing in the world so invisible as a monument."[8] But Heap of Birds argues implicitly that we should not become complacent about these silent remains of an earlier time—they should be called out and reanimated. The wounds should be reopened, punctured anew. The narratives they continue to declaim should be met and challenged—a new confrontation staged. Other histories should be remembered and told. Public artworks are never passive reflections of a coherent community that exists already, waiting to be represented. In representing such histories, Heap of Birds's artworks labor to create a public that is able to acknowledge and account for the past and address the incommensurable differences and unfinished business that remain at the heart of community.

Public History

In 1990, Heap of Birds created *Building Minnesota*, a temporary public art installation that coincided with the exhibition of his traveling exhibition *Claim Your Color* at the Walker Art Center in Minneapolis. The work comprised forty commercially printed aluminum panels installed in a wide four-hundred-foot arc along a section of West River Parkway—on the west bank of the Mississippi River near downtown Minneapolis. Printed in red, each panel commemorates and asks readers to pay respects to (HONOR) an individual Dakota warrior hanged in retaliation for the Dakota War (also known as the Sioux Uprising) of 1862. Each of the forty panels features in Dakota and English the name of an individual warrior, such as Ma-Ka'ta I-na'-zin (One Who Stands on the Earth), above the phrase "DEATH BY HANGING." The panels—memorial markers—were posted at eye level, creating the impression of forty formidable men standing vigil shoulder to shoulder, backs to the river. "They're almost the embodiment of the warrior standing there," Heap of Birds said.[9]

In *Building Minnesota*, Heap of Birds recovered an episode that was foundational for Minnesota, and unpropitious for indigenous people. The Dakota War was precipitated by increasing white settlement in the Minnesota River valley in the 1850s (which had previously been mostly Indian Country), bad faith on the part of U.S. Bureau of Indian Affairs agents, and corrupt and unsympathetic white traders in the region. An 1851 treaty forced the Dakota to cede large tracts of their traditional homelands in Minnesota Territory and accept a reservation along the Minnesota River. In exchange for confinement on the new reservation, the Dakota were to receive government annuities (in cash payments and staple supplies)

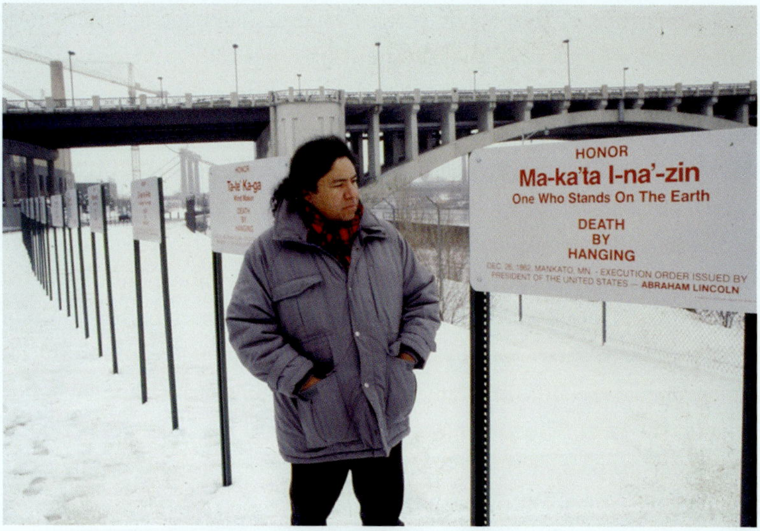

3.2 Edgar Heap of Birds, *Building Minnesota*, 1990. Forty aluminum panels, each 18 × 36 inches. Installed along the Mississippi River in downtown Minneapolis. Artwork © Edgar Heap of Birds.

meant to ease the transformation of traditional cultures based on hunting and gathering to a life of settled agriculture, compatible with white society. In 1858, as Minnesota became the thirty-second state of the United States, the Dakota accepted a further cession of half of the 1851 reservation in exchange for increased annuities. White agents and traders, however, profited as the Dakota starved on their reservation; Dakota society began to collapse, as the new economy undermined traditional culture. In the summer of 1862, late annuity payments—upon which the Dakota now depended—led to violence, as some traders refused to extend credit and open agency warehouses. One was quoted as saying, "So far as I am concerned, if they are hungry, let them eat grass." He was later found killed, his own mouth stuffed with grass. By late summer 1862, hundreds of whites—soldiers and civilians—and Dakota had been killed. A punitive expedition led by Colonel Henry H. Sibley stopped the fighting. Military tribunals, swiftly convened and prosecuted, condemned 303 Dakota men to death. President Abraham Lincoln had hoped to commute all the sentences, but mindful that such an action would be seen as an unwelcome intervention in a state beset by fear of Indian uprising, Lincoln signed the execution order for thirty-eight men to appease angry and fearful whites. The executions took place the day after Christmas 1862 in Mankato, Minnesota. Lincoln's successor, Andrew Johnson, authorized the execution of two more men, who were executed three years later at Fort Snelling, on the bluffs overlooking the confluence of the Minnesota and Mississippi Rivers, south of Minneapolis, in November 1865.

Heap of Birds explained that he was inspired to create *Building Minnesota* by the song "Water in the Rain," written by Minneapolis folksinger Larry Long.[10] The song recounts the Dakota war, and in a lengthy interlude includes elder Amos Owens reciting in Dakota the names of the thirty-eight warriors executed in Mankato, over a recording of a traditional honor song for the dead. The song moved Heap of Birds deeply. "It goes on for a long time. Just hearing that song and thinking about it, you know, that was what Minnesota meant to me at the time."[11]

In a sense, *Building Minnesota* recalls Maya Lin's Vietnam Veterans Memorial in Washington, DC, dedicated in 1982. Like Lin's memorial, *Building Minnesota* lists the names of the dead, and like the DC memorial, *Building Minnesota* became a destination for mourners—members of Minneapolis's urban Native American community and many others who left offerings and made blessings at the site. The Vietnam Veterans Memorial was developed in the midst of a wide-ranging reassessment of America's involvement in Vietnam. The memorial's earthbound minimalist form—a deliberate break from the vertical and heroic tradition of war monuments—was designed to avoid political statement and to effect a coming to terms with the divisive war and the turbulent decades in which it dominated the national consciousness. In creating a monument that abstained from telling Americans how to remember the war—refrained from dictating the terms of its use—Lin's design sought to create a shared experience for a divided public. If the mission and justification for the war remained controversial, the Vietnam Veterans Memorial offered a focus for mourning the dead, irrespective of political perspective.

Like Lin's memorial, *Building Minnesota* also worked to reclaim the dignity of those listed. But Heap of Birds did not refrain from political comment. Heap of Birds effected an even more profound change of perspective than Lin. Unlike the dead and missing soldiers of the Vietnam Veterans Memorial, the honored dead of *Building Minnesota* were not killed in battle, but arrested, tried, and executed by the U.S. government as enemies of the state, even as Lincoln fought to preserve the Union. (Minnesota's application for statehood in 1858 was delayed for several months as it became entangled in the question of whether Kansas would enter the Union as a free or a slave state.) In memorializing the executed Dakota warriors in *Building Minnesota*, Heap of Birds claims and restores their honor as men who fought to preserve their communities and way of life.

The significance of place—acknowledging contemporary Minnesota as the product of complex histories—was central to *Building Minnesota*. Heap of Birds was specific in choosing a site for his installation. Water had a symbolic resonance for him, befitting the warriors he sought to memorialize: "It was about the water, the renewal of the water, and the ceremonial Dakota ways," he said. "I know those warriors were probably trained like I am, you know, and they probably had to live without water for ceremonies lasting four days, you know, to renew the earth, and so I thought that they would respect being by the river, so I put them there."[12]

In choosing the river as a backdrop, Heap of Birds also placed the work at the location of some of the earliest white settlements in Minnesota, a site today dominated by the industries that have made the state prosperous—the mills and granaries that collected the grain grown throughout the upper Midwest, processed it into flour, and packaged and transported it downriver. Heap of Birds recalled, "I had the whole city to choose from, but I kept coming back to that water. . . . I kept coming back to one place, the granary. . . . It had a little plaque there."[13] To place the forty sign panels, Heap of Birds spread forty pounds of white flour in a four-hundred-foot arc, addressing the Gold Medal and Pillsbury flour mills across the river, and acknowledging the commodity to which the warriors were sacrificed. As in other projects in Seattle, New York, and Pittsburgh, Heap of Birds sited *Building Minnesota* in relation to existing public historical markers and memorials: "It [the plaque] was playing up the great shipping channel of the Mississippi, how it was the business hub of America and how the most grain in the world was shipped through there. Then I got to thinking about the land, and movement, and why the Dakotas are thought of being from South Dakota, like no one thinks they're from Minnesota. I didn't either; I thought, 'Well, Sioux are in South Dakota; where else would they be?' And then you find out that they got kicked out of here and all their warriors were executed."[14]

Here, Heap of Birds recalled the tragic history of Dakota removal from

Minnesota, which paved the way for the state's economic ascendancy. After the end of the Dakota War, women, children, and the elderly were held temporarily in an internment camp established on Pike Island, below Fort Snelling. Hundreds died in the poorly designed camp—stricken by infectious diseases—before the survivors were transported en masse to new reservations in the Dakota and Nebraska Territories. Remaining free Dakota in Minnesota were hunted down, the state offering a twenty-five-dollar bounty per scalp. Today the only Dakota reservations in Minnesota are those of Mdewakanton bands, descendants of those who remained neutral or allied with white settlers during the Dakota War.

Today, the Twin Cities of Minneapolis–St. Paul are home to an intertribal community with its own rich history. Native people compose about 2 percent of the population in booming, multicultural Minneapolis, and slightly less than 1 percent in St. Paul. The descendants of many of those Dakota removed in the nineteenth century have returned and live in low-income neighborhoods in the cities, alongside Ojibwe and other tribal peoples who have relocated in search of jobs and better lives than were possible on the reservations the government moved their ancestors to in the nineteenth century. Many families travel back and forth between the cities and the reservation on a regular basis, maintaining a link to home and relations. The intertribal American Indian Movement was formed in 1968 in Minneapolis. The Minneapolis American Indian Center, founded in 1975, is in South Minneapolis, not far from the site of *Building Minnesota*. Heap of Birds saw this urban Indian community as an important collaborator and audience for his artwork; he sought to include Native youth in educational outreach workshops before and during the installation, and welcomed the prayers and offerings at the site as an important component of the piece. Nor is *Building Minnesota* the only memorial to the hanged Dakota warriors: each December 26 since 1987, an intertribal group has carried a feathered staff in a one-hundred-mile memorial relay run from Fort Snelling to Mankato.

Reaching out to the local Native population, Heap of Birds sought to counter forgetting with an expansive project of public history, linking the dispossession of Minnesota's Native peoples to the modern grain processing and transfer facilities that flank the river—the infrastructure that supports Minnesota's wealth—and back to the agency warehouses jealously guarded by white traders during the Dakota War: "It was the largest mass execution in America's history; of course, no one even knows about it, or why it was done," he said. "Then I thought about the land and the shipping, the business aspect of it, and thinking about the Persian Gulf, and the oil business. Commerce was always at the bottom of these situations, you know. It's not some kind of hatred or whatever; it's business, it's money."[15] He sought to link *Building Minnesota* to the global networks of military and industrial power he explored in *American Policy* and other artworks. And as he explained in a later interview, he saw the suppressed memory of the Dakota War as part and parcel of broader historical amnesia, which enables the concentration and misuse of power in contemporary America: "This needed to be brought forward as a hidden grim legacy in American history. Like many official signs, official history contains a heavily biased editorial or outright omission. It is very key to reveal the overall American historical trait, much like the Bush-spun war because of Weapons of Mass Destruction that were never found in Iraq. Fiction is a main method in positions of power."[16] The Dakota War, ultimately, was an episode in a much longer story of American imperialism.

Strong Words

In all his works, Heap of Birds's choice of words is deliberate. Even as his artworks address the past, Heap of Birds has consistently used the present tense and the imperative (or command) for his language-based artworks. As W. Jackson Rushing III writes of *Building Minnesota*, "The word HONOR, which appears at the top of each sign, functions as both directive and descriptor."[17] This tactic highlights the contemporary presence of indigenous peoples, as in *Native Hosts*: "TODAY YOUR HOST IS . . ." Heap of Birds's use of language also contrasts markedly with that of Lawrence Weiner. As Weiner explained to an interviewer, "To use the imperative would be for me fascistic. The tone of command is the tone of tyranny."[18] Often playful in tone and self-referential (as discussed in chapter 2), Weiner's language-based works avoid the "impositional," "directional," or "choreographic." His use of passive voice and the past participle embodies the artist's nondirective and nonhierarchical ethos, as in *SOME LIMESTONE SOME SANDSTONE ENCLOSED FOR SOME REASON / SOME LIMESTONE SOME SANDSTONE INCLOSED FOR SOME REASON*, a 1993 work installed marking the location of the dismantled weight bridge (or vehicle scales) at the entrance to the closed Dean Clough

Mills, formerly the largest carpet factory in the world, and current home of the Studio of the Henry Moore Sculpture Trust in Halifax, England. Memorializing Britain's former industrial might and its once-formidable working class, Weiner's public sculpture was cast of salvaged iron from the derelict scales, and references its original limestone and sandstone foundations, musing on memory and the renovation and recycling that inevitably characterize the built environment. Weiner's intention has been to create noncoercive artworks that give license to the viewer to interact according to their own initiative. An example is his well-known *Declaration of Intent*, a wall text initially created in 1969, which made a radical attempt to break down barriers between artist and audience, between making and beholding, transforming the passive viewer into an active coauthor, at least in theory. Weiner's text reads, "1. The artist may construct the piece; 2. The piece may be fabricated; 3. The piece need not be built; Each being equal and consistent with the intent of the artist the decision as to condition rests with the receiver on the occasion of ownership." Alexander Alberro and Alice Zimmerman write that such works were notable for "attempting to level cultural and social barriers, to communicate across traditional forms of privileged experience in order to address publics different than those traditionally empowered by privilege."[19]

It is perhaps salutary in designing public memorials to imagine an art practice that, as Alberro and Zimmerman suggest, "enfranchises [a new public] as full-fledged cultural participants."[20] But Heap of Birds seems less sanguine on this score. Unlike Weiner's public artwork in Halifax—and unlike Lin's Vietnam memorial—Heap of Birds's temporary monument does not seek to depoliticize history. Weiner's work offered no particular insights on the social and economic forces that precipitated the closing of the Dean Clough Mills, the decimation of the British working class, or the transfer of former industrial properties into the cultural sector. Perhaps Weiner felt no inclination to weigh in on past history, preferring to leave interpretation to viewers. And perhaps Heap of Birds could not imagine that history's struggles had been concluded, at least not for indigenous peoples. Standing on the banks of the Mississippi, he saw a civilization built on the remains of the Indian dead. Other artists who emerged in the post-conceptual 1980s, such as Barbara Kruger or Jenny Holzer, produced works that were often confrontational; Gran Fury did not pull punches, leveling accusations against the government and the medical establishment for ig-

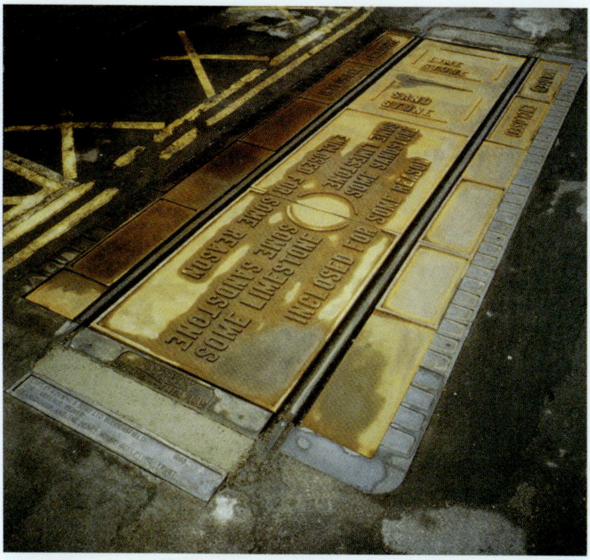

3.3 Lawrence Weiner, *SOME LIMESTONE SOME SANDSTONE ENCLOSED FOR SOME REASON / SOME LIMESTONE SOME SANDSTONE INCLOSED FOR SOME REASON*, 1993. Recast iron. Installation, Henry Moore Studio, Halifax, England. Artwork © 2014 Lawrence Weiner / Artists Rights Society (ARS), New York.

noring the AIDS crisis as it devastated communities. Nor did Heap of Birds feel compelled to avoid what Weiner termed the "impositional." Like other activist artists working in public, Heap of Birds appropriated the voice of state authority—for example, his use in *Building Minnesota* of machine-made aluminum signage, imprinted in impersonal Helvetica. State authority hails us as a subject rather than addressing us as an equal. Heap of Birds appropriated this voice to powerful effect, commanding respect and honor toward those whose histories had been erased. Moreover, artists of Heap of Birds's generational cohort were perhaps more aware than artists of Weiner's generation of the difficulties of engaging in dialogue as equals and across differences. The contemporary public sphere is beset by historical amnesia, with unequal access to means of public address, institutional power, and cultural authority. With their bold, often strident political critique, the neoconceptual artists of the 1980s and 1990s—coming of age amid the neoconservatism of Reagan and Thatcher, in the aftermath of the unfinished struggle for civil rights, and in the foment of the culture wars—seem a world away from Weiner and the radical artists of the 1960s. Even Hans Haacke's politely worded *MoMA Poll* left viewers the option of not participating and just moving along to the next gallery. And, of course, Haacke's artwork took the form of a ballot box—a figure for the presumed free and fair mechanisms of democratic participation. But Heap of Birds recognized that the public sphere was an exclusionary and uneven playing field. What was important to Heap of Birds would not appear on any ballot. Countering historical amnesia demanded strong words.

In a number of public projects since the 1990s, Heap of Birds has engaged in historical research to uncover and make known incidents of injustice against Native peoples, in the manner of *Building Minnesota*—and to frame a new public history. In several locations, Heap of Birds created a public intervention to accompany a gallery or museum exhibition. He created *Mission Gifts*, a temporary signage project organized in conjunction with his traveling exhibition *Claim Your Color* at the San Jose Museum of Art in 1990. Thirty placards placed on the outside of public buses featured printed text in red on a white ground describing what Heap of Birds termed, sardonically, the "gifts" of civilization bestowed on the Native peoples of Alta California by the Spanish friars: "SYPHILIS / SMALL POX / FORCED BAPTISMS / MISSION GIFTS / ENDING NATIVE LIVES."

In 1996, in conjunction with an exhibition of *16 Songs*, his collaboration with Aboriginal Australian contemporary artists, Heap of Birds created *Dunging the Ground*, a temporary installation of two steel panels on the front lawn of the Wadsworth Atheneum in Hartford, Connecticut. Heap of Birds appropriated the title of the work from a statement made by Captain John Mason, commander of the Massachusetts Bay Militia, on the occasion of the Pequot massacre of 1637, a bloodthirsty campaign that eliminated the Pequot as a regional rival to the English in the Northeast. Heap of Birds excerpted for one panel a passage in which Mason, with particular relish, described the rout of the Pequot as the will of the divine:

> THUS WAS GOD CRUSHING
> HIS PROUD ENEMIES
> BURNING THEM UP IN FIRE
> DUNGING THE GROUND
> WITH THEIR FLESH

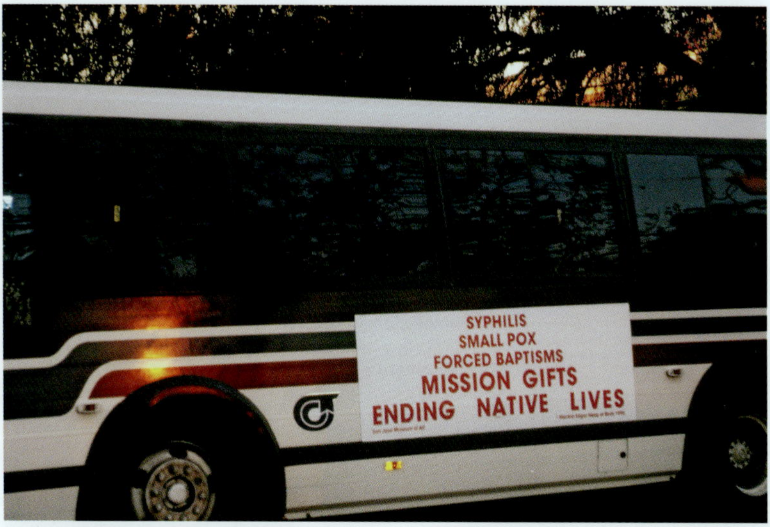

3.4 Edgar Heap of Birds, *Mission Gifts*, 1990. Thirty paper bus signs, each 30 × 90 inches. San Jose, California. Artwork © Edgar Heap of Birds.

IT IS MARVELOUS IN
OUR EYES!

For the other panel, Heap of Birds excerpted Mason's words recounting the burning of men, women, and children—the survivors "RECEIVED AND ENTERTAINED / WITH THE POINT OF THE SWORD"—reproducing them in a seventeenth-century typeface, surrounded by a border of Latin crosses and English crowns. Mason's words are inflammatory enough ("MANY WERE BURNED"); they require no further editorializing on the artist's part. Heap of Birds's sign panels flank a bronze statue of Revolutionary War hero Nathan Hale. Hale, hanged by the British for his activities as a spy, was purported to have uttered as his last words: "I regret that I have but one life to lose for my country." Heap of Birds juxtaposes Hale and the Pequot—martyrs to the English. The Pequot lost many lives, although they are not memorialized in American history.

Heap of Birds reached back into a deeper past in his 2005 project, *Ocmulgee*, a gallery installation at the Atlanta College of Art and outdoor public art on the campus of the Woodruff Arts Center. *Ocmulgee* sought

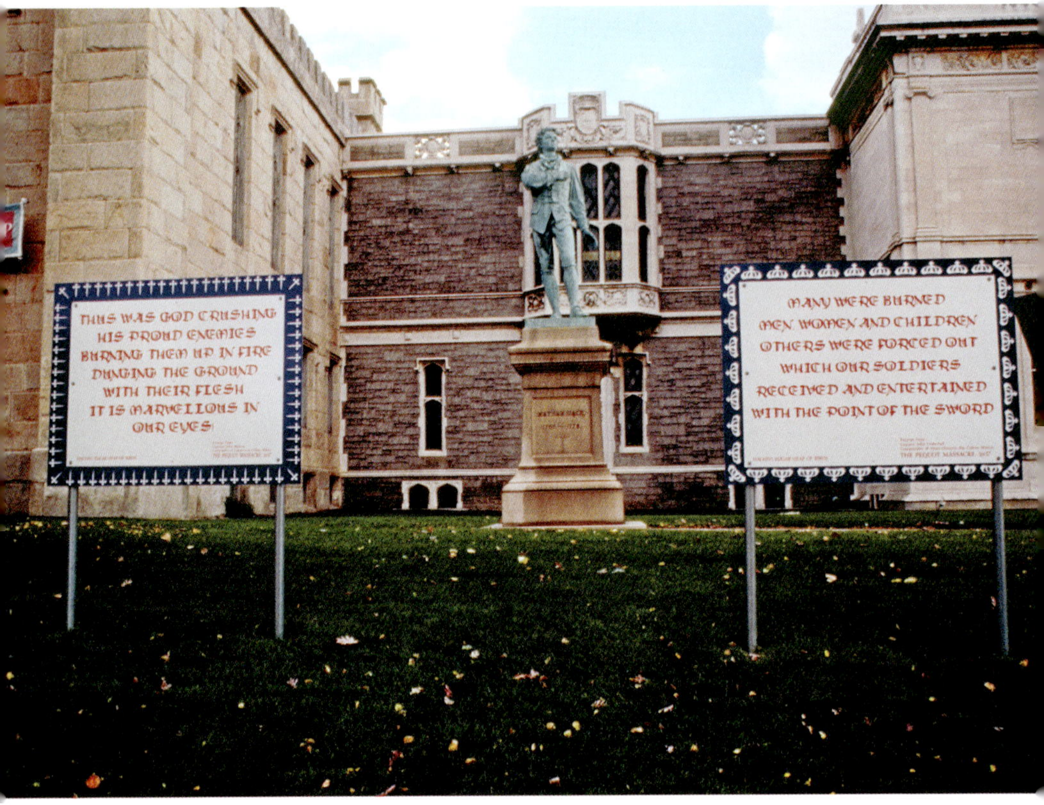

3.5 Edgar Heap of Birds, *Dunging the Ground*, 1996. Two steel panels, each 42 × 60 inches. Wadsworth Atheneum, Hartford, Connecticut. Artwork © Edgar Heap of Birds.

to bring attention to the long history of the Muscogee (or Creek) Nation that traditionally claimed territory in what is now Tennessee, Alabama, and Georgia—including the present-day greater Atlanta metropolitan area—before their forced removal in the nineteenth century. The Muscogee descend from the ancient Mississippian culture that once spanned the entire Southeast from the Ohio Valley to the Gulf of Mexico. Today, the capital of the Muscogee Nation is in Okmulgee in east-central Oklahoma, although descendants of the historic Muscogee also remain closer to ancestral lands in Georgia and Alabama, as well as Florida and Texas. Between 800 and 1500 CE, Mississippian culture built vast urban and temple complexes including Spiro in present-day Oklahoma, Cahokia in present-day Illinois, Moundville in present-day Alabama, and Etowa, just north of Atlanta in present-day Cartersville, Georgia, the most intact Mississippian site in the Southeast. Mississippians produced impressive works of art in ceramic, stone, shell, and metal associated with what is termed the Southern Ceremonial Complex, or Southern Cult. Yet their major sites had been mostly abandoned by the time of Spanish conquistador Hernando de Soto's travels through the region in the 1540s.

Despite its geographical and chronological scope and artistic accomplishments, the Mississippian culture as a chapter of American (pre)history remains largely unknown. Ancient Mississippians left no written records. Much of Mississippian architecture—precisely designed and impressively engineered monumental truncated pyramidal forms built of rammed earth—has deteriorated beyond recognition, or been leveled by rampant development. In the sixteenth century, however, Mississippian buildings still dominated the Southeast, even as the vast woodlands cleared by the ancient agriculturalists had begun to retake the rolling landscape. The earliest Europeans in the region could scarcely believe that the expansive plazas and flanking structures aligned to the cardinal directions had been built by the indigenous people they encountered, their numbers thinned by foreign disease and displaced by land-hungry immigrants. They speculated that the ancient sites must have been created by another race—the Mound Builders, long vanished. As Heap of Birds argued, even the language used to describe the achievements of Mississippian culture is derogatory: the great ancient civilizations of Egypt, the Near East, and Central America built pyramids; indigenous North Americans' architectural monuments are described as mounds.

Heap of Birds sought to reconnect this lost knowledge with the history of the Muscogee Nation, itself a victim of historical amnesia in development-crazy Atlanta, the foremost city of the new Southern economy that has outpaced the aging Rust Belt cities of the Midwest and Northeast since the 1970s. In the gallery at the Atlanta College of Art, Heap of Birds created two large sculptures representing the temple precinct at Ocmulgee, a Mississippian site near present-day Macon, Georgia, that was occupied by Creeks until their forced removal in the nineteenth century, and after which their modern capital city in Oklahoma is named. Contemporary Muscogee still revere the Ocmulgee Old Fields—named a national monument in 1936 but listed by the National Trust for Historic Preservation

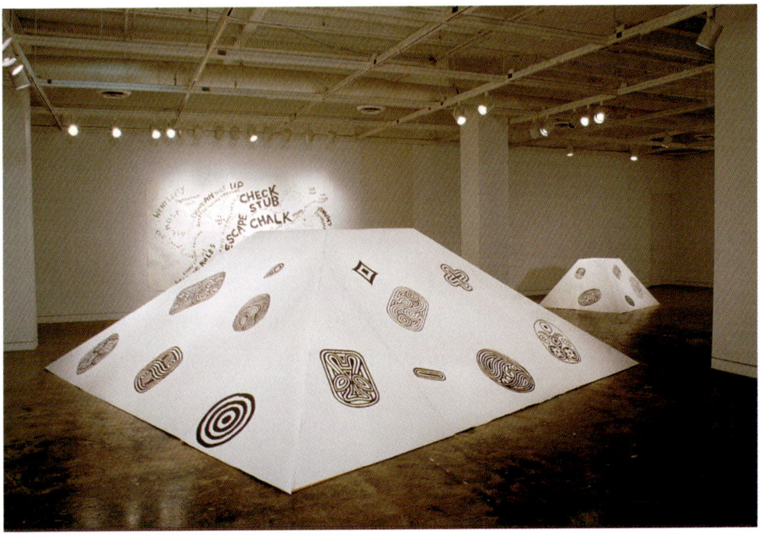

3.6 Edgar Heap of Birds, *Ocmulgee*, 2005. Marker on rag paper over wooden armature, approximately 16 feet square (near left) and approximately 6 feet square (far right). Installation at Atlanta College of Art Gallery. Artwork © Edgar Heap of Birds.

among the most endangered historic places in America—as a sacred site. The two sculptures—the larger approximately sixteen feet square, the smaller six feet square—were built with plywood armatures, covered with white rag paper, and emblazoned with black-and-white designs inspired by Mississippian pottery designs from the Ocmulgee site. Four of Heap of Birds's large marker text drawings hung on the gallery walls.

Outside the gallery, Heap of Birds sited forty-eight metal panels, each twelve by eighteen inches (scaled similarly to No Parking signs), along Peachtree Street and around the Woodruff Arts Center campus in Atlanta's Midtown neighborhood. Targeting pedestrians as well as drivers in the tony neighborhood, the panels repeated a four-part sequence: "DO YOU CHOOSE TO WALK / WERE YOU FORCED TO WALK / TRAIL OF TEARS 1836 / WALK TO OKLAHOMA." In economical phrasing, the panels sought to remind viewers of the removal of Southeastern tribes—the infamous Trail of Tears in the aftermath of the 1830 Indian Removal Act—bitterly remembered by Native people, but largely forgotten by white Southerners. The Indian Removal Act, signed by President Andrew Jackson, mandated the relocation of Cherokee, Chickasaw, Choctaw, Muscogee, and Seminole tribes from traditional homelands east of the Mississippi River to new lands west of the river, beyond the Arkansas Territory, in the newly designated Indian Territory (present-day Oklahoma and southern Kansas). The state name Oklahoma, Heap of Birds wrote in his statement for the exhibition, is a Choctaw word meaning "Red People."

As in other Heap of Birds projects, *Ocmulgee* engaged the important task of memory and reckoning with the past, working to reinsert a Native presence into contemporary Atlanta and, as in *Building Minnesota*, to acknowledge the debt that contemporary Atlanta owes to the descendants of the relocated Muscogee. While most Muscogee had been forced out of Georgia well before 1830, a large number still resided in Alabama. Following the 1832 Treaty of Cusseta, which divided remaining Muscogee lands into individual allotments, many Muscogee were defrauded by white squatters and speculators, leading to the violent outbreak known as the Creek War of 1836—the year Heap of Birds chose to memorialize in his panels—which ended when U.S. secretary of war Lewis Cass ordered the removal of the remaining Muscogee to Indian Territory by military means. Heap of Birds wrote, "We greatly need entrée to the collective past in order to understand the fruits enjoyed by the dominant culture, received as a result of the 1836 plunder of the Creek and Muscogee Nations."[21] (Also, 1836 is the year that the U.S. Supreme Court, ignoring the protests of John Ross and other prominent Cherokees, ratified the illegitimate Treaty of New Echota, which had been signed in 1833 by a small faction of the tribe, finalizing Cherokee removal.)

On the Trail of Tears, dispossessed Native Americans marched many hundreds of miles. In Atlanta, a city dominated by the car, Heap of Birds chose to emphasize the theme of walking, resonating ironically with the presence of exercise walkers around the arts center campus. The theme of walking resonated as well with the monumental bronze edition of Rodin's *The Shade* (1880), itself a memorial donated by the French government to the city's High Museum at the Memorial Arts Center (today the Woodruff Arts Center) in honor of 106 Atlanta residents who died in a plane crash at Orly Airport in Paris in 1962 while on a museum-sponsored sightseeing trip. Rodin's solitary male nude has been described as a figure of resur-

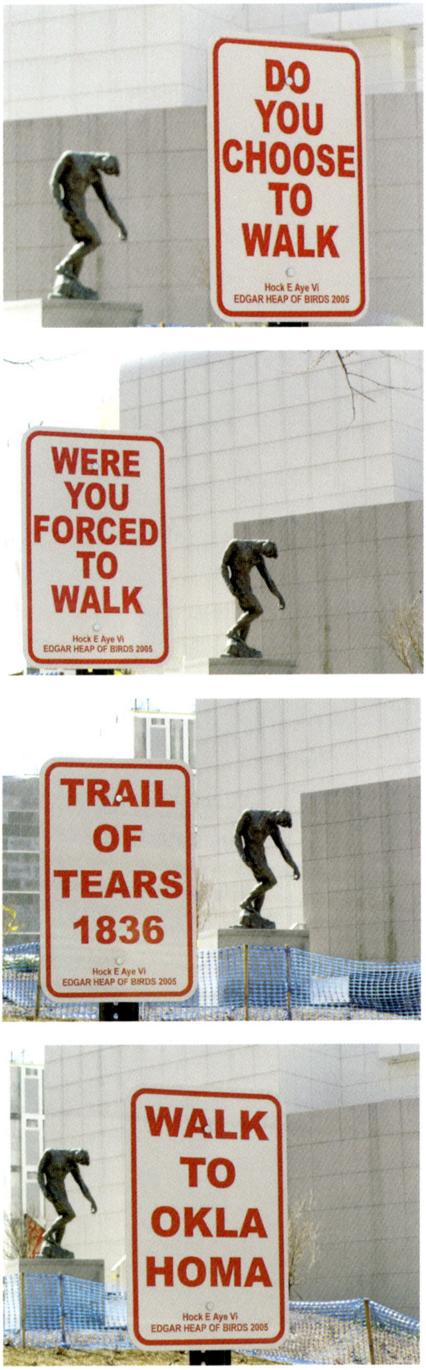

3.7 Edgar Heap of Birds, *Ocmulgee*, 2005. Forty-eight steel panels, each 12 × 18 inches. Atlanta, Georgia. Artwork © Edgar Heap of Birds.

rection, befitting its memorial function; in the context of Heap of Birds's panels, it was transformed into a figure of exhaustion, slumped and bedraggled, making his way to a new home in an unknown land.

Heap of Birds described walking as an "instrument of torture perpetrated upon many tribal peoples as the United States inflicted brutal removal policies."[22] The tribes of the Southeast endured the Trail of Tears in the aftermath of the 1830 Indian Removal Act. There are many such stories of forced relocation, as Indian lands became attractive to white settlers and developers. But Heap of Birds also linked walking to other histories, describing it as a task undertaken as "a necessity for the urban underprivileged, as leisure time exercise, as historic remembrance and as an act of protest." One reviewer doubted the artwork would have an impact "because of Atlantans' general failure at the art of walking."[23] But Heap of Birds's intervention resonated with local history in powerful and positive ways. In the American South it is difficult to think of walking without invoking the historical memory of the civil rights movement. As in *Dunging the Ground*, Heap of Birds thus highlighted and compared an episode in indigenous history to a more widely known American story. To be sure, the work of Dr. King and other civil rights pioneers and martyrs remains, like the business of reckoning with the indigenous past, unfinished. But the struggle for African American emancipation and enfranchisement has become, nonetheless, the dominant racial narrative in the United States—part of the great national bildungsroman of freedom and equality. The histories of the Dakota, Pequot, Muscogee, and others remain largely unknown, not yet part of a shared cultural inheritance. Still, Heap of Birds concluded on an optimistic and spiritual note. He wrote in his artist's statement for the exhibition: "The spirits of Ocmulgee return to usher forth these supportive notions of walking and astronomical renewal. They serve as reminders of the revered ways of the past, which offer respect to the star-lit heavenly bodies above and equal treatment of those human bodies we share."[24]

Opening the Archive: *Wheel*

Heap of Birds's public artworks engage in a historical project that seems to exemplify what Foster terms an archival impulse, in which "artists seek to make historical information, often lost or displaced, physically present . . .

in a gesture of alternative knowledge or counter-memory."[25] But Heap of Birds's project further complicates notions of history, or of historicity embedded within Western modernity, that imply a continual forward momentum and notions that significant moments of transformation leave their mark as part of a written record, an archive. To be sure, this is a standard biased implicitly against the historical memories of many non-Western traditions. Like artists such as Renée Green or Fred Wilson, whose artworks critique historical representations of African American experience, Heap of Birds's artworks and public interventions have examined and occasioned dialogue about the meaning of history as a mode of knowledge making. Heap of Birds's projects have also challenged—if implicitly—history's archival bias. In the research he undertakes to develop his projects, Heap of Birds taps conventional written sources, as well as oral histories and indigenous knowledge—resources that are not in the archive, or which figure in the archive only refracted through the lens of Western modernity. What constitutes history then? Who owns it? Who claims the privilege to narrate the past? Whose telling has power, and in what forms? Whose voices comprise the archive, and what is missing from the archive? How have the experiences of marginalized communities—other voices—been distorted in the archive? Who has access to the archive and the knowledge it produces, and the power claimed by those in its possession? The notion of the archive itself—a project of the European Enlightenment, to be sure—has been a tool of domination. Definitions of historicity and the archive, what constitutes knowledge, have been used to deny that the less powerful even possessed a history—that is, agency and intentionality exercised across time—of their own. When Heap of Birds asserts that it is the "POINT OF SWORD WHO OWNS HISTORY," he reminds us that the privilege of authoring the narrative, defining the shared inheritance, accrues to the powerful. This has been particularly insidious in a settler society such as the United States. How does our understanding of the past—the product of a historically asymmetrical settler-indigenous power dynamic—shape our shared present and determine our common future? And in a world in the throes of globalization, what can history teach, and to whom?

The monumental *Wheel*, Heap of Birds's first commission for a permanent public sculpture, was dedicated on June 21, 2005 (the summer solstice), on the grounds of the Denver Art Museum (DAM), the culmination of a decade-long process. In terms of years in planning and its aesthetic departure from his previous works, *Wheel* is Heap of Birds's most ambitious undertaking to date. It may also be his most poignant. Located in Denver, Colorado—in what was once the traditional homeland of the Cheyenne and Arapaho Nations—*Wheel* commemorates a long history of Native peoples in the West, and memorializes the victims of the 1864 Sand Creek Massacre, which took place 186 miles to the southeast near the town of Eads, Colorado. Ten vertical forms—each twelve feet tall and notched at the top in a Y-form, resembling a forked tree trunk—in red porcelain enamel over steel frames mark the contour of a circle forty-eight feet in diameter in a grassy lawn adjacent to the entrance to the museum's 1971 North Building, designed by Gio Ponti. The vertical red sculptural forms are inscribed with a combination of graphic elements—abstract forms, line drawings, and text, written in the style of Heap of Birds's wall lyrics and marker drawings. The circular space defined by the sculpture echoes a concave exterior wall of the museum, on which the phrase "NAH-KEV-HO-EYEA-ZIM" (in Cheyenne: "We are always returning back home again") is spelled out in raised letters. Heap of Birds refers to the circle as a space reclaimed for the Cheyenne and Arapaho, after lands along the Front Range of the Rocky Mountains guaranteed by the 1851 Fort Laramie Treaty were lost.[26] Rushing describes *Wheel* as a "commingling of ancient belief systems, awareness of colonial history, and hope for healing and renewal."[27] The sculpture looks back to a turbulent history and predicts a redeemed future, even as it posits the notion that life and history, in keeping with Plains spiritual beliefs, are ultimately cyclical.

Implicit in the project is a critique of notions of historicity and the archive. As Heap of Birds explained shortly after the dedication of *Wheel*, the artwork was an attempt to rewrite a history of the West from an indigenous point of view. "There was an absence of history that native people have been in control of," he said. "We're really sort of moved out of all the history or we're painted in a very bizarre way where no one really knows what happened. So it's kind of a rebuttal for me—going on record to describe what I think history really is." Noting that the artwork engaged "some difficult issues perhaps," Heap of Birds said that his intention was to bring to light the experience of the Cheyenne and other Native peoples in the West.[28] "I want people to understand the history of their nation," he explained. "So much history has been hidden in Colorado."[29]

Unlike *Building Minnesota*, which marked the industrial corridor of the Mississippi River in downtown Minneapolis as a site of Native American

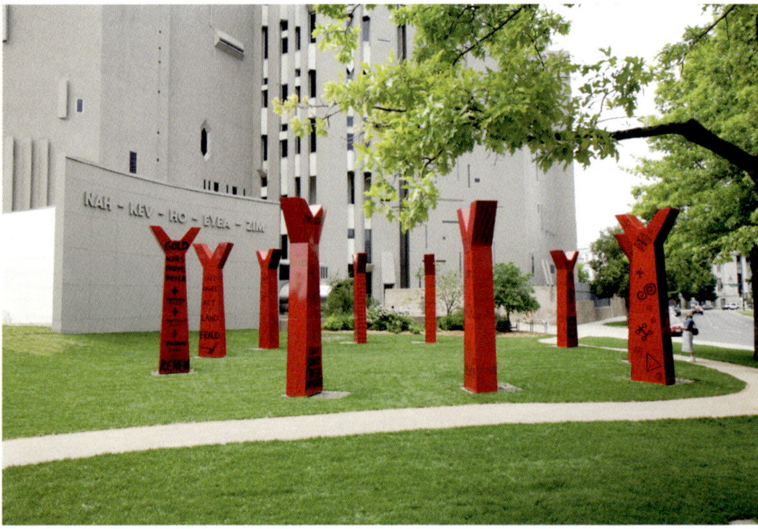

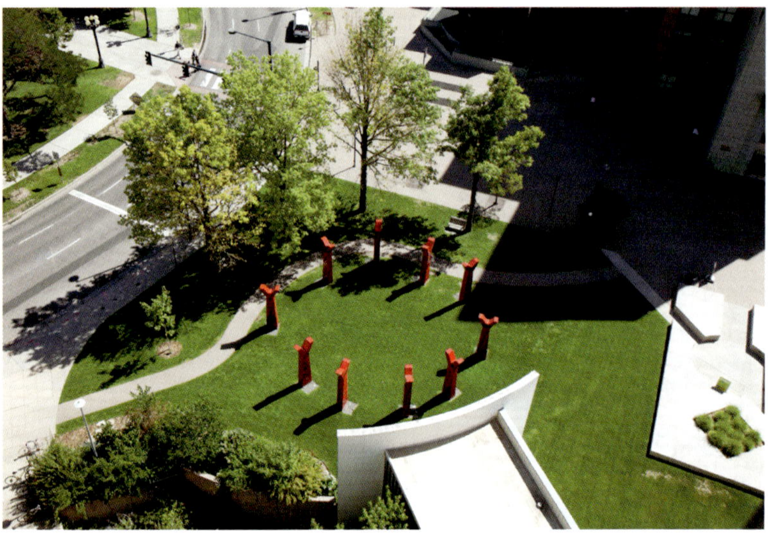

3.8–3.9 Edgar Heap of Birds, *Wheel*, 2005. Porcelain on steel, 48-foot diameter, each form 24 × 24 × 144 inches. Denver Art Museum Collection: funds from Charles J. Norton by exchange, and funds from the Bonfils-Stanton Foundation, the AT&T Foundation, the National Endowment for the Arts, and the Douglas Society, 1997.1452. Artwork © Edgar Heap of Birds. Photograph © Denver Art Museum.

history, *Wheel* is sited amid beaux arts monuments and architecture and contemporary artworks in a developing arts district adjacent to Denver's City Beautiful–era Civic Center Park (comparable to the arts campus where Heap of Birds installed his public signage in Atlanta). *Wheel* shares civic space with *Lao-Tzu*, a looming, welded-steel sculpture by Mark di Suvero, and *The Yearling*, a sculpture depicting a horse incongruously placed atop an oversized chair by Donald Lipski at the Denver Public Library across a pedestrian plaza from the museum (itself an iconic, sculptural design by architect Michael Graves), as well as *Big Sweep* by Claes Oldenburg and Coosjie van Bruggen, and a Deborah Butterfield sculpture of a horse on the grounds of the museum, which comprise the 1971 Gio Ponti building and the Frederic C. Hamilton building by Daniel Libeskind, opened in 2006. The outdoor sculpture collections at DAM and the Denver Public Library serve as a focus for the ongoing redevelopment of the Golden Triangle neighborhood (so named for the gold that first lured pioneers to Denver), a once elegant Victorian district that had become by the 1980s a neighborhood of used car dealerships and bail bondsmen. Now the city's premiere cultural destination, the area is home to the Byers-Evans House, the Colorado Historical Society, and the Clyfford Still Museum (showcasing the American abstract expressionist, to whom Heap of Birds's *Neuf* paintings are sometimes compared), as well as a number of galleries and several luxury condominium developments, in addition to the museum and library.

Claiming pride of place outside one of the museum's main entrances and opposite Civic Center Park, *Wheel* offers a pointed contrast to *Shoot-Out*, a twelve-by-twenty-foot painted-aluminum and steel outdoor sculpture by American artist Red Grooms (b. 1937), perched atop the museum's restaurant to the south. Originally planned in 1982 for the courtyard of a privately developed condominium complex directly west of downtown Denver on land owned by the University of Colorado and adjacent to the Denver Center for the Performing Arts, *Shoot-Out* was commissioned with the input of Diane Vanderlip, DAM's curator of modern and contemporary art. Grooms's sculpture depicts an armed struggle between stereotypical cowboy and Indian protagonists, leading to complaints from some prospective condominium buyers. A plan to relocate the sculpture to a nearby traffic island on the University of Colorado's Auraria campus was received with protests from university faculty and students and local Native American leaders, who criticized its cartoonish style and reliance on demeaning and hackneyed Hollywood images. However, the pop artist Grooms routinely worked with such images, depicting all of his characters in cartoonish style; the cowboy in *Shoot-Out*, for example, is depicted metonymically by a ten-gallon hat and a bandolier of bullets. Art historian Erika Doss writes that the work "is clearly a caricature: an irreverent lampoon of a B-grade Hollywood Western, a pop art version of Mel Brooks's 1974 Western spoof, *Blazing Saddles*."[30] Protesters failed to appreciate Grooms's whimsy. Following a contentious rally and a counter-demonstration mounted by local artists, the board of regents of the University of Colorado voted unanimously to remove the sculpture from the campus. Grooms's sculpture was relocated to an enclosed sculpture garden in DAM's Gio Ponti building until 1996, when it was moved to a rooftop terrace. In 2007, as part of renovations to the North Building, *Shoot-Out* was moved again, onto the roof of the museum's restaurant, where it is barely visible from the site of Heap of Birds's sculpture. In its new location—perhaps chastened by the solemn gravitas of *Wheel*—it has not caused the slightest stir.[31]

Wheel also shares a psychic and semiotic space with another, older reminder of the atrocities at Sand Creek. On the nearby grounds of the state capitol, the Colorado Soldiers Monument honors Civil War dead. A bronze plaque on the 1909 monument lists Sand Creek as the last of twenty-one Civil War battles and engagements fought by Colorado troops in New Mexico, Indian Territory, Missouri, and Colorado between 1861 and 1865. The monument had long been a focus for the outrage of Native Americans in Colorado, and a destination for numerous anti–Columbus Day demonstration marches organized by American Indian Movement activists. The monument had also been a source of embarrassment for others in the state. In 1998, state senator Bob Martinez introduced a resolution that Sand Creek be removed from the memorial, arguing, "Sand Creek was not a battle between the North and the South. . . . Sand Creek was a disgrace."[32] The resolution passed unanimously, as did a similar resolution one year later in the state house of representatives.

Moreover, the monument, designed by John D. Howland and modeled by Jakob Otto Schweizer, features a standing portrait of an armed Union soldier, which American Indian Movement activists claimed was a portrait of army colonel John Milton Chivington, "the fighting preacher" known for boasting, "I have come to kill Indians, and believe it is right and honor-

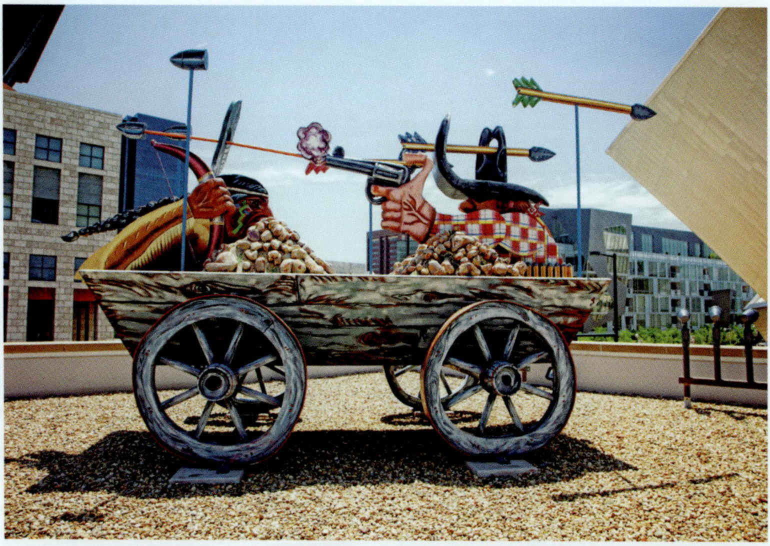

3.10 Red Grooms, *Shoot-Out*, 1982. Denver Art Museum Collection: gift of Lawrence Street Ventures, 1985.819. Artwork © 2014 Red Grooms / Artists Rights Society (ARS), New York. Photograph © Denver Art Museum.

able to use any means under God's heaven to kill Indians."[33] Chivington led the combined troops of the Colorado Militia in the brutal attack on Black Kettle's camp at Sand Creek. Howland, the monument's designer, was himself a veteran of the First Colorado Cavalry (he has not been identified as playing a role in the massacre), and later served as secretary to the Indian Peace Commission, which negotiated the Medicine Lodge Treaty of 1867, establishing the first reservations on the Plains. Chivington is listed on the monument's base, with Colonel John P. Slough, as leading the First Colorado Cavalry, along with three other leaders of state military units that fought in the Civil War. However, the soldier is not identified as Chivington. Indeed, the monument is dedicated to all Colorado Civil War soldiers. If the monument were a portrait of Chivington, it would likely say so, as in the nearby Pioneer Monument (sculpted by Frederick MacMonnies in 1911), which includes an equestrian portrait of a rifle-toting Colonel Christopher Houston "Kit" Carson, another infamous Indian killer who oversaw the 1864 Long Walk, which removed the Diné (Navajo) Nation from their traditional homelands to internment at Bosque Redondo (Fort Sumner) in southeastern New Mexico.

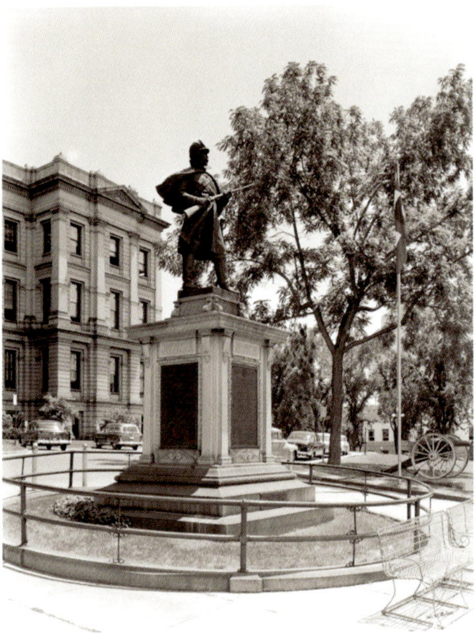

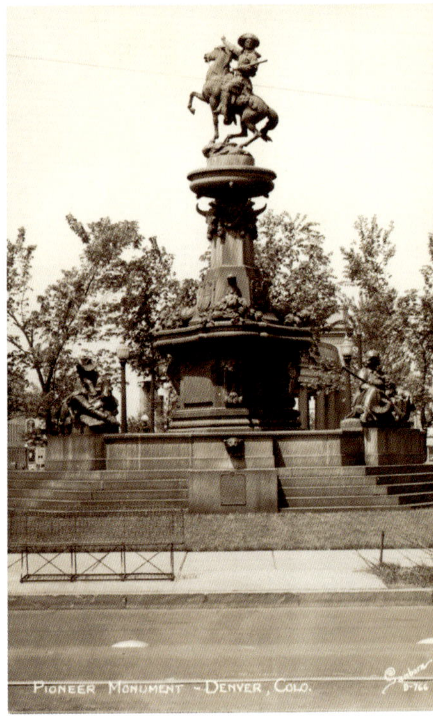

3.11 John D. Howland and Jakob Otto Schweizer, Colorado Soldiers Monument, 1909. Colorado State Capitol, Denver. History Colorado, Stephen H. Hart Library, scan #10037235, Denver, Colorado.

3.12 Frederick MacMonnies, Pioneer Monument, 1911. Civic Center Plaza, Denver, Colorado. Postcard. History Colorado, Stephen H. Hart Library, accession #93.101.19, Denver, Colorado.

Ultimately, legislators chose to leave the monument intact as a testimony to the state's troubled history; an additional plaque was added in 2002 to contextualize the 1909 statue: "The controversy surrounding this Civil War Monument has become a symbol of Coloradans' struggle to understand and take responsibility for our past. . . . By designating Sand Creek a battle, the monument's designers mischaracterized the actual events. Protests led by Native Americans and others throughout the twentieth century have since led to the widespread recognition of the tragedy as the Sand Creek Massacre."

The process for *Wheel* began in 1996, when the museum solicited proposals from nine contemporary Native artists for a public sculpture on the museum's grounds. Heap of Birds's proposal was selected because, as DAM curator of Native arts Nancy Blomberg explained, "the subject matter of his work really spoke to Colorado history."[34] Heap of Birds's original proposal for *Wheel* was actually much broader in its range of references, citing ancient and contemporary structures from a variety of indigenous cultures from the west and Central America: pre-Columbian stelae from Oaxaca, Mexico; circular subterranean kivas built by Anasazi or Ancestral Pueblo peoples in the Southwest; Plains medicine wheels; and the contemporary Earth Renewal or Sun Dance lodge used by Cheyenne and other Plains Indians. As the plan came together, Heap of Birds narrowed his focus to Plains traditions. The first design included twelve standing tree forms—modeled closely after the Earth Renewal lodge; this was later reduced to ten, rendering the sacred form secular and making a more universal reference, an abstract enclosure that recalls the various, circular ritual spaces used by indigenous peoples. Nevertheless, Heap of Birds's design resonates most profoundly with the Plains Earth Renewal lodge and monuments such as the Bighorn Medicine Wheel in north-central Wyoming, an important heritage and spiritual site for Plains people. A circle of stones eighty feet in diameter, with twenty-eight radial spokes radiating from a central stone cairn, the Bighorn Medicine Wheel is linked conceptually to the contemporary Earth Renewal lodge; both are cosmic diagrams, aligned to the four directions and the summer solstice. Plains nations, Heap of Birds notes, share a "unified religious kinship" around the medicine wheel and the Earth Renewal ceremony. The linkage to Cheyenne-Arapaho history specifically is also made clear by Heap of Birds's original proposal, which would have inscribed the names of ninety-seven families who were camped at Sand Creek in 1864. This memorial wall, recalling the listing of American dead in Lin's Vietnam Veterans Memorial and Heap of Birds's honoring of murdered Dakota warriors in *Building Minnesota*, was ultimately abandoned in favor of the optimistic—and more universal—phrase in Cheyenne, "We are always returning back home again," reclaiming the site, and Colorado, for Native people. Construction began at a groundbreaking ceremony during DAM's Tenth Annual Friendship Powwow on Saturday, September 11, 1999, with a blessing from Cheyenne and Arapaho spiritual leaders preparing the site to accept the sculpture.

For the ten tree forms, Heap of Birds drew inspiration from the forked branches he saw used in simple shelters, makeshift supports for cooking pots. They suggest improvised structures—they might support a horizontal roof beam—and speak to the resourcefulness of traditional indigenous cultures; Heap of Birds described the form as "symbolic of our inherent strength."[35] (Heap of Birds has also suggested the upraised limbs of the tree forms represent the Cheyenne chiefs, their arms outstretched in a gesture of blessing and offering to the Cheyenne people.)[36] Three different tree forms are used in the sculpture, each slightly different in design. In the Earth Renewal lodge, each structural member is meaningful, chosen specifically and aligned to the cosmos. The central pole "holds up the universe," Heap of Birds explained, although *Wheel* lacks a center pole; it and the roof beams are to be imagined by the sculpture's intended audience, Native people who will reclaim their ancestral homeland. "It is our wish," Heap of Birds wrote in his proposal, "that today's Native brothers and sisters shall spiritually finish the roof by offering their own creative actions inherent in their significant everyday lives."[37] The entire structure is aligned with the summer solstice; if one observes from a vantage point at the sixth tree, the sun rises in the space between the first and tenth tree on the longest day of the year.

Each of the tree forms is covered in a unique palimpsest of symbols, line drawings, words, and acronyms baked into the surface of the red enamel. The effect is similar to Heap of Birds's wall lyrics and marker drawings but also incorporates graphic elements utilized in a manner similar to the pyramids he built for *Ocmulgee*, borrowed from indigenous sources such as petroglyphs from ancient sites and drawings traditionally made by Plains men on hides and in ledger books. The text and images thus reference indigenous practices of marking space and time; the sculpture references native histories and indigenous knowledge, alongside but not subordinated to the history of settler state–Indian relations, as narrated by Western historiography and marked by the dates of treaties and federal legislation. Histories share space—the linear time of Western modernity as measured by years and a progressive drive toward recognition and equality intersect with an indigenous conception of time as cyclical—"always returning back home."

Tree one begins the sequence with a pattern of petroglyphs and other abstract forms, drawing from the Ancestral Puebloan cultures of the ancient Southwest, as well as the spiral motif, which reappears throughout

Wheel, a symbol of perseverance and return—an optimistic motif that sets a hopeful tone and reminds viewers of the story of renewal that the sculpture ultimately highlights. Tree two depicts Bent's Fort, an important site of exchange for early Anglo-American traders, Cheyenne and Arapaho people, and their Indian allies, built along the Arkansas River in present-day southeastern Colorado, midway between Missouri and New Mexico along the old Santa Fe Trail. A symbol of mutually beneficial coexistence and cooperation—Buffalo hides harvested by Comanche and other Plains people were traded by Cheyenne and Arapaho middlemen to an eager U.S. market—the fort was abandoned and destroyed after a devastating cholera outbreak in 1849. The period of peaceful trade ended as the Plains descended into decades of bloodshed, as U.S. settlers pushed westward across Plains nations' traditional hunting territories. A pattern of question marks seems to ask what might have happened if trade relations between the United States and the sovereign nations of the Plains had been nurtured and sustained.

Tree three—titled *Cheyenne and Arapaho Massacres*—depicts a pattern of wound-like train tracks, suggesting the period following the Mexican-American War of 1846–48, as westbound routes for commercial expansion were developed, cleaving the Central Plains and beginning the painful process of moving Cheyenne, Arapaho, and other Plains peoples onto reservations. Tree four examines the gold rush that followed the discovery of gold at Pike's Peak in 1858, an event that brought an influx of commercial interests into the region, leading to the establishing of the Colorado Territory in 1861 (followed by statehood in 1876), and the resulting dispossession of the Ute (Yutah) Nation.

In tree five, Heap of Birds's narrative picks up in the reservation period, as Plains peoples were forced into new lives and U.S. government policies attempted, through the Dawes General Allotment Act of 1887, to assign individual farm plots to formerly migratory peoples. Tree six displays an array of acronyms representing the myriad programs and organizations established by the U.S. government and other groups to address the new situation of Native peoples in the late nineteenth and twentieth centuries. Heap of Birds likens Indians' relationship with the federal government to a "bittersweet marriage."[38] Many organizations were created to inculcate a culture of dependency in once-sovereign peoples, hastening their assimilation into the American mainstream. Other acronyms, such as N.A.R.F.

(Native American Rights Fund, headquartered in Colorado), refer to organizations that continue to assert and defend the legal and political rights of indigenous people and communities.

The final four trees assert the resilience and resistance of Native peoples in the present. Tree seven is dedicated to the American Indian Religious Freedom Act of 1978, which established the right of Native Americans to pursue their traditional spiritual practices, such as the Native American Church (in which peyote is a sacrament) and other traditional beliefs, which were brutally repressed throughout much of the nineteenth and twentieth centuries. The resurgence of Native spirituality is also linked to an earlier moment of spiritual resistance—the Ghost Dance of the last decade of the nineteenth century, which united many of the tribes of the Western United States in an attempt to drive white invaders out of Indian Country. The Ghost Dance is represented on tree seven by the abstract symbols that participants believed (wrongly) would protect them from U.S. troops' bullets. Tree eight thematizes Native perseverance in the face of oppressive institutions such as the compulsory boarding schools through which the U.S. government sought to indoctrinate and assimilate Native youth. The tree also highlights the 1990 Native American Graves Protection and Repatriation Act, a landmark legal victory of indigenous peoples in the struggle to regain control of physical remains and priceless objects of cultural heritage. Tree nine, *Indigenous Global Allies*, links organizations such as the American Indian Movement—represented by an inverted American flag—to international organizations devoted to indigenous rights. The tenth and final tree highlights Native renewal and growth, documenting rebounding population figures and educational and professional achievements by contemporary Native people. While one critic described the message of *Wheel* as "unmistakably, perpetually negative," Heap of Birds's tenth tree and the message "We are always returning back home again" are affirmative and positive, looking forward to a revitalized future for Native people and culture, connecting the circle back to the beginning of the sequence and the spiral of life and renewal.[39] As poet and critic Dean Rader writes, "Flowing both circuitously and vertically, *Wheel* seems to stretch in all directions, an aesthetic compass, a map of both historical and interior landscapes leading us concurrently outward and inward."[40]

Highlighting its connections to indigenous notions of time and history, Heap of Birds linked *Wheel* specifically to the solstice, the end of the old and the beginning of the new year for Plains people, when the ceremony of the Earth Renewal takes place. "We start over," he said at the dedication ceremony, "start fresh, today."[41] Blomberg predicted that *Wheel*'s message of renewal and return would become a focus for community: "We envision this as a vital and active place where groups—especially American Indians—can come together for community renewal and solstice celebrations."[42] More than fulfilling the hopes of Heap of Birds and the museum, *Wheel* has become a destination for local Native communities. The sculpture was a stopping point for the second Longest Walk in 2008, a commemoration of the 1978 march from Alcatraz Island in San Francisco to Washington, DC, in support of Native rights and indigenous sacred sites. Also in 2008, forty Cheyenne and Arapaho youth from Montana, Wyoming, and Oklahoma undertook a three-day run from the Sand Creek Massacre site to Denver, ending their trek with a candlelight vigil at *Wheel* on November 28, the day after Thanksgiving and the day before the anniversary of the massacre on November 29, 1864. The Friday vigil coincided with the first Native American Heritage Day in 2008, a new national civic holiday; and Colorado governor Bill Ritter proclaimed November 27–29, 2008, Sand Creek Massacre Spiritual Healing Run Memorial Days. An additional plan, partly funded by the Colorado Historical Society, hopes to create a monument in Denver to army captain Silas Soule, of the First Colorado Calvary, who disobeyed orders from Chivington to fire on the Cheyenne and Arapaho camp at Sand Creek, later testifying against his commanding officer, and who was ultimately ambushed and murdered by a militia member loyal to Chivington.[43] And in 2011, apologizing for Chivington's leadership in the Sand Creek Massacre, the United Methodist Church's General Commission on Christian Unity and Interreligious Concerns announced a $50,000 grant to develop an educational center at the Sand Creek Massacre National Historic Site, which has since 2007 been managed by the National Park Service. Indeed, rather than a negative and divisive presence for Native and non-Native citizens of Colorado, *Wheel* has become a focal point for revisiting and acknowledging the state's tragic histories—for coming to terms with the past.

Telling New Histories: *Most Serene Republics*

In 2007, at the Fifty-Second Esposizione Internazionale d'Arte in Venice, Italy (popularly known as the Venice Biennale—the oldest and most prestigious of the recurrent international exhibitions of contemporary art), Heap of Birds created *Most Serene Republics*, a temporary site-specific artwork sponsored by the Smithsonian Institution National Museum of the American Indian (NMAI) and installed in four locations around the city.[44] Heap of Birds's descriptions as he planned the project focused on the need to recover lost Native American perspectives, which are absent in the archive and missing in Eurocentric histories. "It is a human right to have a voice and be heard," he wrote. "So often our Native American heritage is represented by silent faces, stoic in their repression. My work in Venice begins with a belated honoring of those Native spirits who died in Europe as part of the Wild West spectacles."[45]

Like other Heap of Birds public artworks, *Most Serene Republics* addressed its local context, making links to broader histories. The name "most serene republic"—Serenissima Repubblica—was bestowed on Venice during its independence. The appellation is ironic given the city's tumultuous history, some of which is evoked by Heap of Birds's interventions, which play on stories of the city as a destination for Native American traveling performers in the nineteenth century as well as evoking the city's past status—now expired—as a world power. The signage for *Most Serene Republics* made use of green text, in addition to the artist's signature red, in a nod to the Italian flag. Moreover, the artwork engaged with histories of travel, tourism, and exotic encounters with otherness, and the vagaries of cultural translation in a global context. Heap of Birds's interventions at the Biennale invoked Native American experiences of travel and participation in popular culture—the touring Wild West shows of the nineteenth century were compared to the contemporary global art marketplace and linked North American Native histories to global histories of power and domination. Indian reservations were compared to Jewish ghettoes, and Europe's Crusades were juxtaposed with the project of empire in North America. Curator Kathleen Ash-Milby described Heap of Birds's project for the Biennale as a "compelling microcosm of the world history of the creation of republics or nation-states through acts of aggression, displacement, or replacement of populations and cultures."[46] Indeed, Heap of Birds used the platform of the Biennale to address the political debacles of the present day, and as an indigenous historian and critic in his own right.

Most visitors to the Biennale first encountered Heap of Birds's artwork as they traveled to the exhibition, passing through the international arrivals area at Marco Polo International Airport in Venice. Near passport control and customs, Heap of Birds installed a banner that implicitly compared the Biennale to Buffalo Bill's popular Wild West shows of the late nineteenth century, in which Native Americans toured Europe as an exotic spectacle. Bordered by a pattern of Latin crosses and shields, Heap of Birds's panel instructed those arriving in the city to view the Biennale to remember (in Italian: RAMMENTARE) the Native performers—"SHOW INDIANS"—who died while traveling Europe with Buffalo Bill Cody's Wild West show. The panel identifies women—in the Lakota language, *Nastona* ("our daughters")—as well as men, *Numshim* ("our grandfathers"). In its memorial function, the airport panel and the entirety of *Most Serene Republics* might be seen to echo *Building Minnesota*. But while the Dakota warriors honored in *Building Minnesota* were executed in retaliation for their efforts defending the communities and homelands, the performers remembered in *Most Serene Republics*—many of whom were former combatants—are perhaps more tragically ambivalent figures as they were participants in a transnational circuit of production and exchange, whereby indigenous cultural heritage was unhinged from traditional senses of place and became, in effect, a global commodity.

Significantly, Buffalo Bill's show Indians were not the first Native American people to travel to the Old World, or to die there, far from home. In 1493, a small group of indigenous people returned with Columbus as exotic curiosities; in 1617, Pocahontas traveled to England; in 1846, the American artist and entrepreneur George Catlin toured Europe with his Indian Gallery and a party of Plains men. For his 2005 Biennale exhibition, also sponsored by NMAI, Luiseño artist James Luna created an installation and performance that memorialized Pablo Tac, a young Luiseño who, embracing Catholicism, traveled to Rome at the age of ten in 1832 to study for the priesthood, and who died there nine years later, having begun work on a Luiseño dictionary, and having written a history of the Spanish missions in California.

Heap of Birds chose to focus on the Wild West show Indians because they had traveled to Venice—a striking photograph by Paolo Salviati shows

Buffalo Bill and an entourage posed picturesquely in a gondola on the Venice Lagoon, the Cathedral of San Marco visible in the background—and performed in nearby Verona.[47] In 1887, Cody's first trip overseas to England had been wildly popular; in 1889–90, the troupe embarked on a second, extended tour, which included continental Europe and Italy, where the famous photo in the Lagoon was taken. Moreover, the Native men, women, and children who traveled with Cody were Plains people—Oglala Lakota from Pine Ridge, South Dakota. More than sixty Native American performers and their families traveled with the Wild West show. Heap of Birds suggests that these performers performed "under duress."[48] During the late 1880s and early 1890s, tensions on the Northern Plains had reached a fever pitch, with the outbreak of murderous violence and government crackdown a daily threat for Native people. After the 1890 massacre at Wounded Knee, Cody (working with the U.S. secretary of the interior) hired Ghost

3.13 Edgar Heap of Birds, banner at Marco Polo International Airport, Venice, Italy, installed as part of *Most Serene Republics*. Venice Biennale, 2007. Photo by Fotostudio Comin. Courtesy of the National Museum of the American Indian, Smithsonian Institution. Artwork © Edgar Heap of Birds.

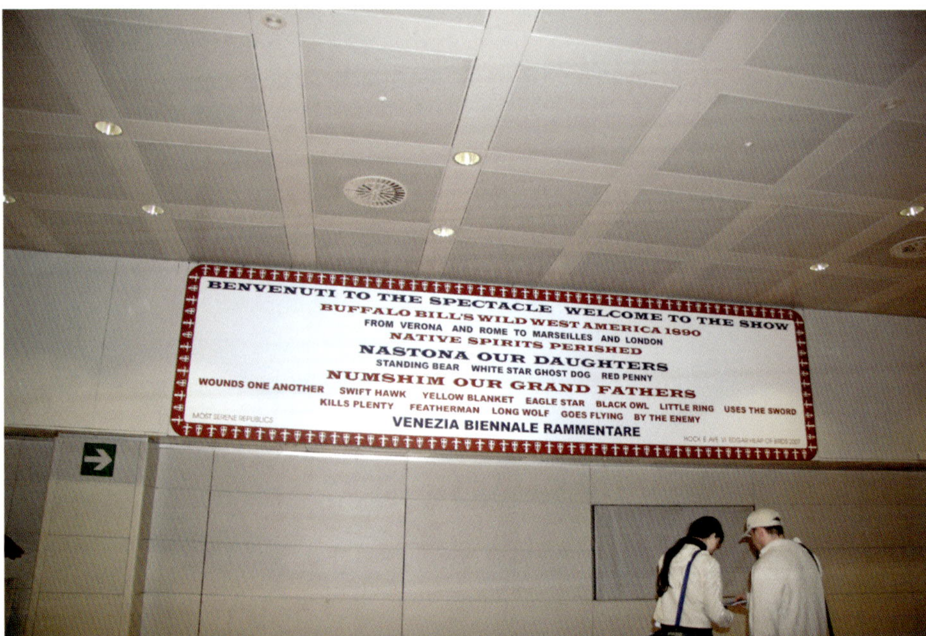

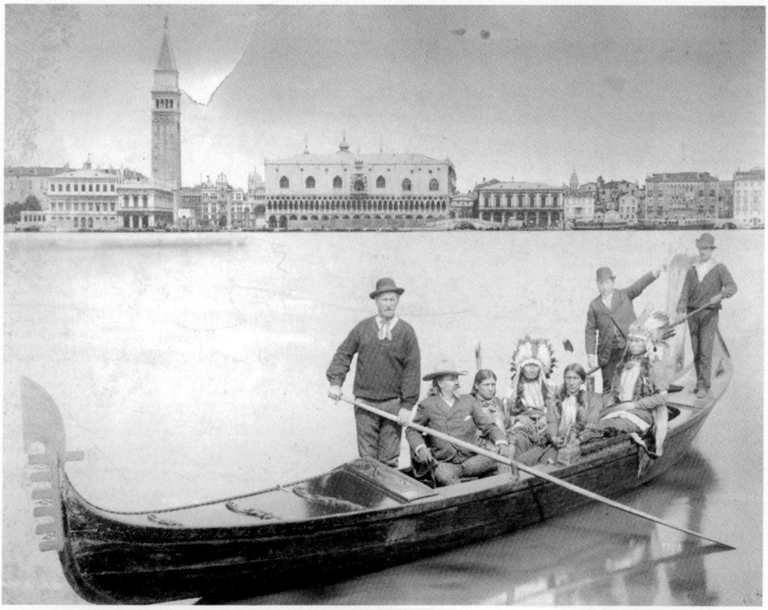

3.14 Paolo Salviati, *Buffalo Bill Cody and Native American Performers Touring Venice, Italy*, 1889. Photograph. Denver Public Library, Western History Collection, NS-136.

Dancers imprisoned at Fort Sheridan—former combatants who were given the choice of touring and performing or serving the remainder of their sentences. Surely, for many, the opportunity to perform and represent their people—to live as warriors, even if only as a simulation—was preferable to living for another half year under guard. Twenty-three warriors and their families chose to join the tour. We can only assume that the experiences of the former combatants-turned-reenactors were complicated and conflicted. Cody's performance included theatrically flaunting the scalp and headdress of Yellow Bonnet, purportedly taken by Cody himself at the 1876 Battle of Little Big Horn. And yet it was a shrewd choice; the warriors sought to make the best for their families of an unlivable situation as the life that they knew was thrown into crisis, and the world was in flux.

The second location in which Heap of Birds chose to intervene was along the Viale Garibaldi, between Giardini Napoleonici and Via Garibaldi, near the Giardini Pubblici, the location of the permanent national pavilions that are the centerpiece of the Biennale. Here, Heap of Birds installed sixteen panels, imploring passersby to "Honor the Dead" and to "Remember" (RAMMENTARE) the show Indians. One panel listed fifteen names; each of the others listed the individual names of twelve adults and three children.

The location was a broad, heavily treed pedestrian walkway (there are no streets open to automobile traffic in Venice's old city center) and lined with substantial eighteenth-century houses. Ash-Milby noted that this location was "a place rife with both symbolic and literal reference to the end of Venetian independence."[49] The sense of space along the Viale Garibaldi contrasts with the rest of the medieval city—the leafy lane was the creation of Napoleon Bonaparte, who directed that the existing neighborhood be razed to make way for a grand processional avenue. The stately character of the neighborhood conceals a tumultuous history; Napoleon's conquest of the city brought to a close the period in which Venice was a sovereign republic.

Heap of Birds installed eight more panels in a third location, the Giardini Reali (or Royal Gardens) adjacent to the iconic Piazza San Marco. Like the Viale Garibaldi, the Giardini Reali was also created at the behest of Napoleon, who mandated that the existing neighborhood be cleared and space reconfigured to create a vista of the Grand Canal from his imperial palace. At this site, Heap of Birds was also attentive to earlier histories of displacement and narratives of sovereignty usurped, seeking to link these episodes to the recovered Native experiences of his Biennale project.

Here, in the small public park, Heap of Birds's panels were set among shrubs behind a row of benches. Each bordered with a pattern of fitched crosses ("associated with war and religious zeal," according to Ash-Milby), the panels alluded to Venice's involvement in the Crusades, as well as the artistic and nautical achievements of the republic, which Heap of Birds suggested were dependent on the medieval campaigns of conversion and plunder.[50] A panel that read "CRUSADES OF STOLEN GOODS" referred to the Fourth Crusade, in the thirteenth century, during which time Venice sacked and looted the city of Constantinople. Ash-Milby writes, "The treasury of San Marco was formed with precious objects—silver, gold, reliefs, sculpture—torn from palaces and churches throughout Constantinople in the sacking of the city in 1204 during the Fourth Crusade."[51] The Venetians' participation in the crusade was motivated not by Christian zeal (it was an anomaly—the city had not participated in previous crusades)

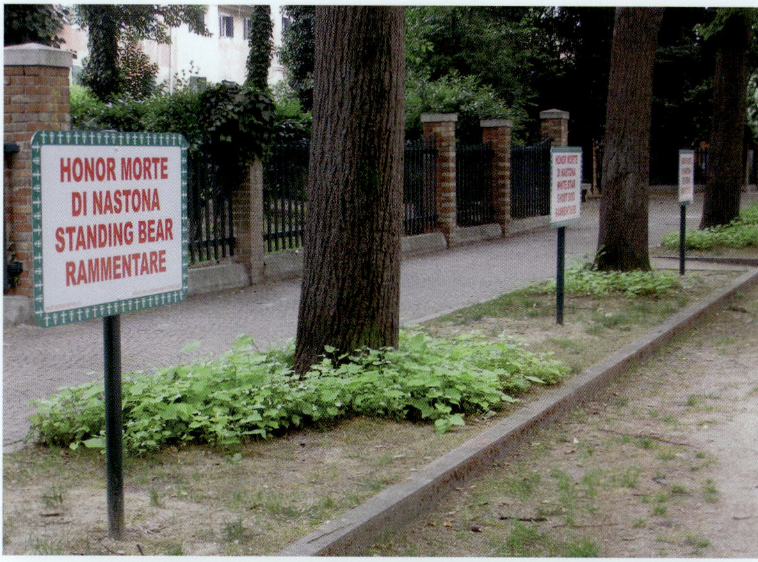

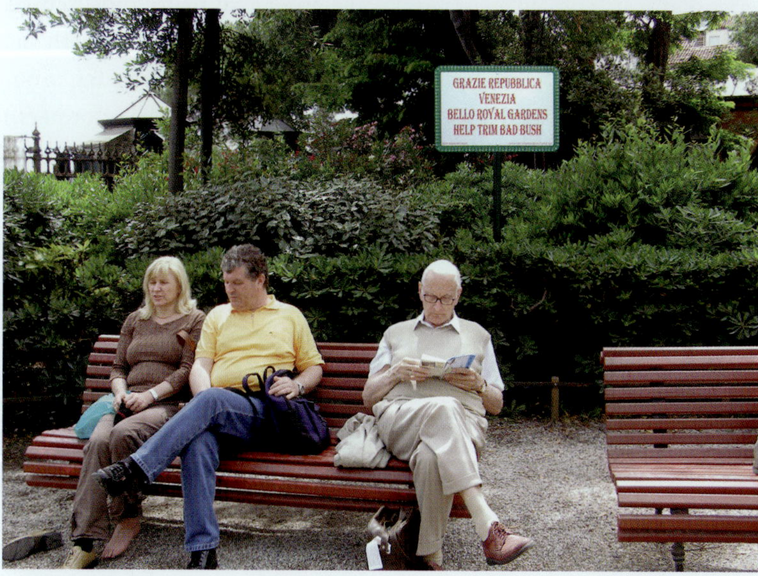

3.15 Edgar Heap of Birds, panels along Viale Garibaldi installed as part of *Most Serene Republics*, 2007. Sixteen steel panels, each 24 × 36 inches. Venice Biennale. Artwork © Edgar Heap of Birds.

3.16 Edgar Heap of Birds, signage in the Giardini Reali installed as part of *Most Serene Republics*, 2007. Eight steel panels, each 24 × 36 inches. Venice Biennale. Artwork © Edgar Heap of Birds.

but by a desire to settle scores with the rival city of Zara (or Zadar), across the Adriatic on the Dalmatian coast of present-day Croatia, precipitating massive, wanton destruction. A panel that read "LET FOUR HORSES RUN HOME" referred to a grouping of four gilded copper statues of classic Greek manufacture that are emblematic of the traffic in stolen treasures that filled Venice's coffers when the city was at its height. The four horses formerly stood at the Hippodrome in Constantinople. In the eighteenth century, Napoleon had the sculptures dismantled and shipped to Paris. They were repatriated in the nineteenth century, but to Venice, not to Turkey or Greece. For Heap of Birds, gilded copper horses serve as an allegory for Native cultures that were uprooted and showcased for eager audiences in Europe—once proud and formidable Plains warriors "paraded throughout Europe as the trophies of American conquest"—as well as the human remains that have yet to be repatriated.[52] (As a fourth location, *Most Serene Republics* also included an artist's multiple—a printed tote bag—and a series of placards placed on *vaporettos*, the water taxis that shuttle tourists between Venice's many islands and the mainland, emblazoned with the slogan "CARRY SHOW INDIANS REMAINS BACK HOME," speaking to ongoing efforts to locate and repatriate the remains of the fallen performers.)

In all of the Giardini Reali panels, Heap of Birds drew parallels with American history, as well as with contemporary politics. One panel made reference to the fact that Venice was the site of Europe's first Jewish ghetto—the Ghetto Nuovo, created in 1516 to confine a formerly integrated and multiethnic Jewish population that had lived in the city for generations—drawing a parallel with Indian reservations in the United States. A panel imploring visitors to "HELP TRIM BAD BUSH" brought the project full-circle to the present. As Heap of Birds explained, "The history of Venice, its Republic (Empire) and cultural dealings have a broad application to power relations in the world today. Often we see history as an isolated and obsolete set of facts, particularly in a tourist zone. We may find it fitting to reveal these forgotten relationships and make a correlation to events, struggles, and triumphs of today."[53]

In addition to being a memorial, *Most Serene Republics* is a meditation on place and power. Two of the three locations in which Heap of Birds installed panels—the Viale Garibaldi and the Giardini Reali—were sites at which Napoleon had destroyed the existing urban fabric to create new spaces befitting his reign. At all the sites, Heap of Birds sought to lay bare

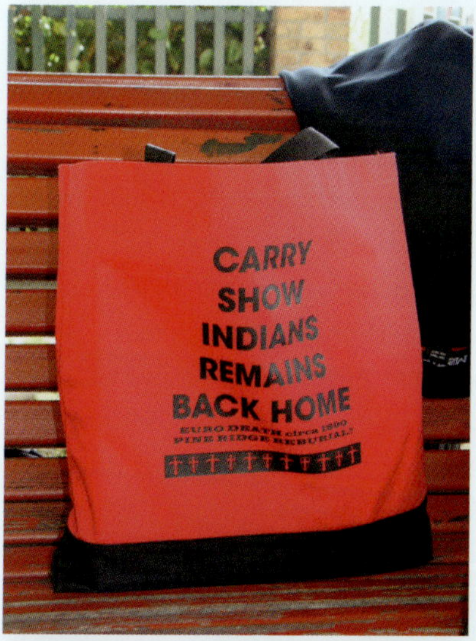

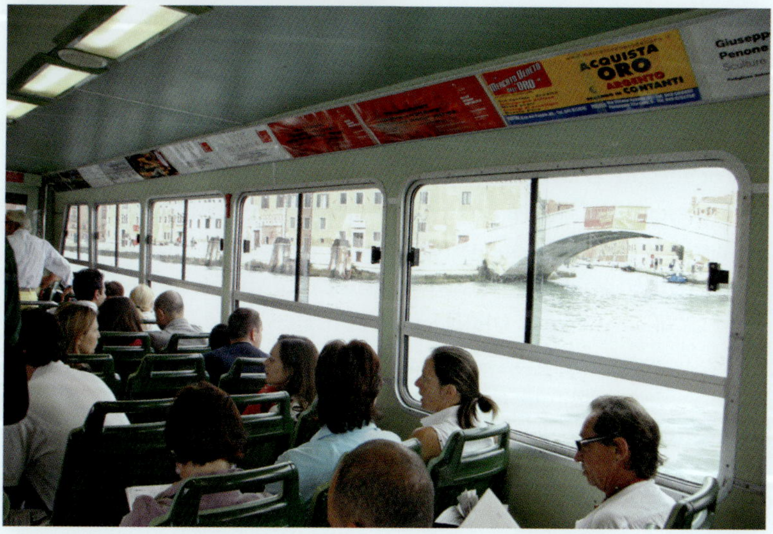

3.17 Edgar Heap of Birds, tote bag created for *Most Serene Republics*, 2007. Printed canvas. Venice Biennale. Photo by Fotostudio Comin. Courtesy of the National Museum of the American Indian, Smithsonian Institution. Artwork © Edgar Heap of Birds.

3.18 Edgar Heap of Birds, placard for *vaporettos* (water taxis) created for *Most Serene Republics*, 2007. Venice Biennale. Photo by Fotostudio Comin. Courtesy of the National Museum of the American Indian, Smithsonian Institution. Artwork © Edgar Heap of Birds.

layers of historical geography, adding his own psychogeographical exploration of the site as a location of Native American experience and a point in a global itinerary that he himself was now following. (After its installation in Venice, *Most Serene Republics* was installed in Verona, where Cody's troupe had performed in a Roman-era amphitheater; the exhibition, in modified form, has continued to travel.) He sought to make linkages between the end of Venetian sovereignty and the lost sovereignty endured by Native peoples in the Americas—Cody's performers, in particular—whose removal was likewise necessitated by the territorial ambitions of an expansionist imperial power. As Heap of Birds said of the foundations of nation-states and empires, "The nature of their creation is to eclipse or absorb previous societies and governmental groups."[54]

In *Most Serene Republics*, Heap of Birds sought to connect these hidden layers and lost narratives. This might be seen as analogous to the renaming of places and the erasures of memory and history by European settler-colonials in the New World (or by Napoleon himself as he sought to remake Venice more to his liking). Heap of Birds was motivated, as Ash-Milby writes, to uncover "hidden histories of Venice."[55] However, *Most Serene Republics* operated not just by revealing, but through a process of allegorical layering. Heap of Birds mapped the suppressed historical experiences of Native American people onto an existing site of erased memory—Napoleon Bonaparte's remade districts of medieval Venice, which figured another historical episode of displacement, effacement, and loss of sovereignty. Did Heap of Birds's layered historical allegories efface those other histories? If so, *Most Serene Republics* might be seen as more aggressive in tone than other, comparatively passive minimalist or conceptual memorials, such as those by Maya Lin or Lawrence Weiner. Lin's Vietnam memorial declined to command viewers to show respect; Heap of Birds's imperative—RAMMENTARE—does exactly that. In *SOME LIMESTONE*, Weiner made exclusive use of the past tense to describe the materiality of the physical monument, which is itself composed of the physical remains of a lost artifact—it has literally become the fabric of the new monument—and declines to contextualize and historicize its destruction, effacement, and remaking, only alluding to its preservation "for some reason." In theory, at least, Weiner leaves it to the viewer's individual initiative to assign agency. If Heap of Birds's project for many viewers effectively displaced Venetian history—claiming spaces for the remembrance of the dead Native performers from Cody's troupe and their families—these displacements and erasures are never complete; they are only ever partial. They remain open to contestation, as Heap of Birds himself has sought to do in other series such as *Native Hosts*, in which suppressed indigenous claims to territory, sovereignty, and history are given voice.

An interesting precursor—and illuminating contrast—to *Most Serene Republics* is a project for the 1984 Biennale by Lothar Baumgarten, a German artist who has often explored the suppressed histories of the indigenous peoples of the Americas. Prefiguring Heap of Birds's project (as well as artworks by Cai Quo Qiang, Santiago Sierra, Fred Wilson, James Luna, and other artists who have explored the histories of non-Europeans in the city), Baumgarten mapped Venice Lagoon on a marble floor in the German exhibition pavilion, superimposing the names of the rivers of the Amazon basin. In doing so, Baumgarten referenced an auspicious incident in 1499, when Amerigo Vespucci first sighted the coast of South America, the continent that would bear his name. The Italian cartographer saw houses built by indigenous South Americans along the shore on stilts and named the place after the city it reminded him of—Venezuela, or Little Venice—as critic Craig Owens wrote, "thereby obliterating its Indian name and instituting in its place a *proper* (i.e., Spanish) name." Citing the "violence implicit in this—or any—act of denomination," Owens noted that the act of naming, or "semiotic warfare," when in the service of imperial ambitions also obscures the traces of its own violent act.[56]

Owens suggested that Baumgarten's overlay of the Amazon basin onto the urban fabric of Venice was allegorical—two places and histories brought into a relationship—rather than violent, as in Vespucci's case or any other act of imperial nomination. To accrete layers—as happens in any place that is inhabited over any period of time, as in an urban environment—is a process of allegorizing. The addition of new layers does not displace earlier layers, but allows both to occupy the same space, as registers in dialogue, each being deepened, augmented, and transformed by the presence of another history. Owens argued that Baumgarten's new map did not obliterate the old psychogeographies of the lagoon, unlike Napoleon's creation of the Giardini Reali, which destroyed an earlier accretion of layers or concretion of value—an earlier place. Baumgarten's addition of a new layer modeled a way in which different histories might coexist. Similarly, *Most Serene Republics* brought Native North Ameri-

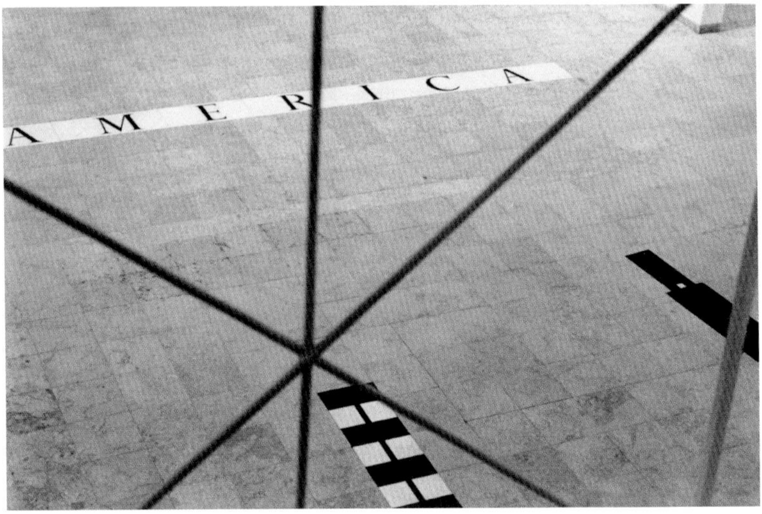

3.19 Lothar Baumgarten, AMERICA *Señores Naturales*, 1983–84. Installation at the Forty-First Venice Biennale, 1984. Artwork © 2014 Lothar Baumgarten / Artists Rights Society (ARS), New York.

can and European histories into dialogue. Heap of Birds's overlay of Native experiences—and in particular the histories of Native Americans in Europe—onto the already layered urban palimpsest of Venice connected two histories of place and power.

Most Serene Republics differs from *Wheel* in its relationship to the local context. *Wheel* sought to reclaim lost territory as a site of remembrance for Native people in the Western United States; *Most Serene Republics*, in its allegorical layering, invoked, but ultimately remained silent on, the topic of Venice's own traumatic histories. Heap of Birds was deliberate in his decision to place key elements of the project at sites that call up—for an informed viewer—the city's experience of living under foreign rule. But this was not a primary objective, it seems. Some degree of historical specificity risks disappearing. Perhaps that degree of layering—or allegorizing—is unrealizable in the festival atmosphere of the Biennale. The Venice that founded the "first ghetto" and profited from "crusades of stolen goods" predominates—an imperial power like the United States. Venice is a useful foil for Heap of Birds—it locates in a specific psychogeography the story of the Lakota performers who traveled with Cody, and who perished while overseas, far from home, and allows Heap of Birds to suggest something of what a world history that refused to make Europe the center of the story might look like.

But ultimately, in its memorial function, *Most Serene Republics* has a goal similar to *Wheel*'s. Heap of Birds described his goals for the Venice project in terms of "renewal and reconciliation" and a desire for healing and restoration of honor and harmony.[57] A consistent organizing principle that runs through the separate components of *Most Serene Republics* is the number four, as in Heap of Birds's other projects. He placed interventions in four locations: the airport, Viale Garibaldi, the Giardini Reali, and on the *vaporettos*. Panels were placed in multiples of four: eight in the Giardini Reali, sixteen along the Viale Garibaldi. Across Heap of Birds's diverse practice, the number four links the work of history back to ceremony and the Earth Renewal in particular, the four directions, and the ongoing series of abstract *Neuf* (four) paintings. The symmetry of the number four, and the way an arrangement of four equal elements marks a place as the axis and center, suggests that Heap of Birds sought to create a sense of balance, to offer a resolution to the painful histories of Native people. The number four, for Heap of Birds and for traditional Plains cultures, is also linked powerfully to notions of renewal and the human commitment to ensure renewal through mindful attention to the performance of ritual—in cycles of four, each year after four seasons have passed. The cyclical nature of time when measured by the annual return of the seasons, marked by the solstice, contrasts markedly with Western modernity's conception of time—of history and of historicity—as forward motion punctuated by transformative events. Layering an indigenous sense of time, wherein the return of "SHOW INDIAN REMAINS BACK HOME" happens alongside other histories—other times—ensures renewal and continuity. We are always returning back home again.

4

GENERATIONS

New Growth

In central London in 2012, Heap of Birds installed a banner at Camley Street Natural Park, a two-acre urban nature reserve in the borough of Camden in a former industrial site, wedged between Regent's Canal and a busy railway; the new Eurostar departs from a station at nearby St. Pancras. Heap of Birds had been invited to participate in *Wild New Territories*, an exhibition of artworks focused on themes befitting the reclaimed coal yard—urban ecology and habitat restoration, the threat of ecosystem collapse, and need for environmental stewardship. Along a busy roadway, Heap of Birds's thirty-foot-long banner read, "25 MILLION RED INDIAN LIVES LOST!"

Heap of Birds's intervention, based on consultation with demographers and historians, reminded viewers of the human toll that accompanied the rise of England as a global power—and of Europe and its colonial proxies—during the era of discovery and conquest. (The exhibition traveled to Vancouver and Berlin over the following year.) London and other cities that benefited from the extraction of resources in the Americas and other colonial endeavors now grapple with the burden of environmental remediation—reckoning with nearly two centuries of exploitive and damaging

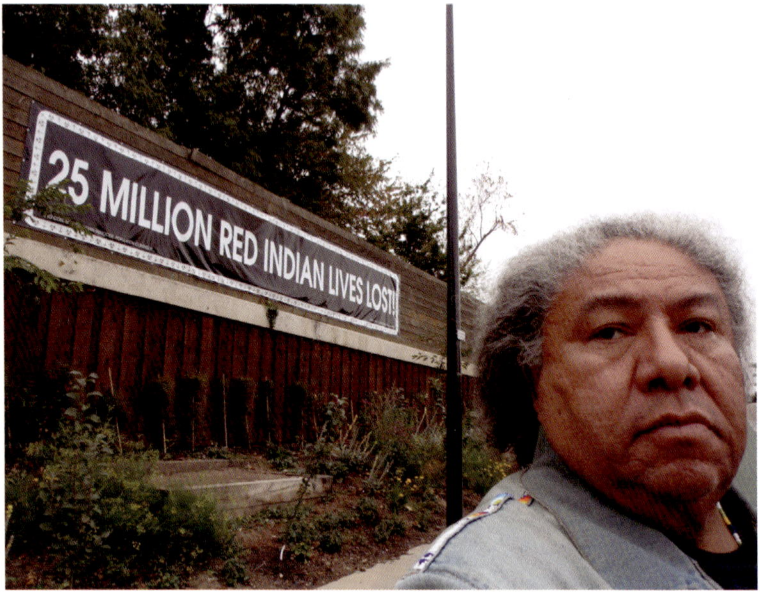

4.1 Edgar Heap of Birds, *25 Million Red Indian Lives Lost!*, 2012. Vinyl banner, 5 × 30 feet. London. Artwork © Edgar Heap of Birds. Created for the exhibition *Wild New Territories* in London in 2012, Heap of Birds's banner featured text surrounded by a border composed of fitched crosses and the international symbol for biohazard, linking histories of empire to contemporary issues of environmental health.

land use patterns that have blighted industrial centers. But even amid the greening of former brownfields such as Camley Street Natural Park—a site of new growth—Heap of Birds suggested there was accounting yet to be done. In the perspective of the Cheyenne and other indigenous peoples, interconnections between the human and natural world have always been apparent; for Heap of Birds, an ecological view necessitates an equal attention to issues of cultural preservation and renewal, to the needs of human communities. The exhibition was dutifully mindful of the environmental issues related to global population growth. But to bracket off environmental from human histories is bad faith. In smaller text at the bottom edge of the banner, Heap of Birds added the words "EURO CONTACT, RED INDIAN GENOCIDE, POPULATION CONTROL?"

Yet, while the historical imperative—his archival impulse—is foregrounded in the London installation, and the work is located in a place of renewal, where the costs of England's old industrial order are being addressed, looking to the past is for Heap of Birds never undertaken for its own sake. Rather, a countermemory of empire is asserted so that it might offer a point of departure. A return to the past, offering a record of lives lost, might make possible a new beginning, a point of departure at the very spot where the high-speed trains embark for Paris and Brussels, the capital of the European Union, connecting a new generation of Londoners to the new economies in the world beyond. Any such departure must acknowledge the past and its costs—global travelers should reckon with the burdens of history for all the world's peoples.

For many years, Heap of Birds's work has acknowledged that new growth requires that the past be accounted for. There is no renewal if the past is not honored, or if histories are suppressed. Travelers passing through Purchase, New York, in 1988 might have seen Heap of Birds's installation that mimicked a typical highway mile marker, asking if New York had been "PURCHASED?" or perhaps "STOLEN?" Accounting for this history makes possible another question: might these lands, home to the Six Nations of the Iroquois Confederacy, be "RECLAIMED?"

The historical imperative in Heap of Birds's art differentiates his work from much of that made under the banner of relational aesthetics (or social practice) during the past two decades, described by curator Nicolas Bourriaud as "an art that takes as its theoretical horizon the sphere of human interactions and its symbolic context."[1] But while this may seem to correspond with Heap of Birds's practice, which attempts to make a puncture in the social fabric rather than offering an illustration or an aesthetic response to a situation, according to Bourriaud relational art as exemplified by Rirkrit Tiravanija and Liam Gillick breaks from the work of previous generations in its attitude toward social change and historical agency. Bourriaud writes that relational artists are concerned with "learning to inhabit the world in a better way," focusing more on the immediate present than on the past or future. As Bourriaud writes, "It seems more pressing to invent possible relations with our neighbors in the present than to bet on happier tomorrows."[2] And while imagining possible relations—presumably more humane and ethical—with one's neighbors is positive, much of the work of Tiravanija and the other artists championed by Bourriaud declines to grapple with questions of power and historical agency, throwing out the baby of progressive social change—of justice—with the lukewarm

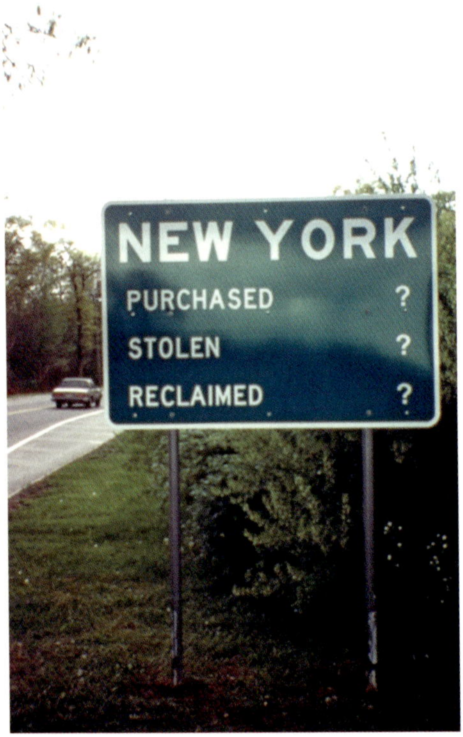

4.2 Edgar Heap of Birds, *Reclaim*, 1988. Steel panel, 24 × 36 inches. Purchase, New York. Artwork © Edgar Heap of Birds.

avant-gardist bathwater of the old notions of futurity and utopianism. In Tirvanija's artworks and staged events, community is affirmed and reified, never punctured.[3]

As Terry Smith has argued, citing Boris Groys, contemporary artists have broken modernism's "contract with the future."[4] Indeed, Heap of Birds's art has also ditched the avant-garde's contract with the future—the future having always been the jealously guarded property of the powerful anyway; notions of futurity having always been aligned with Western modernity's belief in its own historical telos. In the cosmologies of the Cheyenne and other indigenous peoples, time is never an arrow (or a bullet). It is always a circle, a wheel. In California, the local Tongva people have added their own interpretation of Heap of Birds's signature reversed text in *Native Hosts*, resonating with the artist's belief that renewal is made possible by facing the past. Julia Bogany, a tribal educator who consulted with Heap of Birds for his project and taught him the names of villages and other sacred sites in the Los Angeles area, has said that, for her, revers-

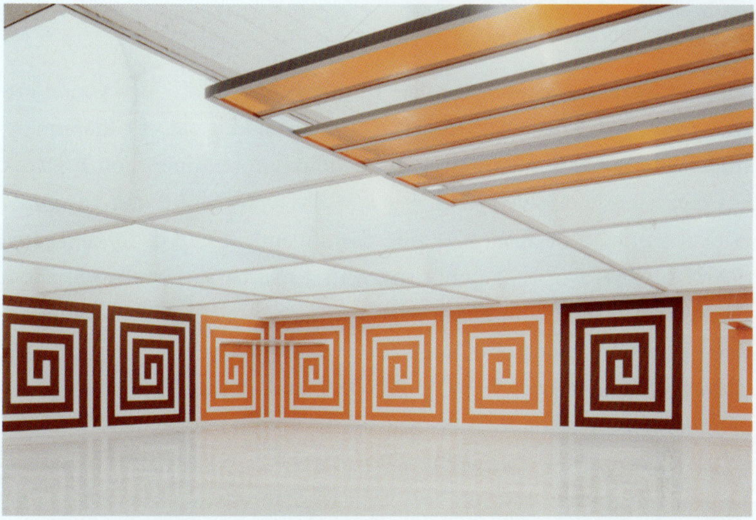

4.3 Liam Gillick, *Post Discussion Revision Zone #1–#4/Big Conference Centre 22nd Floor Wall Design*, 1998. Aluminum, Plexiglas (four colors), four panels, 240 × 240 cm. Collection CNAM-Centre Pompidou, Paris. Photo: J. Brasille. Courtesy of the artist and Villa Arson, CNAC, all rights reserved. With thanks to the Casey Kaplan Gallery. Artwork © Liam Gillick. Gillick's sculptures are designed as platforms or backdrops for potential conversations. He describes *Big Conference Center Limitation Screen* as an object that "helps to define a location where individual actions are limited by rules imposed by the community as a whole." In Claire Bishop, "Antagonism and Relational Aesthetics," *October* 110 (fall 2001): 59.

ing the word "CALIFORNIA" means that "everything comes back around again."[5] We are always returning back home. Again.

Heap of Birds's artwork—thoroughly contemporary and also based on indigenous understandings of culture as a strategy of community renewal and defense—resonates with what Anishnaabe writer Gerald Vizenor has termed "survivance," a neologism that brings together the terms "survival" and "resistance," asserting that Native people have persevered not as passive victims, but as active historical agents.[6] Vizenor's postmodern and indigenous critical literary and cultural theory is itself an analogue for Heap of Birds's practice as a contemporary artist—global in purview and engaged with the institutions of the contemporary art world, while remaining rooted in indigenous knowledge and values.

Global Collaborations

Heap of Birds has been a traveler in many art worlds. As a young artist, he sought connection with the world beyond his native Oklahoma—studying in London and traveling throughout Europe. Since then, his work has consistently engaged with issues in the wider world and has found critical purchase in diverse locales. Significantly, Heap of Birds created one of his first works of public art with a text-based installation about the apartheid regime in South Africa, compared to the histories of Native peoples in the United States. For the exhibition *American Policy* at Cleveland State University in Ohio in 1986, student volunteers made hand-painted signs based on Heap of Birds's design, with the text "OH! / THOSE SOUTH AFRICAN / HOMELANDS / YOU IMPOSE / U.S. INDIAN RESERVATIONS." (Heap of Birds would revisit the topic three years later in his home state with *Apartheid Oklahoma* in 1989, comparing the Sooner land rush to displacement of black and colored populations in South Africa.) Amid a climate of campus protest, as student activists across the United States pressed American university trustees to divest from South African investments, Heap of Birds's artwork drew connections between racist government policies at home and abroad, locally and globally.

Heap of Birds's global projects—often collaborations—have focused on renewal as a theme as he connects Cheyenne ceremony to the efforts of indigenous artists in other locations. In Australia in 1994, Heap of Birds created *16 Songs* with Aboriginal artists from the Tandanya National Aboriginal Cultural Institute in Adelaide and the Boomali Artists' Cooperative in Sydney. For *16 Songs*, he selected sixteen words or short phrases to present as gifts to his Aboriginal hosts, connoting renewal and linking his own Cheyenne ceremonial tradition with that of his local collaborators. Heap of Birds chose the words—or songs—during his participation in the Earth Renewal. Heap of Birds sees commonality in the cyclical, seasonal ceremonies that are practiced in indigenous and tribal groups around the world.[7] Read together, his words become a poem of hope, connection, and perseverance:

SKY
EARTH
OFFERING

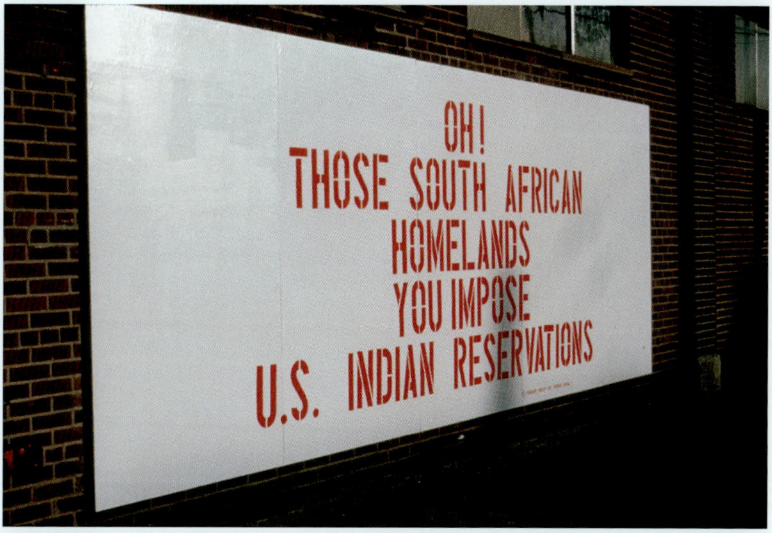

4.4 Edgar Heap of Birds, *South African Homelands*, 1986. Hand-painted mural, 8 × 20 feet. Cleveland State University, Ohio. Artwork © Edgar Heap of Birds.

PATIENCE
TREES
STRENGTH
SING
NEW GROWTH
GREEN
FOUR
AWARENESS
RESISTANCE
SOLSTICE
FOR EVERYONE
DANCE
WATER

Each song was received by an urban Aboriginal artist, who produced an individual artwork to be shown alongside Heap of Birds's words. Waanyi artist Gordon Hookey created *New Growth*, a painting in which silhouetted figures set brush fires to clear the earth—a process of destruction and renewal—with Sydney's iconic Harbour Bridge and Opera House in the

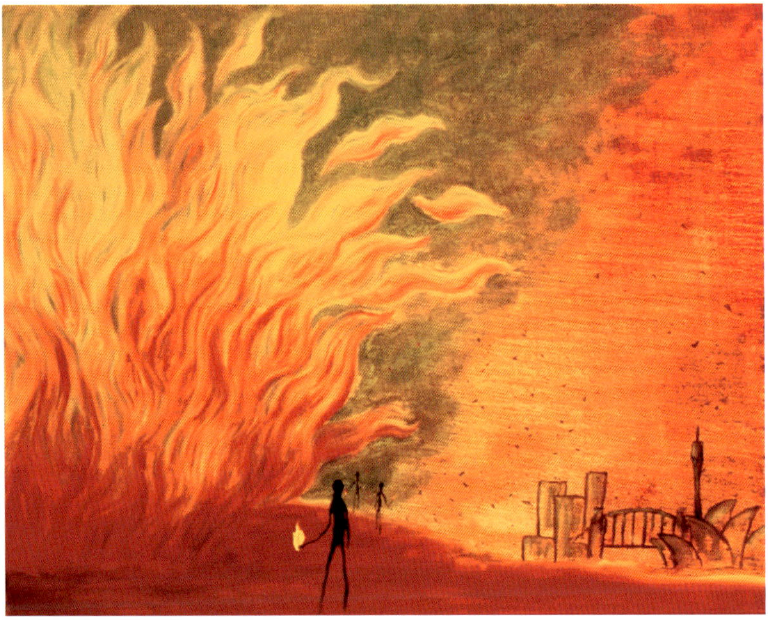

4.5 Gordon Hookey, *New Growth*, 1994. Acrylic on canvas, 24 × 30 inches. Artwork © Gordon Hookey.

background, the sky blazing red and filled with a swirl of smoke and cinders. Settler-colonial Australia displaced the land's Aboriginal inhabitants. In Hookey's painting, Aboriginal Australians return to clear and reclaim the landscape; the earth is renewed to begin again.

The exhibit *16 Songs* traveled from Australia to the United States, with showings at the University of North Texas Art Gallery, Denton, Texas; the Cleveland Art Institute in Cleveland, Ohio, as part of the exhibition for which Heap of Birds created *American Leagues*, his jab at the Cleveland Indians' cartoon mascot Chief Wahoo; and the Wadsworth Atheneum in Hartford, Connecticut, where it was shown in conjunction with *Dunging the Ground*, his public artwork that addressed the seventeenth-century massacre of the Pequot by English settlers. Each time *16 Songs* was exhibited, it linked local to global indigenous issues, as one reviewer noted, "pointing up a common bond of travails concerning sovereignty and civil rights at opposite sides of the globe."[8]

In 2002, Heap of Birds undertook *Eagles Speak*, a project that linked Narragansett, Pequot, and Wampanoag artists in New England—tribes that had intermarried historically with African Americans—with black artists from South Africa. The exhibition title referred to the eagle—a key personage in the Earth Renewal, sacred to Native North Americans and a symbol of power and perseverance in southern Africa—and a global conversation between indigenous peoples. Heap of Birds spoke of his collaborations with indigenous artists in Africa and Australia and explained how he hoped the exhibition at the Rhode Island School of Design in Providence, which traveled to other locations including Cape Town, South Africa, would make visible that relationship:

> Collaboration has been so natural; I don't pursue it. Indigenous artists tend to be very welcoming to each other and to respect one another. We share a disadvantaged perspective from being colonized, which is a unifying factor. Reservation life in Oklahoma is similar to life in Australia for Aboriginal artists. If I am in a township in South Africa or if I am in Zimbabwe, there is a certain kind of style of living and circumstance of domination that has to be struggled through. I think artists who work hard to deal with the market system of art in the world and still speak their mind and get their work done share in the same struggle. In *Eagles Speak*, I hope to articulate this experience to the public. Artists are some of the best people to put forward that issue and to demonstrate that we have this alliance. Indigenous populations should align together. We can present artwork that has an affinity, and we can learn from each other. I hope it will encourage more collaboration worldwide.[9]

For the exhibition, Heap of Birds brought together multimedia works by Pequot-Wampanoag artist Everett Tall Oak Weeden, Narragansett-Wampanoag artist Cynthia Listens to the Wind Ross-Meeks, and Thembinkosi Goniwe from Cape Town. He included his own drawings of eagles based on an early twentieth-century Cheyenne shield and on a carved stone eagle from Zimbabwe c. 1200 CE. On the significance of the eagle, he explained:

> We [Cheyenne] have been living with the eagle and its value system for hundreds of years. As I travel the world, I am looking for things that are shared by many, such as the stars above us. Once, I was in Botswana in a boat on a river. It was raining. I saw a big fish eagle sitting on the reeds near me. I had this vision that as I travel and witness other cultures

> and bring them to my culture, it is like eagles talking to each other. An eagle from a ceremony in Oklahoma could speak to the eagles in Africa. Then I went to Great Zimbabwe and did some research on rock art, and I found these wonderful carved stone eagles that were the prominent symbols of freedom in that culture.[10]

He also included a marker drawing of accumulated airport codes (see the introduction) and installed it with a collection of bottles of blackstrap molasses, which he described as "symbols of brutal rum and sugar commerce and the triangle slave trade era from Africa to the Caribbean and the Americas."[11] While in an earlier era of globalization, peoples from the Americas and Africa interacted only via the trade in human slaves and commodities—a destructive system in which indigenous people participated only at the point of a sword or gun—contemporary artists come together to speak of shared experiences, and to draw from one another's strengths.

Eagles Speak also included outreach to local communities—particularly children—a gesture that has been part of Heap of Birds's practice for many years. While creating *Building Minnesota*, Heap of Birds held educational workshops with urban Indian youth in Minneapolis. In Providence, he offered an art workshop for children at the public library in Fox Point—an inner-city neighborhood with a vibrant community of Afro-Portuguese Cape Verdean immigrants and with children from the Narragansett reservation; in Cape Town, he spoke to community members at the Metropolitan Gallery, the Association for Visual Arts. In workshops with children, Heap of Birds has taught the history of teepee construction and symbolism in Plains Native cultures and has had students make and decorate their own teepee model. The teepees made by children in Providence, Rhode Island, traveled to Cape Town, South Africa, where they were exhibited with work by Heap of Birds and other artists. The artworks created by Providence children traveled to Africa for exhibition—a contemporary art world version of the triangular flow in people and merchandise and a positive reimagining of the brutal trade that made colonial Providence a wealthy commercial hub. As Heap of Birds explained, "I will bring the work of the children to South Africa. We'll have this full circle from Providence to Cape Verde—where a lot of the Fox Point kids are from—to South Africa and back again."[12] At the Bandung Institute of Technology, Java, Indonesia, in 2005, Heap of Birds collaborated with students to cre-

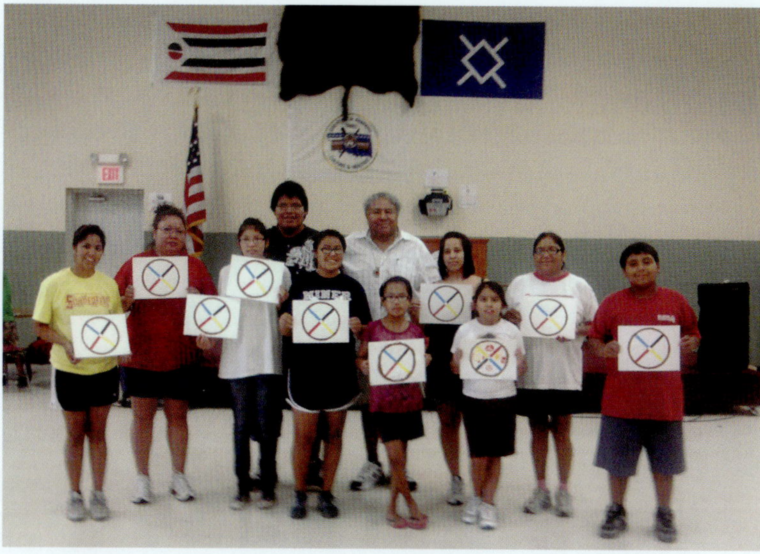

4.6 Edgar Heap of Birds poses with Cheyenne and Arapaho youth for art program, 2013.

ate *Thursdays*, a language-based installation. Heap of Birds invited the students to interpret four hundred of his phrases in whatever form they chose—echoing his process with artists in Sydney. He has also led workshops with youth on the Cheyenne-Arapaho reservation, explaining the design and meaning of the Plains medicine wheel. In conjunction with his projects in Claremont, California, in 2013, Heap of Birds repeated the workshop assignment he used in Providence with Native students at the Sherman Indian High School in nearby Riverside. Heap of Birds speaks often of closing the circle—bringing the work back to local audiences and communities—engaging populations that have often been depicted in artworks, but have rarely been participants or coauthors.

In 2011 Heap of Birds participated in *Digital Natives*, a public project in Vancouver, British Columbia, where he has often worked, which is also the site of a permanent installation of his *Native Hosts* series (2007). Curated by Lorna Brown and Clint Burnham and coinciding with commemoration of the 125th anniversary of the founding of the city of Vancouver, the project made use of an electronic billboard located near the historic Burrard Street Bridge, conventionally used to broadcast commercial advertisements. Recalling the 1982 project in which artists were invited to create content for the Spectacolor billboard in Times Square, New York, artists contributed tweets (140-character digital text messages) that interrupted the regularly programmed advertising. Contributions were translated into Kwak'wala, hən'q'əmin'əm'/Musqueam, and Skwxwú7mesh, languages spoken by the region's original indigenous inhabitants. Messages commented on the history of the site and billboard, language and digital communications, and the histories—indigenous, settler, and immigrant—of Vancouver. Selected texts authored by indigenous youth in outreach workshops and global audiences who spoke back to the project via Twitter were also included in the broadcasts.

Of the sixty messages authored for the project, two were censored by the billboard's owner, including Heap of Birds's contribution: "IMPERIAL CANADA AWARDED SEX ABUSE TO NATIVE YOUTH BY THE BLACK ROBES NOW PROUDLY BESTOWS BRONZE SILVER GOLD MEDALS WITH INDIAN IMAGE." Heap of Birds's text pointed to the history of Jesuit missionaries' notorious treatment of indigenous communities—and the irony of Canada's indigenous heritage being highlighted on medals for the 2010 Olympic Games when the national past remains an unsettled account. The other censored message—"Your grandparents' unacknowledged debts return to you as rage against the car in front," contributed by Canadian novelist Larissa Lai—also raised issues of unresolved histories, albeit in more abstract terms. Seen as inflammatory, the messages were not broadcast. In protest, the exhibition's organizers printed all the messages as lawn signs, including those by Lai and Heap of Birds, and deployed them along the grassy median on Burrard Street.

Like the outreach workshops for Native youth, the project's title evidenced a concern for future generations. The term "digital natives" commonly refers to individuals born into a culture of universal computer literacy. Yet while the phrase "digital natives" invokes a millennial generation fluent in the means of electronic communications and social networks and unburdened by the past, it masks inequalities in access to hardware and high-speed connections that make the promises of the digital age unattainable in some communities, including urban indigenous enclaves and reservations. Not all are born digitally equal, as it were, even in the flat world.

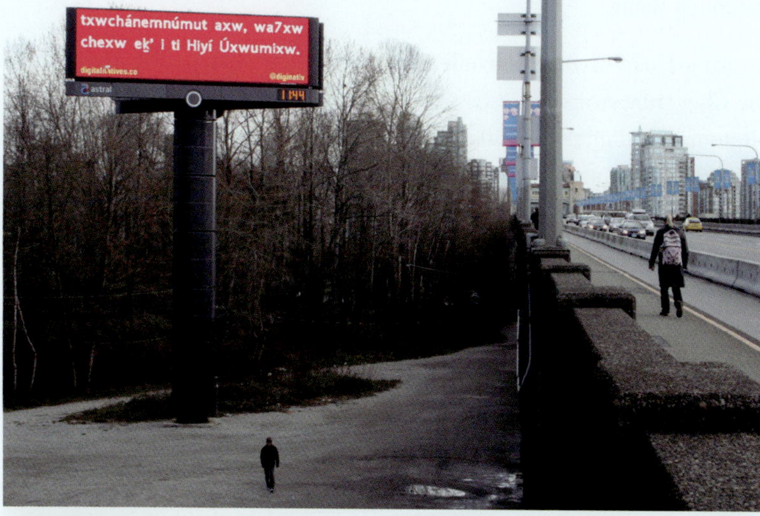

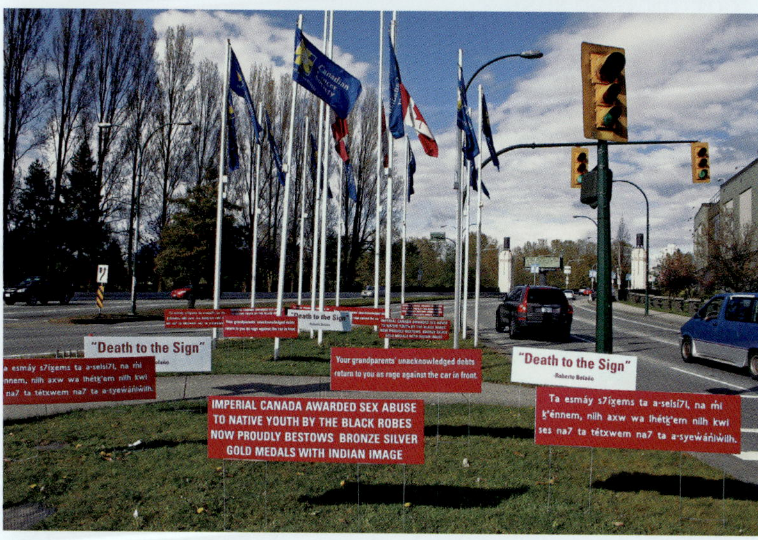

4.7 *Digital Natives*, broadcast on electronic billboard, Vancouver, British Columbia, 2011. Photo © Barbara Cole. Info: digitalnatives.othersights.ca.

4.8 Temporary signs installed on a Burrard Street traffic median in protest when messages by Heap of Birds and Larissa Lai were censored by the billboard's owners. Vancouver, British Columbia, 2011. Photo © Barbara Cole.

Returning Home

In 2013, Heap of Birds unveiled his first permanent public artwork on the Cheyenne-Arapaho reservation in Oklahoma. The piece is a diptych photomural, digitally printed on vinyl and installed in the newly renovated public gymnasium in Canton, a predominantly Arapaho community. The eight-by-eight-foot murals feature large-scale, high-resolution images of Cheyenne-Arapaho beadwork medallions with a morning star motif, a symbol of renewal, against blue backgrounds. For the first panel, Heap of Birds adapted the text from an Arapaho Ghost Dance song—words that were sung at the end of the nineteenth century as Native people struggled to keep their cultures and communities intact and hoped for a future in which balance would be restored and the earth would be made new again:

WHIRLWIND
COTTONWOOD SONG
TURTLE GAVE GIFT
MORNING STAR FLY
CIRCLE BOUNDARIES OF SKY

The second panel speaks to the enduring bonds between the longtime neighbors and allies the Cheyenne and Arapaho, and looks to the future of the tribes:

CHEYENNE
AND ARAPAHO
PROUD PAST
FUTURE STRONG

The Canton murals mark a return of sorts for Heap of Birds—to his reservation home but also to traditional Plains art forms. As a student, he made abstract artworks based on beadwork patterns in his grandmother's moccasins and other traditional arts. Heap of Birds abandoned that path, choosing abstract painting and text-based forms. He did not believe that traditional forms were obsolete, but believed that contemporary art was more effective in delivering the messages he wanted to communicate as an artist.

Plains beadwork is itself a powerful symbol of what Vizenor terms "survivance." Sequestered on reservations where it was presumed that Native

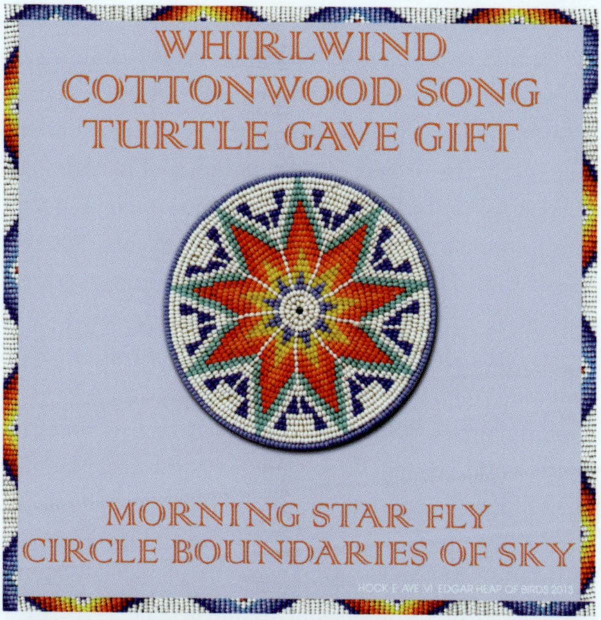

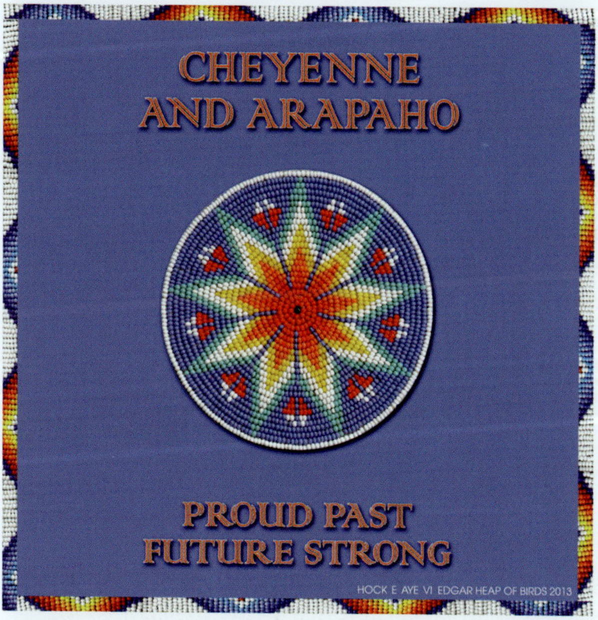

4.9–4.10 Edgar Heap of Birds, murals in Canton, Oklahoma, 2013. Two digital prints on vinyl, 8 × 8 feet each. Artwork © Edgar Heap of Birds.

cultures would finally die away, Native women launched a remarkable renaissance of traditional arts, including textile weaving, ceramics, and beadwork. Confinement on reservations had the effect of codifying distinct tribal styles as expressions of identity and pride. Particular attention was lavished on items made for the next generation, such as elaborately decorated cradle boards, clothing, and dolls. Native women produced objects for home and community use, but also for an eager intercultural marketplace. Formerly sacred arts were secularized and commercialized, but, in contradiction of all expectations, traditional arts blossomed.

For Heap of Birds, the beadwork was a symbol of Native creativity and a call for renewal: "With these two large scale digital murals for the newly renovated Canton gym I wish to honor beadwork artists who have passed on to the spirit world," he told those gathered at the dedication ceremony for the murals. "In this honoring I also want to excite and encourage our tribal youth to take up the beadwork traditions and explore, as well as expand, what beadwork can become today. I challenge the youth to build upon our elders' artistic accomplishments and lead us all visually to a new level."[13]

The murals in Canton mark a return for Heap of Birds, his artwork installed in public view on his own Native land. But he has never left the reservation. He returns often to visit family, to teach, and to participate in ceremony. For sixteen summers, Heap of Birds worked to renew the earth for his community, even as he has traveled through many art worlds as he pursues his career. He is always returning back home again.

From the perspective of the hilltop and the Earth Renewal lodge, the idea of coming home as giving back and of keeping balance recognizes, as Julia Bogany noted, that "everything comes back around again" and ensures survivance. Time and history might be seen as a spiral, a circular return and a continual renewal, a different type of investment in a different idea of futurity. New growth requires respectful attention to ceremony. This is a shift in perspective if we are accustomed to art's histories being written as if they are, like the modernist project, directed toward the future. Terry Smith and others have suggested that our faith in the future has lapsed. Nicolas Bourriaud claims that artists have ceased to "bet on happier tomorrows." If this is true, it would have us living purely in the now of contemporaneity, at the end of history, with no investment in setting

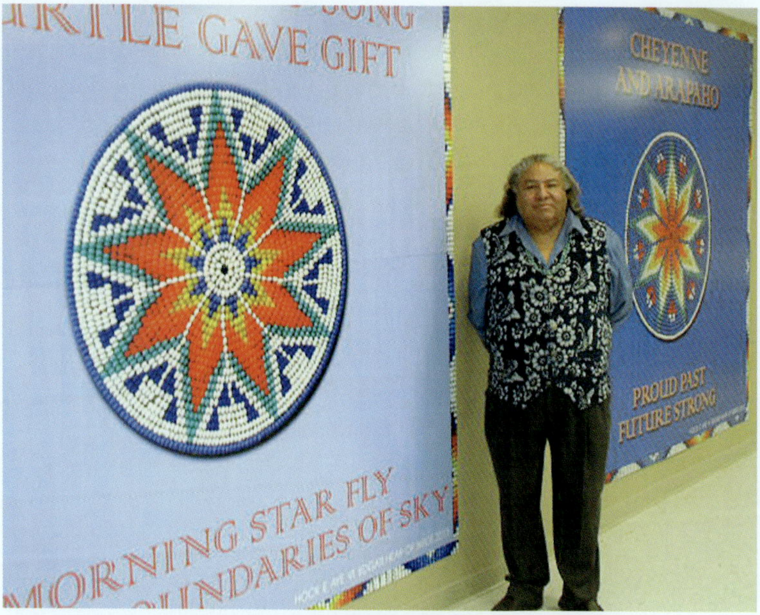

4.11 Edgar Heap of Birds poses with his artwork at the dedication ceremony in February 2013. Artwork © Edgar Heap of Birds. The creation and installation of the artwork was supported by Cheyenne and Arapaho Culture and Heritage and the tribally owned Canton Lucky Star Casino.

right history's injuries and injustices, no imperative to restore or to strike a balance, or to open the archive to allow other histories to be narrated, from other perspectives.

And there are many nows, of course. Keith Moxey suggests the term "heterochrony" to convey the sense of multiple temporalities and the incommensurable experiences of time in multiple locations and from multiple positionalities. But another of Moxey's terms is also relevant: "anachrony," which refers to artworks' "capacity to create their own time for attentive beholders."[14] The Earth Renewal ceremony—the source of Heap of Birds's perspective and the grounding for his practice as an artist—has such capacity. It is a time machine; it creates time.

At the conclusion of the Earth Renewal ceremony, the music and dance reach a crescendo; the energy pouring forth seems like it might cause the lodge, which Heap of Birds described as a spacecraft, to rise above the prairie and carry those assembled into the evening sky. As the final cycle of sixteen songs reaches its end, the dancers bolt out of the enclosure, toward the four directions, and run into the arms of their families and friends, elated and exhausted. The work of the ceremony is finished for the year; the dancers will come back to this hilltop next summer.

NOTES

Introduction

1 Important work on Edgar Heap of Birds has appeared primarily in essays and exhibition catalogs. See Kathleen Ash-Milby and Truman T. Lowe, eds., *Edgar Heap of Birds: Most Serene Republics* (Washington, DC: National Museum of the American Indian, Smithsonian Institution, 2009); Jeanette Ingberman, Papo Colo, Jean Fisher, Lowery Stokes Sims, and Hachivi Edgar Heap of Birds, *Claim Your Color*, exhibition catalog (New York: Exit Art, 1989); Kate Morris, "Picturing Sovereignty: Landscape in Native American Art," in *Painters, Patrons, and Identity: Essays in Native American Art to Honor J.J. Brody*, ed. Joyce M. Szabo (Albuquerque: University of New Mexico Press, 2001), 187–209; Kate Morris, "Reading between the Lines: Text and Image in Contemporary Native American Art," *American Indian Art Magazine* 34, no. 2 (spring 2009): 52–59; W. Jackson Rushing III, "Street Chiefs and Native Hosts: Richard Ray (Whitman) and Hachivi Edgar Heap of Birds Defend the Homeland," in *Green Acres: Neo-colonialism in the U.S.*, ed. Christopher Scoates (St. Louis: Washington University Gallery of Art, 1992), 23–36; W. Jackson Rushing III, "'In Our Language': The Art of Hachivi Edgar Heap of Birds," *Third Text* 19, no. 4 (July 2005): 365–84; Nancy J. Blomberg, ed., *[Re]inventing the Wheel: Advancing the Dialogue on Contemporary American Indian Art* (Denver: Denver Art Museum, 2008); and Shanna Ketchum, "Native American Cosmopolitan Modernism(s): A Re-articulation of Presence through Time and Space," *Third Text* 19, no. 4 (July 2005): 357–64. I have written about Heap of Birds: Bill Anthes, "Contemporary Native Artists and International Biennial Culture," *Visual Anthropology Review* 25, no. 2 (fall 2009): 109–27; and Bill Anthes, "Ethics in a World of Strange Strangers: Edgar Heap of Birds at Home and Abroad," *Art Journal* 71, no. 3 (fall 2012): 58–77.

2 "Native Hosts," Pitzer College, February 27, 2013. Video, http://vimeo.com/60673043.

3 Benjamin Buchloh, "Conceptual Art 1962–1969: From the Aesthetics of Administration to the Critique of Institutions," *October* 55 (winter 1990): 105–43.

4 Heap of Birds quoted in Nick Blomley, "Artistic Displacements: An Interview with Edgar Heap of Birds," *Environment and Planning D: Society and Space* 22 (2004): 802.

5 Miwon Kwon, *One Place after Another: Site-Specific Art and Locational Identity* (Cambridge, MA: MIT Press, 2002). See chapter 1, "Genealogy of Site Specificity," esp. pp. 24–32.

6 Suzanne Lacy, ed., *Mapping the Terrain: New Genre Public Art* (Seattle: Bay Press, 1995).

7 Jean Fisher, *Heh No Wah Maun Stun He Dun: What Makes a Man*, exhibition catalog (London: Matt's Gallery, 1989), quoted in Lowery Stokes Sims, "Words into Vision: The Art of Hachivi Edgar Heap of Birds," in Ingberman et al., *Claim Your Color*, 18.

8 Lucy Lippard, "Signs of Unrest: Activist Art by Edgar Heap of Birds," in Ash-Milby and Lowe, *Edgar Heap of Birds*, 21.

9 Edgar Heap of Birds, *Sharp Rocks* (Buffalo, NY: CEPA, 1986), n.p.

10 Hal Foster, "An Archival Impulse," *October* 110 (fall 2004): 4–5.

11 Heap of Birds quoted in Susan Shown Harjo, "Gallery Exhibition: Identity Perspectives by Native Artists," *Native Americas* (Ithaca) 19, no. 1 (June 30, 2002): 72.

12 Heap of Birds quoted in Melissa Merli, "Sign Vandals Sad Surprise to 'Native Hosts' Artist," *Champaign-Urbana News-Gazette*, May 17, 2009, G-1.

13 Teresa Ramos, "Tolerance of Racist Action on Campus," *Champaign-Urbana News-Gazette*, May 21, 2009, A-8.

14 Tim Mitchell, "Artist Who Created 'Beyond the Chief' Exhibit to Return to Campus," *Champaign-Urbana News-Gazette*, April 25, 2009, A-2.

15 Melissa Merli, "Campaign Shows Support for Work," *Champaign-Urbana News-Gazette*, June 27, 2009, B-1.

16 Mark Schenk, "Recent UI Graduate Accused of Stealing Signs Last Weekend," *Champaign-Urbana News-Gazette*, June 19, 2009, B-1.

17 Tim Mitchell, "More Signs Near Native American House Vandalized, *Champaign-Urbana News-Gazette*, May 7, 2009, A-2.

18 Melissa Merli, "Artist Questions Value Placed on Stolen Signs—State Listed Worth under $300, Making Charge a Misdemeanor," *Champaign-Urbana News-Gazette*, June 27, 2009, B-1.

19 Travis McDade, "Prosecutor Limited by Law on Art Theft," *Champaign-Urbana News-Gazette*, July 5, 2009, C-5.

20 Mark Schenck, "Man Gets Court Supervision for Stealing Art," *Champaign-Urbana News-Gazette*, July 30, 2009, B-2.

21 The narrative art customarily made by Plains men persevered as captured Cheyenne and other combatants were detained in a military prison at Fort Marion, Florida, following the Red River War of 1874 and into the reservation period of the twentieth century, representing significant community events as well as individual accomplishments (see chapter 2).

22 Heap of Birds quoted in John Brandenburg, "Artistic Weapons Defend Indian Culture," *Daily Oklahoman*, Art and Entertainment, April 14, 1985, n.p.

23 Heap of Birds, *Sharp Rocks*, n.p.

24 Néstor García Canclini, *Art beyond Itself: Anthropology for a Society without a Story Line*, trans. David Frye (Durham, NC: Duke University Press, 2014), 47.

25 Rushing, "'In Our Language,'" 369.

26 Mónica Amor with Okwui Enwezor, Gao Minglu, Oscar Ho, Kobena Mercer, and Irit Rogoff, "Liminalities: Discussions on the Global and the Local," *Art Journal* 57, no. 4 (winter 1998): 29.

27 Kwon, *One Place after Another*, 156–57.

28 Terry Smith, *Contemporary Art: World Currents* (London: Laurence King, 2011). See also Anthes, "Contemporary Native Artists and International Biennial Culture"; Nancy Marie Mithlo, "'We Have All Been Colonized': Subordination and Resistance on a Global Arts Stage," *Visual Anthropology* 17 (2004): 229–45; Nancy Marie Mithlo, "Reappropriating Redskins: *Pellerossasogna* (Red Skin Dream); Shelley Niro at the 50th La Biennale di Venezia," *Visual Anthropology Review* 20, no. 2 (fall 2004): 22–35; National Museum of the American Indian, *Vision, Space, Desire: Global Perspectives and Cultural Hybridity* (Washington, DC: Smithsonian Institution, 2006); and Judith Ostrowitz, *Interventions: Native American Art for Far-Flung Territories* (Seattle: University of Washington Press, 2009).

29 Shari M. Huhndorf, *Mapping the Americas: The Transnational Politics of Contemporary Native Culture* (Ithaca, NY: Cornell University Press, 2009), 3.

30 Steven Durland, "Call Me in '93: An Interview with James Luna," *High Performance* 14, no. 4 (winter 1991): 34–39, quoted in Paul Chaat Smith, "Luna Remembers," in *Everything You Know about Indians Is Wrong* (Minneapolis: University of Minnesota Press, 2009), 95.

31 Heap of Birds, lecture, University of San Francisco, May 5, 2010.

32 Thanks to Jane Blocker for suggesting that Heap of Birds's description might serve as a guiding metaphor for this book, conceived as an intervention into the emerging historiography of contemporary art.

33 Heap of Birds, conversation with the author, Concho, Oklahoma, July 24, 2010.

34 Heap of Birds quoted in Blomley, "Artistic Displacements," 803.

35 Bill Anthes, *Native Moderns: American Indian Painting, 1940–1960* (Durham, NC: Duke University Press, 2006).

36 For example, see Hal Foster et al., "Questionnaire on 'The Contemporary,'" *October* 130 (fall 2009): 3–124; Terry Smith, *What Is Contemporary Art?* (Chicago: University of Chicago Press, 2009); and Richard Meyer, *What Was Contemporary Art?* (Cambridge, MA: MIT Press, 2013).

37 Pamela Lee, *Chronophobia: On Time in the Art of the 1960s* (Cambridge, MA: MIT Press, 2006); Jennifer L. Roberts, *Mirror Travels: Robert Smithson and History* (New Haven, CT: Yale University Press, 2004).

38 Christine Ross, *The Past Is the Present; It's the Future Too: The Temporal Turn in Contemporary Art* (London: Continuum, 2012), 3.

39 Smith, *What Is Contemporary Art?*, 3–4.

40 Smith, *What Is Contemporary Art?*, 5.

41 Ross, *The Past Is the Present*, 4.

42 Keith Moxey, *Visual Time: The Image in History* (Durham, NC: Duke University Press, 2013), 16.

43 Moxey, *Visual Time.*

44 Geeta Kapur, *When Was Modernism: Essays on Contemporary Cultural Practice in India* (New Delhi: Tulika, 2000).

45 Moxey, *Visual Time*, 20.

46 Terry Smith, "Contemporary Art and Contemporaneity," *Critical Inquiry* 32 (summer 2006): 703, emphasis in original.

47 Clement Greenberg, "Avant-Garde and Kitsch," in *Clement Greenberg: The Collected Essays and Criticism*, vol. 1, ed. John O'Brian (Chicago: University of Chicago Press, 1986), 8, emphasis in original.

48 Boris Groys quoted in Terry Smith, "Introduction: The Contemporaneity Question," in *Antinomies of Art and Culture: Modernity, Postmodernity, Contemporaneity*, ed. Terry Smith, Okwui Enwezor, and Nancy Condee (Durham, NC: Duke University Press, 2008), 7.

49 Smith, "Contemporary Art and Contemporaneity," 703.

50 Ross, *The Past Is the Present*, 6.

1. Land

1 Heap of Birds quoted in Diana Nemiroff, Robert Houle, and Charlotte Townsend-Gault, *Land Spirit Power: First Nations at the National Gallery of Canada* (Ottawa: National Gallery of Canada, 1992), 149.

2 Heap of Birds quoted in Dorothy Shinn, "Taking Aim at Chief Wahoo: American Indian's Billboard Labeling Tribe Mascot Racist Doesn't Fly," *Akron Beacon Journal*, December 22, 1996, E5.

3 Edgar Heap of Birds, *Sharp Rocks* (Buffalo, NY: CEPA, 1986).

4 Jaune Quick-to-See Smith, "Curator's Statement," in *Our Land / Ourselves* (Albany: University Art Gallery, State University of New York at Albany, 1990), v–vi.

5 George Longfish and Joan Randall, "Landscape, Landbase and Environ-

ment" (unpublished typescript, 1984), quoted in Lucy Lippard, *Mixed Blessings: New Art in a Multicultural America* (New York: Pantheon, 1990), 109.

6 Heap of Birds quoted in Nick Blomley, "Artistic Displacements: An Interview with Edgar Heap of Birds," *Environment and Planning D: Society and Space* 22 (2004): 799.

7 Arjun Appadurai, *Modernity at Large: Cultural Dimensions of Globalization* (Minneapolis: University of Minnesota Press, 1996), 180–81.

8 Vine Deloria Jr. and Clifford Lytle, *The Nations Within: The Past and Future of American Indian Sovereignty* (New York: Pantheon, 1984), 8.

9 Deloria and Lytle, *The Nations Within*, 12.

10 Robert Allen Warrior, *Tribal Secrets: Recovering American Indian Intellectual Traditions* (Minneapolis: University of Minnesota Press, 1995), xxi.

11 Warrior, *Tribal Secrets*.

12 Taiaiake Alfred, *Peace, Power, Righteousness: An Indigenous Manifesto* (Oxford: Oxford University Press, 1999), 55–58.

13 Jolene Rickard, "Sovereignty: A Line in the Sand," in *Strong Hearts: Native American Visions and Voices*, ed. Peggy Roalf (New York: Aperture, 1995), 51–59.

14 Jolene Rickard, "Visualizing Sovereignty in the Time of Biometric Sensors," *South Atlantic Quarterly* 110, no. 2 (spring 2011): 467.

15 Rickard, "Visualizing Sovereignty," 468.

16 Hannah Arendt, *The Origins of Totalitarianism* (1951; repr., New York: Harcourt Brace Jovanovich, 1973), 232. See also Jolene Rickard, "The Local and the Global," in *Vision, Space, Desire: Global Perspectives and Cultural Hybridity*, ed. National Museum of the American Indian (Washington, DC: Smithsonian Institution, 2006), 59–67.

17 An important critical touchstone for many of these writers, including Rickard, is Māori theorist Linda Tuhiwai Smith's *Decolonizing Methodologies: Research and Indigenous Peoples* (London: Zed, 1999).

18 Rickard, "Visualizing Sovereignty," 471.

19 Rickard, "Visualizing Sovereignty," 472.

20 Rickard, "Visualizing Sovereignty," 471.

21 Malcolm Andrews, *Landscape and Western Art* (Oxford: Oxford University Press, 1999), 77.

22 Jay Appleton, *The Experience of Landscape* (London: John Wiley, 1975), quoted in Andrews, *Landscape and Western Art*, 18.

23 Heap of Birds quoted in Larry Abbott, "A Conversation with Hachivi Edgar Heap of Birds," in Sarah J. Rogers, *Will/Power: New Works by Papo Colo, Jimmie Durham, David Hammons, Hachivi Edgar Heap of Birds, Adrian Piper, Aminah Brenda Lynn Robinson* (Columbus: Wexner Center for the Arts, Ohio State University, 1992), 49–50.

24 Michelle Raheja, "Reading Nanook's Smile: Visual Sovereignty, Indigenous

Revisions of Ethnography, and Atanarjuat (The Fast Runner)," *American Quarterly* 59, no. 4 (December 2007): 1164.

25 Deloria and Lytle, *The Nations Within*, 8.

26 Charlotte Townsend-Gault, "Hot Dogs, a Ball Gown, Adobe, and Words," in *Native American Art in the Twentieth Century*, ed. W. Jackson Rushing III (London: Routledge, 1999), 125, emphases in original.

27 See, for example, W. Jackson Rushing III, "Street Chiefs and Native Hosts: Richard Ray (Whitman) and Hachivi Edgar Heap of Birds Defend the Homeland," in *Green Acres: Neo-colonialism in the U.S.*, ed. Christopher Scoates (St. Louis: Washington University Gallery of Art, 1992), 23–36; and Kate Morris, "Picturing Sovereignty: Landscape in Native American Art," in *Painters, Patrons, and Identity: Essays in Native American Art to Honor J.J. Brody*, ed. Joyce M. Szabo (Albuquerque: University of New Mexico Press, 2001), 187–209.

28 Heap of Birds quoted in Nemiroff, Houle, and Townsend-Gault, *Land Spirit Power*, 149.

29 Heap of Birds's initial proposal included twelve panels, but the installation was limited to six by the mayor's office. Lucy Lippard, "Signs of Unrest: Activist Art by Edgar Heap of Birds," in *Edgar Heap of Birds: Most Serene Republics*, ed. Kathleen Ash-Milby and Truman T. Lowe (Washington: National Museum of the American Indian, Smithsonian Institution, 2009), 20.

30 Heap of Birds quoted in Deborah P. Work, "'I Reflect, and I Respect'—Art by Hachivi Edgar Heap of Birds Speaks for Native Americans Who Do Not Speak for Themselves," *Sun-Sentinel*, March 13, 1994, 3D.

31 Jean Fisher, "New York Today Your Host Is Shinnecock," in Jeanette Ingberman, Papo Colo, Jean Fisher, Lowery Stokes Sims, and Hachivi Edgar Heap of Birds, *Claim Your Color*, exhibition catalog (New York: Exit Art, 1989), 18.

32 Fisher, "New York Today Your Host Is Shinnecock."

33 Robert L. Pincus, "Heap of Birds Weaves Spell That Sustains Show," *San Diego Union-Tribune*, March 12, 1995, E-1.

34 Heap of Birds, "Sooners Run Over Indian Nations Apartheid Oklahoma," in Ingberman et al., *Claim Your Color*, 16.

35 Heap of Birds, "Insurgent Messages for America" (1986), reprinted in Ingberman et al., *Claim Your Color*, 22.

36 Heap of Birds quoted in Karen Mathieson, "Framing the Issues—Connecting with the City: Pressing Problems Such as AIDS, Racism Are the Focus of Many in Public Artworks," *Seattle Times*, June 20, 1991, K1.

37 Regina Hackett, "Art Is the Connective Thread between Far-Flung Tribal Peoples at Sacred Circle," *Seattle Post-Intelligencer*, February 6, 1998, 16.

38 Regina Hackett, "Seattle Goes 'Public'—the City's Celebration of Art for the People Opens Tonight," *Seattle Post-Intelligencer*, June 27, 1991, C1;

"Public Art, Civil Disappointment: Many Blemishes, Only a Few Bright Spots for SAC's 'In Public' Project," *Seattle Times*, December 31, 1991, D1.

39 Regina Hackett, "Heavyweight Artists Discuss Public Work, Stress Collaboration," *Seattle Post-Intelligencer*, May 20, 1991, C1.

40 David Horsey, "Is It Really Art?—or Is 'In Public' a Program of Self-Indulgent Social Commentary," *Seattle Post-Intelligencer*, July 28, 1991, D1.

41 Heap of Birds, "In Honor of Rain Forest," *Caliban* 8 (1990): 80.

42 W. Jackson Rushing III, "'In Our Language': The Art of Hachivi Edgar Heap of Birds," *Third Text* 19, no. 4 (July 2005): 381.

43 Kwame Anthony Appiah, *Cosmopolitanism: Ethics in a World of Strangers* (New York: Norton, 2006), xv.

44 Timothy Morton, *Ecology without Nature: Rethinking Environmental Aesthetics* (Cambridge, MA: Harvard University Press, 2007).

45 Notably, Hudson's voyage was not the first by a European up the waterway that would bear his name. As artist Matthew Buckingham writes, "Far from being the first, Hudson was one of the last Europeans to arrive before European colonization. Indeed, there seems to have been little surprise when one of the first Indigenous people he met on his voyage spoke to him in French." Matthew Buckingham, "Muhheakantuck—Everything Has a Name," *October*, no. 120 (spring 2007): 173. Buckingham's essay is the text of the voice-over from his artwork of the same name, a thirty-eight-minute, 16 mm color film projection with sound. Buckingham's artwork was first exhibited in 2004, in *Watershed: The Hudson Valley Art Project*, in Beacon, New York, curated by Diane Shamash for Minetta Brook.

46 Jennifer McGregor, *The Muhheakantuck in Focus*, exhibition brochure (New York: Wave Hill Glyndor Gallery, 2009).

47 Heap of Birds, lecture, University of San Francisco, May 5, 2010.

48 Benjamin Genocchio, "The River's Meaning to Indians, before and after Hudson," *New York Times*, September 6, 2009, WE10.

49 Heap of Birds, lecture, University of San Francisco, May 5, 2010.

50 Heap of Birds, e-mail to author, January 20, 2011.

2. Words

1 Thanks to Stephen Glass for unpacking this etymology.

2 Edgar Heap of Birds, *Sharp Rocks* (Buffalo, NY: CEPA, 1986), n.p.

3 Kate Morris, "Reading between the Lines: Text and Image in Contemporary Native American Art," *American Indian Art Magazine* 34, no. 2 (spring 2009): 52.

4 Heap of Birds, *Sharp Rocks*, n.p.

5 Heap of Birds quoted in John Brandenburg, "Indian Artist 'Pointing toward Home' with Exhibit," *Daily Oklahoman*, September 8, 1983, News.

6 Johanna Drucker, "The Art of the Written Image," in *Figuring the Word: Essays on Books, Writing and Visual Poetics* (New York: Granary, 1998), 57.

7 Victor Burgin, "Situational Aesthetics" (1969), in *Art in Theory, 1900–2000: An Anthology of Changing Ideas*, 2nd ed., ed. Charles Harrison and Paul J. Wood (London: Blackwell, 2002), 894.

8 Liz Kotz, *Words to Be Looked At: Language in 1960s Art* (Cambridge, MA: MIT Press, 2007), 4.

9 Kotz, *Words to Be Looked At.*

10 Sol Lewitt, "Paragraphs on Conceptual Art" (1967), in Harrison and Wood, *Art in Theory*, 846.

11 Lucy Lippard, "Introduction to 557,087" (1969), in *Conceptual Art: A Critical Anthology*, ed. Alexander Alberro and Blake Stimson (Cambridge, MA: MIT Press, 1999), 178.

12 Lucy Lippard, preface to *Six Years: The Dematerialization of the Art Object from 1966 to 1972* (Berkeley: University of California Press, 1997), 7–8.

13 Rosalind Krauss, *A Voyage on the North Sea: Art in the Age of the Post-medium Condition* (London: Thames and Hudson, 2000).

14 Michel Foucault, *Power/Knowledge: Selected Interviews and Other Writings, 1972–1977*, ed. and trans. Colin Gordon (New York: Pantheon, 1980).

15 Rancière's key work is *Disagreement: Politics and Philosophy*, trans. Julie Rose (Minneapolis: University of Minnesota Press, 1999); see also Jacques Rancière, *The Politics of Aesthetics: The Distribution of the Sensible*, trans. Gabriel Rockhill (London: Continuum, 2004).

16 Hulleah Tsinhnahjinnie, Jimmie Durham, George Longfish, and Jaune Quick-to-See Smith also made use of text extensively in their work. See Morris, "Reading between the Lines."

17 Michael Brenson, "Art People: Art Lights Up Times Square," *New York Times*, June 25, 1982, C26. Colab had first used the billboard for their joint exhibition with the South Bronx alternative gallery Fashion Moda, the Times Square Show, which was installed in a former massage parlor in the seedy Midtown Manhattan neighborhood in 1980.

18 Jaune Quick-to-See Smith made a similar decision to incorporate source texts, as Kate Morris writes, out of concern "that her audience was not grasping the full range of information and meaning that her paintings endeavored to convey." Morris, "Reading between the Lines," 54.

19 Heap of Birds quoted in James Auer, "Indian Artist Blends Images to Challenge Viewers," *Milwaukee Journal*, December 18, 1994, Features, 1.

20 Michael Winerip, "Computerized Billboard Brightens Up Times Sq. with Art-of-the-Month," *New York Times*, August 26, 1983, B1.

21 Heap of Birds, *Sharp Rocks*, n.p.

22 Heap of Birds, *Sharp Rocks*, n.p.

23 Ruth B. Phillips, "Show Times: De-celebrating the Canadian Nation, Decolonizing the Canadian Museum, 1967–1992," in *Rethinking Settler Co-*

lonialism: History and Memory in Australia, Canada, Aotearoa New Zealand, and South Africa, ed. Annie E. Coombes (Manchester: Manchester University Press, 2006), 121–39.

24 Heap of Birds, artist's statement from *Imperial Canada*, 1988, quoted in Lowery Stokes Sims, "Words into Vision: The Art of Hachivi Edgar Heap of Birds," in Jeanette Ingberman, Papo Colo, Jean Fisher, Lowery Stokes Sims, and Hachivi Edgar Heap of Birds, *Claim Your Color*, exhibition catalog (New York: Exit Art, 1989), 6.

25 Heap of Birds, e-mail to author, October 8, 2010.

26 Jean Fisher, "Edgar Heap of Birds," *Artforum* 26, no. 5 (January 1988): 116–17.

27 Caliban has also been employed by other contemporary Native artists, most notably Jimmie Durham, in his *Caliban Codex* (1992). See Laura Mulvey, Dick Snauwaert, and Mark Alice Durant, *Jimmie Durham* (London: Phaidon, 1995).

28 Heap of Birds quoted in Brandenburg, "Indian Artist 'Pointing toward Home.'"

29 Heap of Birds, "Life as Art: Creating through Acts of Personal and Cultural Renewal," in *[Re]inventing the Wheel: Advancing the Dialogue on Contemporary American Indian Art*, ed. Nancy J. Blomberg (Denver: Denver Art Museum, 2008), 29. Heap of Birds's comments resonate with Jaune Quick-to-See Smith, who added text to her paintings for similar reasons: "I began to see that what I had to say was equally as important as the painting surface. Perhaps more so." Quoted in Lawrence Abbott, ed., *I Stand in the Center of the Good: Interviews with Contemporary Native American Artists* (Lincoln: University of Nebraska Press, 1994), 216, in Morris, "Reading between the Lines," 54.

30 W. Jackson Rushing III, "In Our Language: The Art of Hachivi Edgar Heap of Birds," *Third Text* 19, no. 4 (July 2005): 370.

31 Janet Catherine Berlo, ed., *Plains Indian Drawings 1865–1935: Pages from a Visual History* (New York: Harry Abrams, 1996); Joyce M. Szabo, *Art from Fort Marion: The Silberman Collection* (Norman: University of Oklahoma Press, 2007).

32 Edgar Heap of Birds, "Life as Art," 30.

33 Quoted in Jamake Highwater, "Heap of Birds," *Native Arts/West*, April 1981, 31, in Rushing, "In Our Language," 370.

34 Heap of Birds, "Life as Art," 30. Heap of Birds mentions that, years later, he was sent a reprint from a Fort Marion newspaper that reported on the Cheyenne prisoners "sunning themselves on the beach like lizards." He had not been aware of the reference. Lecture, University of San Francisco, May 5, 2010.

35 Heap of Birds quoted in Auer, "Indian Artist Blends Images to Challenge Viewers."

36 Heap of Birds, *Sharp Rocks*, n.p.
37 Heap of Birds, *Sharp Rocks*, n.p, emphasis in original.
38 Heap of Birds quoted in Regina Hackett, "Heap of Birds' Effective Show Pares Art to Bare Bones," *Seattle Post-Intelligencer*, December 9, 1986, C5.
39 Quoted in Heap of Birds, *Sharp Rocks*, n.p.; a longer version of the account of Moving Behind (Mrs. Black Hawk) is in Theodore A. Ediger and Vinnie Hoffman, "Some Reminiscences of the Battle of Washita," *Chronicles of Oklahoma* 33 (1955): 137–41, digital.library.okstate.edu/chronicles/v033/v033p137.pdf.
40 Edgar Heap of Birds, "Living upon a Grave: American Policy / Native Hosts," *Whitewalls*, no. 23 (fall 1989): 79.
41 Rushing, "In Our Language," 369.
42 Heap of Birds quoted in Hackett, "Heap of Birds' Effective Show."
43 Rushing, "In Our Language," 369.
44 Heap of Birds, e-mail to author, November 30, 2013.
45 Hackett, "Heap of Birds' Effective Show."
46 Shanna Ketchum, "Native American Cosmopolitan Modernism(s): A Rearticulation of Presence through Time and Space," *Third Text* 19, no. 4 (July 2005): 357–64.
47 Rushing, "In Our Language," 373.
48 Heap of Birds, "Henaae Nane Hetane, *What Makes a Man*, Solo Exhibition Proposal" (unpublished typescript, n.d.).
49 Heap of Birds, "Henaae Nane Hetane."
50 Fisher, "Edgar Heap of Birds," 116.
51 Heap of Birds, "Henaae Nane Hetane."
52 Heap of Birds, "Henaae Nane Hetane."
53 Edgar Heap of Birds, "Living upon a Grave," 78.
54 Heap of Birds, e-mail to author, November 30, 2013.
55 Jo Ortel, "Exhibition Review of Continuum: 12 Artists at the George Gustav Heye Center, Part 1," *American Indian Art Magazine* 30, no. 1 (winter 2004): 74.
56 Heap of Birds, e-mail to author, September 16, 2010.
57 Susan Snodgrass, *Tell Your Self*, exhibition brochure (Sydney: Art Gallery of New South Wales, 1994), n.p.
58 Heap of Birds, e-mail to author, November 30, 2013.
59 Heap of Birds, *Crosses for Diné/Tepoztlan* (unpublished artist's statement, 2009).
60 Heap of Birds, *Words, Trees, Chiapas* (unpublished artist's statement, 2009).
61 Heap of Birds, *Water Desert Words* (unpublished artist's statement, 2010).
62 Heap of Birds, *Water Desert Words*.

3. Histories

1 Heap of Birds quoted in "Indian Artist's Entry at Festival Shows History Belongs to Those Who Rewrite It," *Pittsburgh Post-Gazette*, June 19, 1992, A1.

2 "Indian Artist's Entry at Festival."

3 Annie E. Coombes, "Introduction: Memory and History in Settler Colonialism," in *Rethinking Settler Colonialism: History and Memory in Australia, Canada, Aotearoa New Zealand, and South Africa*, ed. Annie E. Coombes (Manchester: Manchester University Press, 2006), 1–2.

4 Benedict Anderson, *Imagined Communities: Reflections on the Origin and Spread of Nationalism*, rev. ed. (London: Verso, 1991).

5 Ruth B. Phillips, "Settler Monuments, Indigenous Memory: Dismembering and Re-membering Canadian Art History," in *Monuments and Memory, Made and Unmade*, ed. Robert S. Nelson and Margaret Olin (Chicago: University of Chicago Press, 2003), 284.

6 Jean Fisher, "Remembering the Future: Tradition and Modernity in the Work of Hock E Aye Vi Edgar Heap of Birds," in *Edgar Heap of Birds: Most Serene Republics*, ed. Kathleen Ash-Milby and Truman T. Lowe (Washington, DC: National Museum of the American Indian, Smithsonian Institution, 2009), 42.

7 Hal Foster, "An Archival Impulse," *October* 110 (fall 2004): 5.

8 Robert Musil, "Monuments," in *Posthumous Papers of a Living Author*, trans. Peter Wortsman (Brooklyn: Archipelago Books, 2006), 64.

9 Heap of Birds quoted in Mark Fischenich, "Sooner Artist Wants Sculpture at Site Where Indians Hanged," *Tulsa World*, June 9, 1991, A21.

10 Larry Long, "Water in the Rain (Dakota Oyate)," on *Run for Freedom / Sweet Thunder*, Flying Fish Records, 1987.

11 Edgar Heap of Birds quoted in Lawrence Abbott, ed., *I Stand in the Center of the Good: Interviews with Contemporary Native American Artists* (Lincoln: University of Nebraska Press, 1994), 34.

12 Heap of Birds quoted in Abbott, *I Stand in the Center of the Good*, 35.

13 Heap of Birds quoted in Abbott, *I Stand in the Center of the Good*, 34.

14 Heap of Birds quoted in Abbott, *I Stand in the Center of the Good*, 34.

15 Heap of Birds quoted in Abbott, *I Stand in the Center of the Good*, 34.

16 Heap of Birds quoted in Nick Blomley, "Artistic Displacements: An Interview with Edgar Heap of Birds," *Environment and Planning D: Society and Space* 22 (2004): 805.

17 W. Jackson Rushing III, "'In Our Language': The Art of Hachivi Edgar Heap of Birds," *Third Text* 19, no. 4 (July 2005): 377.

18 Weiner quoted in John Anthony Thwaites, "Lawrence Weiner: An Interview and an Interpretation," *Art and Artists* (London), August 7, 1972, 23,

quoted in Alexander Alberro and Alice Zimmerman, "Survey," in Alexander Alberro, Alice Zimmerman, Benjamin Buchloh, and David Batchelor, *Lawrence Weiner* (London: Phaidon, 1998), 49.

19 Alberro and Zimmerman, "Survey," 50.

20 Alberro and Zimmerman, "Survey," 67.

21 Heap of Birds, "Artist's Statement," in *Ocmulgee*, exhibition brochure (Atlanta: Atlanta College of Art Gallery, 2005).

22 Heap of Birds, "Artist's Statement," *Ocmulgee*.

23 Cathy Byrd, "Atlanta," *Art Papers* 29, no. 4 (July–August 2005): 39.

24 Heap of Birds, "Artist's Statement," *Ocmulgee*.

25 Foster, "An Archival Impulse," 4.

26 Heap of Birds, e-mail to author, November 30, 2013.

27 Rushing, "'In Our Language,'" 384.

28 Heap of Birds quoted in Kyle MacMillan, "Denver Art Museum Rolls Out 'Wheel,'" *Denver Post*, June 24, 2005, FF-05.

29 Heap of Birds quoted in Mary Voelz Chandler, "The Forest and the 'Trees': Spokes of 'Wheel,'" *Rocky Mountain News*, May 31, 2005, 8D.

30 Erika Doss, *Memorial Mania: Public Feeling in America* (Chicago: University of Chicago Press, 2010), 341.

31 Stephen Terence Gould, "Bravery, Art and Politics," *Denver Post*, January 7, 2007, E-06.

32 "Editing a War Memorial," *Rocky Mountain News*, August 8, 1998, 69A.

33 Dee Brown, *Bury My Heart at Wounded Knee: An Indian History of the American West* (New York: Macmillan, 1971), 86–87.

34 Katrina Martin, "Art Museum Sculpture Celebrates Native Culture," *Denver Post*, September 12, 1999, B-01. The site of *Wheel* had previously been occupied by other site-specific artworks, most recently *Acoma Garden*, created in 1994 by eco-artist Meg Webster for the exhibition *Visions of America: Landscape as Metaphor*. The name of Webster's artwork recalled the historic pueblo in New Mexico but actually referenced Acoma Street, which bordered the museum to the east before the construction of the pedestrian plaza linking the museum and Denver Public Library. Webster created the garden using indigenous plants in what she described as the "demilitarized zone"—an active construction area during the building of the Michael Graves addition to the library, completed in 1995.

35 Denver Art Museum, *Wheel*, exhibition brochure, 2005.

36 Heap of Birds, e-mail to author, November 30, 2013.

37 Heap of Birds, "*Wheel*: Proposal for Outdoor Signature Sculpture for the Denver Art Museum" (unpublished manuscript, 1998).

38 Heap of Birds quoted in Blomley, "Artistic Displacements," 806.

39 Gould, "Bravery, Art and Politics."

40 Dean Rader, *Engaged Resistance: American Indian Art, Literature, and Film from Alcatraz to the NMAI* (Austin: University of Texas Press, 2011), 205.

41 Heap of Birds quoted in Mary Voelz Chandler, "Celebrants Turn Out for 'Wheel,'" *Rocky Mountain News*, June 22, 2005, 14A.
42 Nancy Blomberg quoted in Clara Ricciardi, "New Outdoor Sculpture Installed at DAM," *La Voz Nueva* 31, no. 25 (June 22, 2005): 21.
43 Carol Berry, "Cheyenne and Arapaho Tribal Members Commemorate Sand Creek Ancestors," *Indian Country Today* 28, no. 28 (December 17, 2008): 6.
44 While not sited in the main Giardini Pubblici, *Most Serene Republics* was one of thirty-four off-site exhibitions listed as *eventi collateralli*—collateral events—recognized by the commissioner and published in the official guide to the Biennale.
45 Heap of Birds, *Most Serene Republics*, exhibition brochure (Washington, DC: National Museum of the American Indian, Smithsonian Institution, 2007).
46 Kathleen Ash-Milby, "Most Serene Republics: Remembering and Reconsidering Histories," in Ash-Milby and Lowe, *Edgar Heap of Birds*, 58.
47 *Most Serene Republics* was also installed in Verona, after the closing of the Venice Biennale, near the amphitheater where the troupe performed.
48 Heap of Birds quoted in Ash-Milby, "Most Serene Republics," 64.
49 Ash-Milby, "Most Serene Republics," 66–67.
50 Ash-Milby, "Most Serene Republics," 78.
51 Ash-Milby, "Most Serene Republics," 75.
52 Heap of Birds quoted in Ash-Milby, "Most Serene Republics," 51.
53 Heap of Birds quoted in Ash-Milby, "Most Serene Republics," 77.
54 Heap of Birds quoted in Ash-Milby, "Most Serene Republics," 73.
55 Ash-Milby, "Most Serene Republics," 51.
56 Craig Owens, "Improper Names," *Art in America* 74, no. 10 (October 1986): 129, emphasis in original.
57 Heap of Birds quoted in Ash-Milby, "Most Serene Republics," 78.

4. Generations

1 Nicolas Bourriaud, "Relational Aesthetics" (1998), in *Participation*, ed. Claire Bishop (Cambridge, MA: MIT Press, 2006), 160.
2 Nicolas Bourriaud, *Relational Aesthetics* (Paris: Presses du Réel, 1998), 13, 45, quoted in Claire Bishop, "Antagonism and Relational Aesthetics," *October* 110 (fall 2001), 54.
3 See Bishop, "Antagonism and Relational Aesthetics," for a key critique of relational aesthetics.
4 Terry Smith, "Contemporary Art and Contemporaneity," *Critical Inquiry* 32 (summer 2006): 681–707.
5 Julia Bogany, lecture at Pitzer College, Claremont, California, August 30, 2013.
6 Gerald Vizenor, *Manifest Manners: Narratives on Postindian Survivance* (Lin-

coln: University of Nebraska Press, 1994); and Gerald Vizenor, *Survivance: Narratives of Native Presence* (Lincoln: University of Nebraska Press, 2008).

7 Jacquelyn Lewis-Harris, *Hachivi Edgar Heap of Birds and Artists of Tandanya and Boomali: 16 Songs / Issues of Personal Assessment and Indigenous Renewal*, Saint Louis Art Museum, November 14, 1995–January 6, 1996.

8 Eleanor Charles, "Connecticut Guide," *New York Times*, November 10, 1996, CN16.

9 Heap of Birds quoted in *Art ConText*, RISD Museum, Exhibition Notes, no. 17 (spring 2002): n.p.

10 Heap of Birds quoted in *Art ConText*.

11 *Eagles Speak*, exhibition announcement, Association for Visual Arts, Cape Town, South Africa, 2002.

12 Heap of Birds quoted in *Art ConText*.

13 Heap of Birds quoted in Rosemary Stephens, "World Renown Artist Dedicates Art Murals for New Community Gym," *Cheyenne and Arapaho Tribal Tribune* 8, no. 8 (February 15, 2013): 6. In honor of the occasion, Cheyenne and Arapaho governor Janice Prairie Chief-Boswell signed a proclamation declaring January 31 to be Hock E Aye Vi Little Chief Edgar Heap of Birds Day.

14 Keith Moxey, *Visual Time: The Image in History* (Durham, NC: Duke University Press, 2013), 174.

BIBLIOGRAPHY

Abbott, Lawrence, ed. *I Stand in the Center of the Good: Interviews with Contemporary Native American Artists*. Lincoln: University of Nebraska Press, 1994.

Alberro, Alexander, and Blake Stimson, eds. *Conceptual Art: A Critical Anthology*. Cambridge, MA: MIT Press, 1999.

Alfred, Taiaiake. *Peace, Power, Righteousness: An Indigenous Manifesto*. Oxford: Oxford University Press, 1999.

Amor, Mónica, with Okwui Enwezor, Gao Minglu, Oscar Ho, Kobena Mercer, and Irit Rogoff. "Liminalities: Discussions on the Global and the Local." *Art Journal* 57, no. 4 (winter 1998): 28–49.

Anderson, Benedict. *Imagined Communities: Reflections on the Origin and Spread of Nationalism*. Rev. ed. London: Verso, 1991.

Andrews, Malcolm. *Landscape and Western Art*. Oxford: Oxford University Press, 1999.

Anthes, Bill. "Contemporary Native Artists and International Biennial Culture." *Visual Anthropology Review* 25, no. 2 (fall 2009): 109–27.

Anthes, Bill. "Ethics in a World of Strange Strangers: Edgar Heap of Birds at Home and Abroad." *Art Journal* 71, no. 3 (fall 2012): 58–77.

Anthes, Bill. *Native Moderns: American Indian Painting, 1940–1960*. Durham, NC: Duke University Press, 2006.

Appadurai, Arjun. *Modernity at Large: Cultural Dimensions of Globalization*. Minneapolis: University of Minnesota Press, 1996.

Appiah, Kwame Anthony. *Cosmopolitanism: Ethics in a World of Strangers*. New York: Norton, 2006.

Ash-Milby, Kathleen, and Truman T. Lowe, eds. *Edgar Heap of Birds: Most Serene Republics*. Washington, DC: National Museum of the American Indian, Smithsonian Institution, 2009. Exhibition catalog.

Berlo, Janet Catherine, ed. *Plains Indian Drawings 1865–1935: Pages from a Visual History*. New York: Harry Abrams, 1996.

Berthrong, Donald J. *The Cheyenne and Arapahoe Ordeal: Reservation and Agency Life in the Indian Territory, 1875–1907*. Norman: University of Oklahoma Press, 1976.

Berthrong, Donald J. *The Southern Cheyennes*. Norman: University of Oklahoma Press, 1963.

Bishop, Claire. "Antagonism and Relational Aesthetics." *October* 110 (fall 2001): 51–79.

Blomberg, Nancy J., ed. *[Re]inventing the Wheel: Advancing the Dialogue on Contemporary American Indian Art*. Denver: Denver Art Museum, 2008.

Blomley, Nick. "Artistic Displacements: An Interview with Edgar Heap of Birds." *Environment and Planning D: Society and Space* 22 (2004): 799–807.

Brown, Dee. *Bury My Heart at Wounded Knee: An Indian History of the American West*. New York: Macmillan, 1971.

Coombes, Annie E., ed. *Rethinking Settler Colonialism: History and Memory in Australia, Canada, Aotearoa New Zealand, and South Africa*. Manchester: Manchester University Press, 2006.

Deloria, Vine, Jr., and Clifford Lytle. *The Nations Within: The Past and Future of American Indian Sovereignty*. New York: Pantheon, 1984.

Dorsey, George A. *The Cheyenne*. Publications of the Field Columbian Museum: Anthropological Series, vol. 9. Chicago: Field Columbian Museum, 1905.

Doss, Erika. *Memorial Mania: Public Feeling in America*. Chicago: University of Chicago Press, 2010.

Drucker, Johanna. *Figuring the Word: Essays on Books, Writing and Visual Poetics*. New York: Granary Books, 1998.

Fisher, Jean. *Heh No Wah Maun Stun He Dun: What Makes a Man*. London: Matt's Gallery, 1989. Exhibition catalog.

Foster, Hal. "An Archival Impulse." *October* 110 (fall 2004): 3–22.

Fowler, Loretta. *Tribal Sovereignty and the Historical Imagination: Cheyenne-Arapaho Politics*. Lincoln: University of Nebraska Press, 2002.

Gárcia Canclini, Néstor. *Art beyond Itself: Anthropology for a Society without a Story Line*. Translated by David Frye. Durham, NC: Duke University Press, 2014.

Gussow, Zachary, Leroy R. Hafen, and Arthur A. Ekirch, Jr., Indian Claims Commission. *Arapaho-Cheyenne Indians, Cheyenne and Arapaho Aboriginal Occupation, Historical Development of the Arapaho-Cheyenne Land Area, Cheyenne and Arapaho Indians, Commission Findings*. New York: Garland, 1974.

Heap of Birds, Edgar. *Sharp Rocks*. Buffalo, NY: CEPA, 1986. Exhibition catalog.

Huhndorf, Shari M. *Mapping the Americas: The Transnational Politics of Contemporary Native Culture*. Ithaca, NY: Cornell University Press, 2009.

Ingberman, Jeanette, Papo Colo, Jean Fisher, Lowery Stokes Sims, and Hachivi Edgar Heap of Birds. *Claim Your Color*. New York: Exit Art, 1989. Exhibition catalog.

Jorgenson, Joseph G. *The Sun Dance Religion: Power for the Powerless*. Chicago: University of Chicago Press, 1972.

Kapur, Geeta. *When Was Modernism: Essays on Contemporary Cultural Practice in India*. New Delhi: Tulika, 2000.

Ketchum, Shanna. "Native American Cosmopolitan Modernism(s): A Re-articulation of Presence through Time and Space." *Third Text* 19, no. 4 (July 2005): 357–64.

Kotz, Liz. *Words to Be Looked At: Language in 1960s Art*. Cambridge, MA: MIT Press, 2007.

Krauss, Rosalind. *A Voyage on the North Sea: Art in the Age of the Post-medium Condition*. London: Thames and Hudson, 2000.

Kwon, Miwon. *One Place after Another: Site-Specific Art and Locational Identity*. Cambridge, MA: MIT Press, 2002.

Lacy, Suzanne, ed. *Mapping the Terrain: New Genre Public Art*. Seattle: Bay Press, 1995.

Lee, Pamela. *Chronophobia: On Time in the Art of the 1960s*. Cambridge, MA: MIT Press, 2006.

Lippard, Lucy. *Mixed Blessings: New Art in a Multicultural America*. New York: Pantheon, 1990.

Lippard, Lucy. *Six Years: The Dematerialization of the Art Object from 1966 to 1972*. Berkeley: University of California Press, 1997.

Mithlo, Nancy Marie. "Reappropriating Redskins: *Pellerossasogna* (Red Skin Dream); Shelley Niro at the 50th La Biennale di Venezia." *Visual Anthropology Review* 20, no. 2 (fall 2004): 22–35.

Mithlo, Nancy Marie. "'We Have All Been Colonized': Subordination and Resistance on a Global Arts Stage." *Visual Anthropology* 17 (2004): 229–45.

Moore, John H. *The Cheyenne*. Cambridge: Blackwell, 1996.

Moore, John H. *The Cheyenne Nation: A Social and Demographic History*. Lincoln: University of Nebraska Press, 1987.

Morris, Kate. "Picturing Sovereignty: Landscape in Native American Art." In *Painters, Patrons, and Identity: Essays in Native American Art to Honor J.J. Brody*, edited by Joyce M. Szabo, 187–209. Albuquerque: University of New Mexico Press, 2001.

Morris, Kate. "Reading between the Lines: Text and Image in Contemporary Native American Art." *American Indian Art Magazine* 34, no. 2 (spring 2009): 52–59.

Morton, Timothy. *Ecology without Nature: Rethinking Environmental Aesthetics*. Cambridge, MA: Harvard University Press, 2007.

Moxey, Keith. *Visual Time: The Image in History*. Durham, NC: Duke University Press, 2013.

Musil, Robert. *Posthumous Papers of a Living Author*. Translated by Peter Wortsman. Brooklyn: Archipelago Books, 2006.

National Museum of the American Indian. *Vision, Space, Desire: Global Perspectives and Cultural Hybridity*. Washington, DC: Smithsonian Institution, 2006.

Nemiroff, Diana, Robert Houle, and Charlotte Townsend-Gault. *Land Spirit Power: First Nations at the National Gallery of Canada*. Ottawa: National Gallery of Canada, 1992. Exhibition catalog.

Ostrowitz, Judith. *Interventions: Native American Art for Far-Flung Territories*. Seattle: University of Washington Press, 2009.

Phillips, Ruth B. "Settler Monuments, Indigenous Memory: Dis-membering and Re-membering Canadian Art History." In *Monuments and Memory, Made and Unmade*, edited by Robert S. Nelson and Margaret Olin, 281–304. Chicago: University of Chicago Press, 2003.

Quick-to-See Smith, Jaune. *Our Land / Ourselves*. Albany: University Art Gallery, State University of New York at Albany, 1990. Exhibition catalog.

Rader, Dean. *Engaged Resistance: American Indian Art, Literature, and Film from Alcatraz to the NMAI*. Austin: University of Texas Press, 2011.

Raheja, Michelle. "Reading Nanook's Smile: Visual Sovereignty, Indigenous Revisions of Ethnography, and Atanarjuat (The Fast Runner)." *American Quarterly* 59, no. 4 (December 2007): 1159–85.

Rancière, Jacques. *Disagreement: Politics and Philosophy*. Translated by Julie Rose. Minneapolis: University of Minnesota Press, 1999.

Rancière, Jacques. *The Politics of Aesthetics: The Distribution of the Sensible*. Translated by Gabriel Rockhill. London: Continuum, 2004.

Rickard, Jolene. "The Local and the Global." In *Vision, Space, Desire: Global Perspectives and Cultural Hybridity*, edited by National Museum of the American Indian, 59–67. Washington, DC: Smithsonian Institution, 2006.

Rickard, Jolene. "Sovereignty: A Line in the Sand." In *Strong Hearts: Native American Visions and Voices*, edited by Peggy Roalf, 51–59. New York: Aperture, 1995.

Rickard, Jolene. "Visualizing Sovereignty in the Time of Biometric Sensors." *South Atlantic Quarterly* 110, no. 2 (spring 2011): 465–86.

Roberts, Jennifer L. *Mirror Travels: Robert Smithson and History*. New Haven, CT: Yale University Press, 2004.

Rogers, Sarah J. *Will/Power: New Works by Papo Colo, Jimmie Durham, David Hammons, Hachivi Edgar Heap of Birds, Adrian Piper, Aminah Brenda Lynn Robinson*. Columbus: Wexner Center for the Arts, Ohio State University, 1992. Exhibition catalog.

Ross, Christine. *The Past Is the Present; It's the Future Too: The Temporal Turn in Contemporary Art*. London: Continuum, 2012.

Rushing, W. Jackson, III. "'In Our Language': The Art of Hachivi Edgar Heap of Birds." *Third Text* 19, no. 4 (July 2005): 365–84.

Rushing, W. Jackson, III, ed. *Native American Art in the Twentieth Century*. New York: Routledge, 1999.

Rushing, W. Jackson, III. "Street Chiefs and Native Hosts: Richard Ray (Whitman) and Hachivi Edgar Heap of Birds Defend the Homeland." In *Green Acres: Neo-colonialism in the U.S.*, edited by Christopher Scoates, 23–36. St. Louis, MO: Washington University Gallery of Art, 1992.

Smith, Paul Chaat. *Everything You Know about Indians Is Wrong*. Minneapolis: University of Minnesota Press, 2009.

Smith, Terry. "Contemporary Art and Contemporaneity." *Critical Inquiry* 32 (summer 2006): 681–707.

Smith, Terry. *Contemporary Art: World Currents*. London: Laurence King, 2011.

Smith, Terry. *What Is Contemporary Art?* Chicago: University of Chicago Press, 2009.

Smith, Terry, Okwui Enwezor, and Nancy Condee, eds. *Antinomies of Art and Culture: Modernity, Postmodernity, Contemporaneity*. Durham, NC: Duke University Press, 2008.

Szabo, Joyce M. *Art from Fort Marion: The Silberman Collection*. Norman: University of Oklahoma Press, 2007.

Vizenor, Gerald. *Manifest Manners: Narratives on Postindian Survivance*. Lincoln: University of Nebraska Press, 1994.

Vizenor, Gerald. *Survivance: Narratives of Native Presence*. Lincoln: University of Nebraska Press, 2008.

Warrior, Robert Allen. *Tribal Secrets: Recovering American Indian Intellectual Traditions*. Minneapolis: University of Minnesota Press, 1995.

INDEX